Islands
of History

Islands
of History

MARSHALL SAHLINS

The University of Chicago Press
Chicago and London

MARSHALL SAHLINS is the Charles F. Grey Distinguished Service Professor at the University of Chicago. Among his many books is *Culture and Practical Reason*, also published by the University of Chicago Press.

The University of Chicago Press, Chicago 60637
The University of Chicago Press, Ltd., London
© 1985 by The University of Chicago
All rights reserved. Published 1985
Printed in the United States of America

94 93 92 91 90 89 88 87 86 85   54321

Library of Congress Cataloging in Publication Data

Sahlins, Marshall David, 1930–
  Islands of History.

  Bibliography: p.
  Includes index.
  1. Oceania—History.   2. Oceania—Civilization.
I. Title.
DU28.3.S24   1985   990   84-8820
ISBN 0-226-73357-2
ISBN 0-226-73358-0 (pbk.)

Contents

Introduction
vii

1
Supplement to the Voyage of Cook; or, *le calcul sauvage*
1

2
Other Times, Other Customs: The Anthropology of History
32

3
The Stranger-King; or, Dumézil among the Fijians
73

4
Captain James Cook; or, The Dying God
104

5
Structure and History
136

Contents

Bibliography
157

Index
173

Introduction

History is culturally ordered, differently so in different societies, according to meaningful schemes of things. The converse is also true: cultural schemes are historically ordered, since to a greater or lesser extent the meanings are revalued as they are practically enacted. The synthesis of these contraries unfolds in the creative action of the historic subjects, the people concerned. For on the one hand, people organize their projects and give significance to their objects from the existing understandings of the cultural order. To that extent, the culture is historically reproduced in action. Later on I cite Clifford Geertz's observation to the effect that an event is a unique actualization of a general phenomenon, a contingent realization of the cultural pattern—which may be a good characterization of history *tout court*. On the other hand, then, as the contingent circumstances of action need not conform to the significance some group might assign them, people are known to creatively reconsider their conventional schemes. And to that extent, the culture is historically altered in action. We can speak even of "structural transformation," since the alteration of some meanings changes the positional relations among the cultural categories, thus a "system-change."

Such are the larger ideas of the essays to follow. They may be summed up in the assertion that what anthropologists call "structure"—the symbolic relations of cultural order—is an historical object.

The assertion explicitly overrides the notional opposition, found everywhere in the human sciences, between "structure" and "history." I have seen among theoreticians of "the world-system," for example, the proposition that since the hinterland societies anthropologists habitually study are open to radical change, externally imposed by Western capitalist expansion, the assumption that these societies work on some autonomous cultural-logic cannot be entertained. This is a confusion between an open system and a lack of system. And it leaves us unable to account for the diversity of local responses to the world system—persisting, moreover, in its wake. World-system theory itself allows for the preservation of satellite cultures, as the means of reproduction of capital in the dominant European order. But if so, from the alternate vantage of the so-called dominated people, European wealth is harnessed to the reproduction and even the creative transformation of their own cultural order.

I bring this up because my book is largely about distant encounters, South Sea incidents of the world system. Sometimes it will appear that the autonomy of the indigenous culture is proved only by the enigmas of the historic response. Take the mytho-practical resistance of the Maori hero, Hone Heke, for instance. In 1845, Hone Heke deployed his warriors to assault—and unintentionally overwhelm—the largest colonial settlement in New Zealand, *as a diversionary tactic*: that is, in order to accomplish the exploit Heke always considered more decisive, and on four different occasions performed, which was to cut down a certain flagpole the British had erected above the town. "Let us fight," he said, "for the flagpole alone." Since it will be necessary, in order to decode Hone Heke's preoccupation with the flagpole, to go back to the origin of the universe, I will leave the further details of the story to chapter 2. But the details would support the position I take here: that the historical issues are not nearly so exotic as such incidents might suggest.

The same kind of cultural change, externally induced yet indigenously orchestrated, has been going on for millennia. Not simply because the so-called primitive societies were never so isolated as an earlier anthropology, obsessed by an evolutionary concern for the pristine, was pleased to believe (cf. Wolf 1982). The dynamic elements at work—including the confrontation with an external world that has its own imperious determinations and with other people who have their own parochial intentions—are present everywhere in human experience. History is made the same general way within a given society as it is between societies.

The bigger issue, as I see it in these essays, is the dual existence and interaction between the cultural order as constituted in the society and as lived by the people: structure in convention and in action, as virtual and as actual. In their practical projects and social arrangements, informed by the received meanings of persons and things, people submit these cultural categories to empirical risks. To the extent that the symbolic is thus the pragmatic, the system is a synthesis in time of reproduction and variation.

If culture is as anthropologists claim a meaningful order, still, in action meanings are always at risk. They are risked, for example, by reference to things (i.e., in extension). Things not only have their own *raison d'être*, independently of what people may make of them, they are inevitably disproportionate to the sense of the signs by which they are apprehended. Things are contextually more particular than signs and potentially more general. They are more particular insofar as signs are meaning-classes, not bound as concepts to any particular referent (or "stimulus-free"). Things are thus related to their signs as empirical tokens to cultural types. Yet things are more general than signs inasmuch as they present more properties (more "reality") than the distinctions and values attended to by signs. Culture is therefore a gamble played with nature, in the course of which, wittingly or unwittingly—I paraphrase Marc Bloch—the old names that are still on everyone's lips acquire connotations that are far removed from their original meaning. This is one of the historical processes I will be calling "the functional revaluation of the categories."

Here is another such process, dependent on what Hilary Putnam (1975) calls "the division of linguistic labor." It again brings up certain differences between sense and reference, the intension of the sign and its extension. The sense of a sign (the Saussurean "value") is determined by its contrastive relations to other signs in the system. Therefore, it is complete and systematic only in the society (or community of speakers) as a whole. Any actual use of the sign in reference by some person or group engages only part, some small fraction, of the collective sense. Apart from the influences of the context, this division of meaningful labor is, broadly speaking, a function of the differences among people in social experience and interest. What is a "fluttering bird (of some kind)" to me is a "diseased sparrow hawk" to you (an ornithologist) and perhaps a "poor thing" to some others (members of the SPCA; Stern 1968). Captain Cook appears as an ancestral god to Hawaiian priests, more like a divine warrior to the chiefs, and evidently something else and less to ordinary men and women (chapter 4). Acting from different perspectives, and with different social powers of objectifying their respective interpretations, people come to different conclusions and societies work out different consensuses. Social communication is as much an empirical risk as worldly reference.

The effects of such risks can be radical innovations. For finally, in the contradictory encounters with persons and things, signs are liable to be reclaimed by the original powers of their creation: the human symbolic consciousness. Now, nothing is tabu, in intellectual principle—not even the concept of "tabu," as we learn from Hawaiian history (in chapters 1 and 5). Metaphor, analogy, abstraction, specialization: all kinds of semantic improvisations are incident to the everyday enactment of culture, with the chance of becoming general or consensual by their sociological take-up in the going order. Meanings are ultimately submitted to subjective risks, to the extent that people, as they are socially enabled, cease to be the slaves of their concepts and become the masters. "'The question is,'" said Alice, "'whether you *can* make words mean so many different things.'" "'The question is,'" said Humpty Dumpty, "'which is to be master— that's all.'"

Still, as in another famous dialogue about the relations of master and slave, this domination involves a certain servitude. One is not free, for example, to name things "just what they are," as Adam did: "it looked like a lion, and it roared like a lion; so I called it, 'lion.'" The improvisations (functional revaluations) depend on received possibilities of significance, if only because they are otherwise unintelligible and incommunicable. Hence the empirical is not known simply as such but as a culturally relevant significance, and the old system is projected forward in its novel forms. It also follows that different cultural orders have their own, distinctive modes of historical production.

Different cultures, different historicities. This is the main point of the second chapter, where I contrast the heroic histories of divine kingships with the "new history" of the populist dispensation, "history from below." I try to show why, for societies of a certain type, the stories of kings and battles are with good reason privileged historiographically. The reason is a structure that generalizes the action of the king as the form and destiny of the society. In the same essay, the mytho-praxis of Polynesian peoples is contrasted with the disenchanted utilitarianism of our own historical consciousness. Or again, the first chapter, on the historical efficacy of love in Hawaii, is another exercise in relativity—with a subtext on "performative" and "prescriptive" structures that perhaps merits some further comment.

This is an ideal-typical distinction about the ways structures are realized in the cultural order and over the historical course. In some respects, the difference between prescriptive and performative structures parallels the Lévi-Straussian contrast of mechanical and statistical models (Lévi-Strauss 1963). The problem centers on the relations between social forms and appropriate acts. I raise the possibility, which seems rarely considered, that such relations are reversible: that customary kinds of acts can precipitate social forms as well as vice versa. For generally in the social sciences we give priority to the institutional forms over their associated practices, in this one direction only, the conduct of the parties concerned following from an existing relationship. Friendship engenders material aid: the relationship normally (as normatively) prescribes an appropriate mode of interaction. Yet if friends make gifts, gifts make friends; or it may be, as Eskimo say, "gifts make slaves—as whips make dogs." The cultural form (or social morphology) can be produced the other way round: the act creating an appropriate relation, performatively, just as in certain famous speech acts: "I now pronounce you man and wife."

Just so, in Hawaii one may *become* a "native," i.e., by right action. Having resided a certain time in the community, even strangers become 'children of the land' (*kama'āina*); the term is not exclusively reserved to the native-born. The example allows me to argue that the interchangeability between being and practice itself depends on communities of meaning, hence the determination in either direction is structurally motivated. An act of a given kind can signify a given status inasmuch as the two have the same final sense. For Hawaiians, to live and eat from a certain land makes a person one in substance with the land, in the same sense that a child is of his parents' substance (in Hawaii, by birth and by nurture). A stranger is thus metamorphosed into a child of the land by equal title to the people "born to" it (as we also might say). It follows that societies such as the Hawaiian—or the Eskimo, or our own—where many relationships are constructed by choice, desire, and interest, and through such aleatory means as love, are not for all that structureless, or even "loosely structured." The effects are systematic, whether the institutional arrangements are created "statistically" by proper action or the action is "mechanically" presupposed by the form.

Nevertheless, the performative and prescriptive structures would have different historicities. We could say that they are differentially "open" to history. The performative orders tend to assimilate themselves to contingent circumstances; whereas, the prescriptive rather assimilate the circumstances to themselves—by a kind of denial of their contingent or evenemential character. I have in mind an ideal contrast between Hawaii, where kinship, rank, property rights, and local affiliation are all open to negotiation, and the standard average Radcliffe-Brownian social structure of corporate descent groups, ascribed statuses, and prescriptive marriage rules (say, Australian Aboriginals). In the Hawaiian case, circumstantial happenings are often marked and valued for their differences, their departures from existing arrangements, as people may then act upon them to reconstruct their social conditions. As society thus organizes itself, it knows itself as the institutional form of historical events. But in a prescriptive mode, nothing is new, or at least happenings are valued for their similarity to the system as constituted. What happens, then, is the projection of the existing order: even when what happens is unprecedented, and whether the recuperative interpretation be successful or in vain. Here all is execution and repetition, as in the classic *pensée sauvage*. By comparison, the Hawaiian order is more active historically, in a double way. Responding to the shifting conditions of its existence—as of, say, production, population, or power—the cultural order reproduces itself in and as change. Its stability is a volatile history of the changing fortunes of persons and groups. But then, it is more likely to change as it so reproduces itself. This because, to express the issue in the most general way, the symbolic system is highly empirical. It continuously submits the received categories to worldly risks, the inevitable disproportions between signs and things; while at the same time, it licenses the historic subjects, notably the heroic aristocracy, to creatively and pragmatically construe the going values. Again in Lévi-Straussian terms, the historical temperature is relatively "hot."

As I say, performative and prescriptive structures are ideal types. Both can be found in the same society, in various local areas of the global order. This also implies that a given society will have certain strategic sites of historical action, evenementially hot areas, and other areas relatively closed. I do not pursue the idea any further in these essays. But perhaps enough is said to make the argument of different cultures, different historicities.

I also argue that events themselves bear distinctive cultural signatures. Captain Cook fell victim to the play of Hawaiian categories, or more precisely to their interplay with his own—which inadvertently led him into dangerous "risks of reference." So one might read chapter 4, "Captain James Cook; or The Dying God," wherein the famous navigator meets his end by transgressions of the ritual status the Hawaiians had accorded him. Originally the Frazer lecture (of 1982), the essay gives a lot of attention to the Hawaiian theory of divine kingship which, together with the British practice of imperialism, produced this "fatal impact." With some confidence, one can even offer a structural solution to the long-standing mystery of who done it?: the identity of Cook's assailant is deducible, in Holmesian fashion, from the elementary categories. In these several respects, the interest of the essay is the vexed problem of the relation between structure and event.

I take into account the usual understandings of accident and order in this relation: the contingency of events, the recurrence of structures. Either one would be insufficient by itself. It is not enough to know that Cook was the "instantiation" of certain cultural categories, any more than it suffices to know that he was suffering from intestinal parasites—which is the historical diagnosis recently offered by a prominent English physician. Yet I try to go beyond the vague idea of a dialectic between words and

worms by a twofold theoretical move. First by insisting that an
event is not simply a phenomenal happening, even though as a
phenomenon it has reasons and forces of its own, apart from
any given symbolic scheme. An event becomes such as it is interpreted. Only as it is appropriated in and through the cultural
scheme does it acquire an historical *significance*. There is no ex-
planatory adequacy between the accident to the *Resolution*'s foremast that brought Cook back to Hawaii, on one side, and the
sinister view the islanders took of all this, on the other—except
in the terms of Hawaiian culture. The event is a *relation* between
a happening and a structure (or structures): an encompassment
of the phenomenon-in-itself as a meaningful value, from which
follows its specific historical efficacy. (I return to this point in the
general discussion of the concluding chapter.) The other move,
perhaps more original, is to interpose between structure and
event a third term: the situational synthesis of the two in a "structure of the conjuncture."

By the "structure of the conjuncture" I mean the practical realization of the cultural categories in a specific historical context,
as expressed in the interested action of the historic agents, including the microsociology of their interaction. (My idea of a
structure of conjuncture thus differs from Braudel's in important
respects, even as it is reminiscent of Raymond Firth's distinction
of a *de facto* "social organisation" from the *de jure* or underlying
"social structure" [see note 11 of chapter 4; and Firth 1959].) It
also avoids the danger, implicit in our naïve phenomenology of
symbolic action (cf. above), of viewing the symbolic process
merely as a fancy version of the old opposition between individual and society. In the present instance, the conjunctural structure of British-Hawaiian contacts shows more complexities than
are allowed in previous treatments (e.g., Sahlins 1981), and it
seems to make Cook's fate more comprehensible. Yet beyond the
analysis of such unusual events, this notion of *praxis* as a situational sociology of meaning can be applied to the general understanding of cultural change. As a description of the social de-
ployment—and functional revaluation—of meanings in action,
it need not be restricted to circumstances of intercultural contact.
The structure of conjuncture as a concept has strategic value in
the determination of symbolic risks (e.g., of reference) and selective reifications (e.g., by the powers-that-be).

The Polynesian theory of divine kingship, or what is the same, the Polynesian theory of life, cosmic as well as social, is more fully discussed in the essay on "The Stranger-King" (chapter 3). Here I highlight the Hawaiian and other systems, especially the Fijian, by a comparison with Indo-European conceptions of sovereignty, invoking the celebrated studies of Dumézil, Frazer, and Hocart. Admittedly the comparison is typological (rather than genetic) and apparently far-fetched; and I would not have dared it had not Dumézil himself explicitly suggested it, in all probability from his reading of Hocart. On the other hand, the cartesian excursion—I mean Ho-cartesian, of course—by its emphasis on the ritual polity as a "life-giving" system, makes an interesting point about the temporal character of structure (diachrony).

If Hocart was a structuralist before the letter, his idea of structure (by my reading) was different from Saussure's. Notably it entails a departure from the Saussurean principle of system as a purely synchronic state, a set of mutually contrasting, thus mutually defining, relations between signs on the plane of simultaneity. For in their most abstract representation, which is cosmology, the categories are set in motion; they unfold through time in a global scheme of life-giving or cultural and natural reproduction. The structure has an internal diachrony, consisting in the changing relations between general categories or, as I say, a "cultural life of the elementary forms." In this generative unfolding, common to the Polynesian and Indo-European schemes, the basic concepts are taken through successive stages of combination and recombination, along the way producing novel and synthetic terms. So in the constitution of kingship and the cultural order, the dynastic heroes, initially male and stranger-invaders, are neutralized and "feminized" by the indigenous people. In the process, the people, originally the female reproductive cum earthly powers, are themselves transformed into a peripheral and protective masculine force. The transformations are mediated by the surrender of a native princess to the immigrant prince, which is alternatively the stranger's fructifying marriage to the earth, hence the neutralization of his dynastic successors as the female descent of the native people. And so on: the further development of the categories is followed out in chapter 4. My suggestion is that we should likewise incorporate the internal diachrony in our notions of "structure," and by so doing avoid certain logical difficulties of the Saussurean view, at least as the latter is commonly adapted to anthropological studies.

A strict Saussurean synchrony entangles us in famous "logical instabilities" of the cultural categories. The Fijian king appears both as male and female; his ritual and political nature is dual, or contextually one or the other. Taken as a synchronic and empirical description, there is little more to make of this: it seems a "permanent ambiguity" or "inherent contradiction" of the system. Yet from the standpoint of a diachronic structure, it is a derivative effect, both principled and logical. There is a more general notion of structure, necessarily temporal, by which the contradiction is at once resolved and rendered intelligible. We might have guessed as much anyhow on logical grounds, for if there is a recurrent ambiguity, there must be a consistent, noncontradictory way of stating this. The structure itself is not contradictory, though it repeatedly reproduces such empirical effects.

We can also then do away with the corollary problem developing in the current formulations of "structure" as extended lists of paired contraries or Saussurean proportions. I mean the tables that read: male is to female, as king is to people, culture is to nature, life to death, and so forth—yin-yang structuralism, without a Book of Changes. These proportions too are logically unstable and contradictable. From another vantage, the king is female rather than male and nature (ferocious outsider) rather than culture. The alternatives come down to this. We can try to develop the structure from (or as) the indefinite set of contextual permutations—in certain specifiable contexts, the king is male, in others female: not only an inelegant solution, but probably hopeless. Or, in contrast to this aporetic endeavor, we can conceive the structure the way it is in abstract cosmic schemes.

The latter solution is at least more powerful logically, since one can then account for the genesis of the contradictions precisely as partial or situational views on the global order, taken from some interested standpoint (either by the ethnographer or the people). It becomes clear that any given proportion (A:B: :C:D) is a partial and interested statement of the structure. It assumes some determinate spectator or subject in a determinate relation to the cultural totality. But the structure properly refers to that totality: it is itself the system of relations between categories, without a given subject (if not the famous transcendental subject). Nor is this conception without historical import. For if we put ourselves in the divine intellectual place of the transcendental subject, i.e., outside the system as commentator, we can see history working through the interested selection of social agents among the numerous logical possibilities—including contradictory possibilities—that are presented in any cultural order. Thus, for example, to return to the Cook essay (chapter 4). To the Hawaiian priests, Cook was always the ancient god Lono, even when he unexpectedly came back; whereas, to the king, the god who appears out of season becomes a dangerous rival. The two Hawaiian parties, out of their own self-conceptions, conceived different (proportional) relations in the same event, whence their own conflict in the structure of the conjuncture whose outcome was Cook's death.

Such are some of the general ideas of the essays to follow. In the final chapter, "Structure and History," I resume these broad understandings with the aim of reflecting critically on some of our own academic categories. I mean the radical binary contrasts by which culture and history are usually thought: past and present, static and dynamic, system and event, infrastructure and superstructure, and others of that intellectual, dichotomous ilk. These oppositions are not only phenomenally misleading, I conclude, but analytically debilitating. They are debilitating if only because other civilizations have better understood their synthesis, and in different ways thus synthesize their historical practice. We have to recognize theoretically, find the conceptual place of, the past in the present, the superstructure in the infrastructure, the static in the dynamic, change in stability.

Anthropology has something to contribute to the discipline of history. The converse also goes without saying. Yet I am not arguing simply for more collaboration between the disciplines. As I put it at one point, "the problem now is to explode the concept of history by the anthropological experience of culture." Nor again will the consequences be one-sided: an historical experience will as surely explode the anthropological concept of culture—structure included.

The reason this Introduction has been so long is that the several essays were written for different occasions, so I was not confident they had sufficient unity as a book. Primarily in the same interest of coherence, I have made some revisions of the pieces already published. Hopefully the redundancies have been reduced. (There are also some clarifications and corrections of the original versions.) Still, as a firmer guarantee of unity, might I suggest that the book be considered more like a cylinder than a linear projection?—that is, having gone through it, the reader could usefully return to this introductory section, which is also by way of a summary.

If there is nonetheless an implicit coherence, as I would like to believe, it is because the papers were written within a relatively short period and in a burst of enthusiasm over the discovery that peoples of the Pacific I had studied indeed had a history. Adopting the timeless stance of the common average "ethnographic present," a kind of occupational and theoretical hazard, I was for a long time functionally ignorant of this history. It is amusing now to read, in Evans-Pritchard no less, long the great and almost exclusive champion of the historical approach, the observation that social anthropologists, "so long as they were investigating such peoples as Australian aborigines or South Sea Islanders, who have no recorded history . . . could ignore history with an easy conscience" (1954:59). It was not an easy conscience but a false consciousness and, given the richness of the archival record, never so easily excusable. Nor do I now think that historians are entitled to ignore these exotic histories just because they are culturally remote and as recorded do not go very far back. On both scores, the histories of South Sea Islanders and other distant civilizations deserve special attention: the recency of the textual record may guarantee an archival abundance not always matched, for example, by medieval Europe; and the texts are wonderfully surprising precisely as they are culturally remote.

These essays will be published simultaneously (more or less) in France by Gallimard and Seuil, on behalf of L'École des Hautes Études en Sciences Sociales. Otherwise, two of the five are not previously published. All were originally written as invited lectures. The occasions were as follows:

Chapter 1, "Supplement to the Voyage of Cook; or, *le calcul sauvage*"; Marc Bloch Lecture, under the auspices of L'École des Hautes Études en Sciences Sociales, Paris, June 1981. (Previously unpublished.)

Chapter 2, "Other times, Other Customs: The Anthropology of History"; Distinguished Lecture of the American Anthropological Association, Washington D.C., December 1982. (Previously published in the *American Anthropologist* 85: 517–544, 1983 [not for further reproduction].)

Chapter 3, "The Stranger-King; or, Dumézil among the Fijians"; Presidential Address, Anthropology Section, Australia-New Zealand Association for the Advancement of Science, Adelaide, May 1980. (Previously published in the *Journal of Pacific History* 16:107–32, 1981.)

Chapter 4, "Captain James Cook; or, The Dying God"; Sir James G. Frazer Lecture, Liverpool University, May 1982. (Previously unpublished.)

Chapter 5, "Structure and History," The Edward Westermarck Lecture, Finnish Academy of Sciences, Helsinki, May 1983. (Previously published in *Suomen Antropologi* 3:118–27, 1983.)

I take the present occasion to warmly thank the people who were especially instrumental in arranging these lectures: M. François Furet, president of L'École des Hautes Études en Sciences Sociales; Mr. William Sturtevant, past-president of the American Anthropological Association; Messrs. Bruce Kaepferer and Chris Healey of Adelaide University; Messrs. J. D. Y. Peel and Neel Bowden of Liverpool University; Mr. Jukka Siikala of the Institute of Sociology in Finland.

There are also others who had vital roles in the writing of the lectures. I am especially grateful to Tina Jolas, Dorothy Barrère, and Greg Dening for their intellectual comfort and aid.

I

Supplement to the Voyage of Cook; or, *le calcul sauvage*

I. Venus Observed: History

7 December 1778. The *Resolution* and *Discovery* were beating against the wind off the north coast of Hawai'i Island.* On this day, Captain Cook finally relented and granted Hawaiian women the right to be loved that they had been demanding since the British first anchored at Kaua'i, January last, discovering these Sandwich Islands to the Western world. At Kaua'i, Cook had published orders prohibiting all intercourse with the local women, for fear of introducing the "Veneral Complaint." But the same pages of his journal that record these orders also convey Cook's sense of their futility (Beaglehole 1967:265–66).[1] Similar measures had already failed at Tonga, and the behavior of the Hawaiian women was even more scandalous. The invitation in their erotic gestures was "unmistakable," chroniclers of the voyage relate, and when refused they "abused us most sincerely" (King Journal: 20 Jan. 1778; cf. Riou Log: 28 Nov. 1779).

---

*In spellings of particular Hawaiian islands, I use the currently acceptable glottal stops ('); whereas, in reference to the archipelago as a whole or in adjectival uses I retain the anglicized Hawaii/Hawaiian. The procedure allows one more easily to distinguish the Hawaiian group from Hawai'i Island proper.

[1] Cook was, with reason, dubious of the ability of his doctors to determine when a man was sufficiently cured to prevent communication of "the Venereal," as well as of the inclinations of his sailors who had the disease to resist the advances of Polynesian women.

David Samwell—surgeon's mate, Welshman, and minor poet—
found "the Young Women . . . in general exceedingly beautiful." They "used all their arts," he said, "to entice our people
into their Houses, and finding [the sailors] were not to be al-
lured by their blandishments, they endeavoured to force them &
were so importunate they would absolutely take no denial" (in
Beaglehole 1967:1083).[2]
    The evidence of what had then transpired was quickly made
known to the British when they returned to the Islands from
Northwest America. At Maui—separated from the events at
Kaua'i by ten months, several islands, and over two hundred
nautical miles—a number of Hawaiian men applied to the ships'
surgeons in great distress: "They had a Clap, their Penis was
much swelled and inflamed" (King in Beaglehole 1967:498).[3] As-

_____

[2] Samwell goes on to say that "it was known that some of those who were on
shore had intercourse with the Women" (Beaglehole 1967:1083). Besides, a party
of about twenty men under Lt. Gore was stranded for two nights and a day on
the island of Ni'ihau, near Kaua'i, during which time there was, almost certainly,
connection between the British and Hawaiian women. Mr. Thomas Edgar, master
of the _Discovery_, credits reports he heard of how at Kaua'i the sailors managed to
smuggle women aboard, despite the officers' surveillance: they dressed the Hawaiian women as men and called them their "Tios" (Log: 24 Jan. 1778). If true,
the men succeeded by employing a kaleidoscopic display of cultural impres-
sions: the English seamen would have deceived their officers by using a Tahitian
concept of 'bond friend' (_tio_), unknown however to their Hawaiian paramours.
For notices of Hawaiian women's importunities during Cook's first visit to
Kaua'i/Ni'ihau (19 Jan.–2 Feb. 1778), see among others: Burney (Journal: 2 Feb.
1778), Samwell (in Beaglehole 1967:1084–85), Zimmermann (1930:68), Clerke
(in Beaglehole 1967:597), and Cook and King (1784, 2:130–31). Hawaiian traditions of this visit unanimously claim that the women's overtures were accepted
by the British (Remy 1861–21; Fornander 1969, 2:162–63; S. Kamakau 1961:94 f).
On the tradition that Captain Cook slept with a Kaua'i ranking woman, see below, note 4.
    The women's amorous demands were repeated during Cook's second visit in
late 1778–early 1779 (e.g., Cook in Beaglehole 1967:265–66; Samwell in Beaglehole 1967:1151, 1152, 1158 et passim; Cook and King 1784, 2:544, 3:10–11;
Ledyard 1963:107–9; Ellis 1782, 2:76, 86, etc.).
    [3] On examination by the _Discovery_'s doctors, eight of twelve men in Hawaiian
canoe met off Maui were determined to have "the Venereal" (Burney Journal: 26
Nov. 1778). A few days later, Mr. King reports that three of ten or twelve Hawaiian men aboard the _Resolution_ were similarly afflicted (Beaglehole 1967:300). The
Oxford English Dictionary specifically determines "clap" as gonorrhea, and cites
an 1803 usage, "a clap," like Mr. King's; hence the possible diagnostic confusion
between syphilis and yaws is apparently not pertinent here.

tonished by the possibility that the disease could spread so rapidly, many of Cook's people refused to believe the Hawaiian allegations that they had been its authors. Still, as surgeon Ellis later reflected, "no people in the world . . . indulge their sexual appetites as much as these" (1782, 2:153). Captain Cook, in any event, now gave up the pretense of a discipline he was powerless to enforce on anyone but himself.[4] By the time the *Resolution* reached the south coast of Hawaii, he was complaining of the difficulty of working the ship with so many women about. Samwell had no complaints: just a wave of the hand, he said, could bring a "handsome Girl" to the deck, "like another Venus just rising from the Waves"; and when the British finally anchored at Kealakekua Bay, "there was hardly one of us that may not vie with the grand Turk himself" (Beaglehole 1967:1154, 1159).

Le'a is the Hawaiian word for it.[5] It is not just the famous *aloha*. *Aloha* can refer to the beloved, but its meaning extends to *pitié* in the Rousseauean sense, the sympathy we feel for the suffering of any sensible being, especially those like ourselves. In this sense, *aloha* suggests a kinship of substance with the other, and a giving without thought of immediate returns. But *le'a* is passion rather than compassion: a relation between beings who are complementary in nature and who—as in a certain famous

[4]There is no empirical substance to the later Hawaiian tradition that Captain Cook slept with the sacred Kaua'i woman, Lelemahoalani, daughter of the ranking chiefess of the Island (Remy 1861:19–21; S. Kamakau 1961:94–96; Fornander 1969, 2:168–69). On the other hand, there is considerable cultural substance to the allegation, insofar as Cook was taken for the annual god of fertility Lono who—as several legendary chiefs also so identified—returns to seek his lost wife (= inseminate the land, cf. chap. 4, below). Hawaiian tradition itself offers such explanation for presenting the native princess to Cook. The dignity which Cook gave himself as a British naval commander rather accords with Hawaiian conceptions of his status, only that it would lead him to a different response to the offer of a chiefly woman. According to Zimmermann, Cook was not much one for divine services and rarely conducted them aboard ship, yet neither would he tolerate any cleric on his vessels (Zimmermann 1930:99–100). Nor was he about to yield to the temptations of the flesh, though quite prepared to allow the lesser ranks to thus make display of their mortal weakness (Beaglehole 1974:390–91). Evidently, there could be only one *Authority* on board a vessel of His Majesty's Navy. Hence if the Hawaiians really did present their sacred woman to Captain Cook because he was a god, we can be sure he refused her—for something like the same reason.

[5]An excellent discussion of *le'a* and Hawaiian sexuality in general may be found in Pukui et al. (1972, 2 [1979]); I have relied considerably upon it.

paradigm of good socialism as good sex—gratify themselves in gratifying each other. The dictionary entry for *le'a* is virtually a poem, and perhaps will help convince you that we are dealing with Hawaiian history, not European fantasy. *Le'a*: "joy, pleasure, happiness, merriment: sexual gratification, orgasm; pleasing, delightful, happy, merry," etc. The causative *ho'ole'a* means 'to extol' or 'praise', as in 'Praise the Lord' (*ho'ole'a i ke Akua*)— which is what Hawaiian women were doing on Cook's ships. *Le'a* also denotes something done thoroughly, as in 'thoroughly cooked' (*mo'a le'a*)—which, in a Polynesian way, is also what they were doing.

The first men who came off to the *Resolution* at Kaua'i in January 1778 had made incantations, apparently to consecrate themselves, before boarding. One of them, in open view of the British, then proceeded to carry off the first thing that came to hand, the ship's sounding line. Halted by bourgeois counterincantations of sacred property rights, he said he was merely taking it to his canoe. Everything transpired as if centuries of Hawaiian sacrifice had finally paid off.[6] And also as if the historical event were the metaphor of a mythical reality. When the English anchored next year at Kealakekua, Hawaiian priests were able to objectify their interpretation of Cook as the Year-God Lono, on his annual return to renew the fertility of the land. In a famous scene at the principal temple, the Great Navigator was made to hold his arms outstretched in imitation of the crosspiece image of Lono, while the priests made the customary offerings.[7] Two

---

[6]Reflecting on the Hawaiians' initial disposition to take from the British whatever came to hand, Cook wrote, "They thought they had a right to everything they could lay their hands upon." But, he adds, "they soon laid aside a conduct, which, we convinced them, they could not persevere in with impunity" (Cook and King 1784, 2:205). Midshipman Gilbert likewise remarked that the Hawaiians "very leisurely" and "without any scruple or hesitation" carried off what they could, and when the British took the things back, "they seemed greatly surprised . . . for they could not believe that we were in earnest but imagined that we would allow them to take what they chose" (Narrative: Jan. 1778). For analogous incidents and comments on the initial moments of contact between Hawaiians and English see King (Log: 20 Jan. 1778), Cook and King (1784, 2:195), Clerk (in Beaglehole 1967:1322), and Dibble (1909:23).

[7]The similarity (or identity) between the rituals Cook was subjected to at Hikiau temple (and elsewhere) and the hānaipū ceremony by which ranking chiefs welcome Lono on his annual procession is discussed in Sahlins (1981; cf. chap. 4, where other details of the New Year or Makahiki ceremonies are also noticed).

years running Cook had made his advent during the Makahiki, New Year festival of Lono, in the classic Frazerian mode of the dying god. As we shall see in a later chapter (4), Cook obliged the Hawaiians by playing the part of Lono to its fatal end.

In the New Year rituals, Lono's regeneration of nature is also symbolized as a sacred marriage, a search for his forsaken wife: beautiful chiefess of ancient lineage who had been captured by a political upstart to sire the succession of living kings. Now at Kealakekua, Samwell had remarked that "the Young Women spend most of their time in singing and dancing, of which they are very fond" (Beaglehole 1967:1181). The allusion is to the famous hula, a dance considered blasphemous for its eroticism by later American missionaries, which is just what made it religious for the Hawaiians (cf. Barrère et al. 1980). It was a practice especially of the New Year. The patron of the dance was Laka, known in ancient chant as sister and wife to Lono (Emerson 1965:24). The hula would sexually arouse the returning god of cosmic reproduction, if it did not more directly signify the copulation of Lono with the living daughters of the goddess. One could say, then, that the sexual practices of Laka's *devotées* aboard Cook's ships were just a change of register. Meanwhile, as Fornander remarks, the British seamen were faithful to the complementary and inverse creed of the buccaneers, that "there is no God this side of Cape Horn" (Fornander 1969, 2:163). The women offered themselves because they thought there was a god, and the sailors took them because they had forgotten it.

4 March 1779. The British ships are again at Kaua'i, their last days in the Islands, some thirteen months since their initial visit. A number of Hawaiian men come on board and under the direction of their women, who remain alongside in the canoes, the men deposit the navel cords of newborn children in cracks of the ships' decks (Beaglehole 1967:1225).[8]

[8]For an analogous behavior observed by the missionary Fison on the Polynesian island of Rotuma, see Frazer (1911, 1:184). Hawaiians are connected to ancestors (aūmakua), as well as to living kinsmen and descendants, by several cords emanating from various parts of the body but alike called *piko*, 'umbilical cord'. In this connection, Mrs. Pukui discusses the incident at Kaua'i:

> "I have seen many old people with small containers for the umbilical cords . . . One grandmother took the cords of her four grandchildren and dropped them into *Alenuihaha* channel, 'I want my granddaughters to travel across the sea!' she told me."

Hommages à Diderot. In the end he was able to put aside his utilitarian explanations of an analogous Tahitian sexuality for one that could perceive in the calculus of practice the premises of a Polynesian theogamy. The *Supplément au voyage de Bougainville* would do as well for Cook. Almost everything the sage Orou says to the naïve French chaplain echoes the words and deeds recorded in the chronicles of Cook at Hawaii:

> More robust and healthier than you, we perceived at first glance that you surpassed us in intelligence, and on the spot we selected several of our most beautiful women and daughters to harvest the seed of a race better than our own. It is a trial that we have made and that could work out to our benefit. We have taken from you and yours the only advantage we could take, and believe me, altogether savage as we are, we also know how to calculate (Diderot 1972 [1772/80]:459–60).

But the Hawaiian women's transcendental calculus of love was not something the British could understand. Neither did it at first merit the title of "prostitution" it was soon destined to receive. The women "were but little influenced by interested motives in their intercourse with us," runs a characteristic journal entry, "as they would almost use violence to force you into their Embrace regardless whether we gave them anything or not" (Beaglehole 1967:1085).[9] Yet the British seamen knew how to repay the services done them; more precisely, they reified the women's embraces as "services" by the gifts they made in return. With transactions such as these, the erotic commerce ceased to repeat tradition and began to make history.

Mrs. Pukui believes that the story of women hiding their babies' *pikos* in Captain Cook's ship is probably true.

"Cook was first thought to be the god Lono, and his ship his 'floating island'. What woman wouldn't want her baby's *piko* there?" (Pukui et al. 1972, 1:184).

[9] "No women I ever met with were less reserved. Indeed, it appeared to me, that they visited us with no other view, than to make a surrender of their persons" (Cook and King 1784, 2:544). "The ladies are very lavish of their favours, but are far from being so mercenary as those of the Friendly [Tongan] or Society Islands, and some of their attachments seem purely the effect of affection" (Ellis 1782, 2:153).

The goods in supply among the British were quickly factored by Hawaiian social demands into men's things and women's things. Pieces of iron and iron tools such as adzes were men's goods. The male category was productive, and the female attractive: bead bracelets, scissors, and the mirrors women wore as necklaces and with which (European travelers remarked for decades) they rarely ceased to regard themselves. (In a comedy by Giraudoux of the same title as this piece, a Tahitian woman consoles her daughter with the observation that: "A mirror is always useful, *ma fille*, even if it doesn't reflect England.") The apparent sexual differences are as Hawaiian values complementary, and resolved in a common finality. They are interrelated modes of human reproduction—which, besides, engage men and women in a common opposition to the divine. For the man the promethean task of wresting the substance of humanity from its divine owners in the form of food. For the woman to attract and transform the divine generative forces—not excluding chiefs with land—into the substance of humanity in the form of children. So also sociologically, Hawaiians knew two alternate ways of creating the relationship of childhood: by 'feeding' or *hānai* (usually glossed as 'adoption') and by birth. It is thus not remarkable that men and women of the people immediately developed a common interest in each other's traffic with the British; or that their own common interest put them in opposition to the Hawaiian powers-that-be.

Men brought their sisters, daughters, perhaps even their wives to the ships. Call it hospitality. Or call it spiritual hypergamy. The sailors showed their gratitude by giving the men iron adzes, beside what they gave the women (Beaglehole 1967: 1152–53, 1182). At the same time, the British trading with Hawaiian men for provisions found these demanding at least part payment in bracelets for their women. A notice of the rates of exchange suggests the relative values Hawaiians were putting on things: a pig that would normally cost the British three good adzes could be had for only one if a woman's bracelet were included in the price (Ellis 1782, 2:158).[10]

[10] For other notices of the relation between Hawaiian women's and men's trade in the early years of European contact, see Portlock (1789:159), Puget (Log: 21 Feb. 1793), Manby (1929 1[1]:14). The domestic traffic in women's services continued into the missionary period:

The rest, as they say, is history. The collective interest in trade developed among men and women of the people set them as a class against their chiefs, whose own interests ran to the goods of status and politics. It also set the people against the tabu system. The chiefs instituted tabus to control and engross the trade on their own behalf—practice not inconsistent spiritually with the *mana* they stood to gain. There were also customary tabu periods each month, when chiefs and priests were in the temples; the sea was then interdicted, and the people supposedly confined to their domestic establishments. But the common people showed themselves willing to transgress the tabus of every kind, defiance in which they were sometimes encouraged by the Europeans (Sahlins 1981).

For on board the ships, the sailors were drawing Hawaiian women into their own conceptions of domestic tranquillity. They invited their lovers to sup, on such foods as pork, bananas, and coconuts. So did the women doubly violate the strictest Hawaiian tabus on intersexual dining. Customarily, men's meals were taken in communion with ancestral gods, and these very foods were the sacrifice, hence at all times prohibited to women. The participation of the women would defile the sacrifier, the offering, and, for that matter, the god. But then, the food tabus never sat on the women with the same force they had for men, being rather the negative imprint of the men's consecration. On the other hand, the Hawaiian *logic* of tabu remained in force on board the ships, with this effect: it consumed the divinity of the foreigner. As men who ate with women, the British soon found themselves desecrated, polluted. They were secularized, and an ethnic cleavage set in between Hawaiians and Europeans that

---

The natives [in eastern Kaua'i] though poor are kind even to extremes; they usually set before us the best of their food, and as a mark of respect the Husband offers his wife, the Father his daughter, and the Brother his sister. We told them there is a God in Heaven who has forbidden such iniquity; they say it is good, but you are strange white men (Whitney Journal: 27 May 1820).

In Cook's time, however, the domestic solidarity of exchange was not complete; there are two notices (Trevenen *MS*; Beaglehole 1967:1227) of women keeping iron tools destined for their men and using them to exchange with other Hawaiians (men or women?) for cloth or feather leis.

was not envisioned, for example, by that Hawaiian who first carried off the *Resolution*'s sounding line. In the ensuing decades, Captain Cook alone was able to preserve his divinity—since the Hawaiians had already sacrificed him. But when Vancouver arrived at Kealakekua fourteen years after Cook, King Kamehameha solemnly requested that none of the English be allowed to enter any Hawaiian temple, lest it be defiled. By contrast, Cook's own people had freely used the principal temple as a place to repair their sails, recruit their sick, and bury their dead. When Vancouver left, King Kamehameha went into seclusion to purify himself because, he explained, "of his having lived in such social intercourse with us, who had eaten and drunk in the company of women" (Vancouver 1801, 3:222). So was the course of history orchestrated by the logic of culture.

There is in all this another essay on the dialectics of structure and practice in the history of the Sandwich Islands. But I have already written about that (Sahlins 1981). I invoke this history here mainly to suggest the role that love has had in making it. The questions it then leads to are again historical and structural. How are we to understand this remarkable expression of eroticism in Hawaii? As a "pattern of culture" it seems worthy of comparison with the militarism of Sioux Indians or the quietism of the Hopi—dare one place an "Aphrodisian" alongside the famous "Dionysian" and "Apollonian"? Beyond that, the Hawaiian order is appropriately placed in that whole family of cultures, including our own, which prefer to sediment structural relations out of pragmatic actions, rather than determining the actions *a priori* from the relations. Here is a serious matter for social thought. For, unable so far to develop any theory of these systems beyond the statistical and the practical, anthropology has risked excluding them from the meaningful and the cultural.

II. Venus Again Observed: The Ethnography of Love

One should respect the observation made by the British that the women who flew precipitously into the arms of the English seamen were not of the highest rank (Cook and King 1784, 3:30–31). On the other hand, within the context of traditional Hawaiian society, the erotic interest knew no such limitations of class

or sex. It engaged men as well as women, chiefs as well as commoners. There was wife-capture as well as husband-capture,
hypogamy as well as hypergamy, homosexuality as well as het-
erosexuality. Famous ruling chiefs were bisexual, but the preoccupation with sex was expressed as much in the virginity en-
joined on certain young persons as in the liberties granted to
others. Sociologically, love was a decisive principle of the form
(or formlessness) of the family, as of its division of labor. It was a
favored means of access to power and property. Rank and tabu
might be gained or lost by it. Indeed, popular heterosexual games
of chance were played for it. Children, at least of the elite, were
socialized in the arts of love. Girls were taught the 'amo'amo the
'wink-wink' of the vulva, and the other techniques that "make
the thighs rejoice." Young chiefs were sexually initiated by older
women, preparing them thus for the sexual conquests that singularly mark a political career: the capture of a senior ancestry.
And all this, of course, was celebrated not only in the flesh, but
in dance, poetry, and song.

What a place for puritanical American missionaries! One of
them complained that Hawaiians had about twenty forms of
what he considered illicit intercourse, with as many different
names in the language; so that if any one term were selected to
translate the Seventh Commandment, it was bound to leave the
impression that the other nineteen activities were still permitted
(Andrews 1836:390–91). The solution was an *ad hoc* phrase, *moe
kolohe*; hence, the vagueness of the Lord's word in Hawaii: "Thou
shalt not sleep [about] mischievously." I am unable to catalog
all twenty of the relevant forms. Sufficient here to take brief
notice of certain public expressions of eroticism in art and the
social order, with a view toward confirming Rudyard Kipling's
dictum that:

> There are nine and sixty ways of constructing tribal lays,
> And every single one of them is right.

A paean to cultural relativism full of transcultural puns and
the hidden meanings in which Hawaiians delight! "Lay": in English, a verse sung and slang for sexual intercourse; the hom-
onymous *lei* of Hawaiian is a wreath of intertwined flowers, and

'flower' (*pua*) is common metaphor for the beloved.[11] Thus the mid-nineteenth-century song, "Hot Fire":

> My flower desired
> For me to braid and bind
> An elegant lei
> For evening time . . .

> Chorus

> Hot fire here within,
> The act of love
> Overpowers my body,
> Throbbing last night.

> Two of us
> Have known the power,
> Peaceful relaxing,
> Making love within my body
> (Elbert and Mahoe 1970:28–29)[12]

The cooling and peace of love appear in another famous song of the era, the title phrase variously translated "We two in the spray," or "You and I, then, for an outburst" (Emerson 1965: 166–67). The last may help explain why the song is nowadays presented to tourists as a Hawaiian war chant. The operative word, *huahua'i*, 'to gush forth' or 'spray' is also 'the sexual climax',

> We two in the spray (*huahua'i*),
> Oh joy two together,
> Embracing tightly in the coolness . . .
> (Elbert and Mahoe 1970:62)

I am following a line of metonymy on peace and coolness that leads, by a logic that seems perfectly Hawaiian, to a song written

[11] I will not pursue further the "nine and sixty ways." And I hope you will pardon me for serving as a (*pauvre*) *esprit* in which *les catégories se pensent*.

[12] The Hawaiian text appears in Elbert and Mahoe (1970); other accessible collections of Hawaiian songs include Emerson (1965); Roberts (1926); and Pukui and Korn (1973).

by King Kalakaua, ostensibly in praise of "the royal liquid"—
gin:

> I throb,
> I throb for liquid,
> I throb for cool liquid . . .
>
> Finally I have known
> Twofold peace;
> We two in peace,
> Liquid splattering on the cliff.
> (*Ibid*.:68)

Hawaiians have special categories of love song (*mele ipo*, *mele aloha*). But it is truly difficult (especially for a foreigner) to determine what a love song is, because it is almost impossible to say
what is not a love song. The oral literature is pregnant with *kaona*, 'hidden meanings', frequently erotic. It is a game all Hawaiians play, often more deftly than Western psychoanalysts, and
the point I make of it is accordingly cosmological rather than
Freudian.[13] If almost anything can remind the Hawaiians of sex

---

[13] Elbert has pointed out that the small number of phonemes and large number
of homonyms and near-homonyms in the Hawaiian language make a specially
fertile field for punning and 'hidden meanings' (*kaona*). On the latter subject,
Pukui et al. (1972:85–86) write:

> Where sexual jokes were concerned, Hawaiians had a natural advan-
> tage. They had always used euphemism, allusion and metaphor in
> their speech. They had a natural aptitude for grasping the *kaona*, the
> "hidden meaning" of a word or phrase. . . . Set to music after the West-
> erners came, the *mele* took full advantage of metaphor. Does the song
> about "Beautiful Kaua'i" really describe an island? Or a beautiful
> woman? Is one really singing about *maka* (the sight [cf. below, the dis-
> cussion of the eye]), of *ka palai* (the ferns) on the moist island? Or of
> *makamaka* (the intimate woman friend) and of her 'ferns' now well
> moistened? Does the song "*Ālika*" tell only of a ship by that name that
> progressed with initial difficulty through a "cold, narrow strait?"
> . . . as Mrs. Pukui puts it, "When the Hawaiians all start giggling,
> then you know it means something else" (Pukui et al. 1972, 2:85–86).

Conversely, not all love songs explicitly so called were devoted to what West-
erners would consider proper objects of such affection. Here are some excerpts
from a composition written about 1860 (AH, Collection of *Meles*) entitled "*He*

is it not because, at least as a condition of possibility, the universe of persons and objects is already charged with immense forces of semantic attraction? The universe is a genealogy, which is to say a total cosmological project of sexual reproduction. This continuity of descent between natural, supernatural, and human beings is what distinguished the Polynesian conceptual scheme, in Lévi-Strauss's view (1963), from the so-called totemism. In a common Maori cosmogony, the original beings are abstract concepts of generation, beginning with *Nothingness* and descending genealogically through such as *Pregnancy*, *Mind*, *Thought*, and *Desire* to arrive at Heaven and Earth (cf. Best 1976 [1924]. Sky Father or Heaven (Rangi) then unites with Earth Mother (Papa) and the gods are born. Tāne the god unites with different female elements to give rise to certain natural phenomena and species. Tāne then unites with the first woman, fash-

---

Mele Aloha i ka Na'auao," 'A Love Song to Wisdom'. It also illustrates the penchant for *kaona*:

E ka na'auao, e aloha 'oe	Oh wisdom, love to you,
Kaikamahine 'ūhā nemonemo . . .	Girl with the smooth and round thighs . . .
'Akahi au a ike i ka lomi a ke aloha,	This is the first time I have known the squeeze of love,
Ke oni kapalili la i ka wai o Pukaiki,	Trembling there in the water of Pukaiki [lit., 'Small-Hole']
Kula ke pene i ka la'i o Wainiha luna,	Swift is thrusting in the peace of upper Wainiha [lit., 'Unfriendly-Water']
Mamau pipili papa'a ka wai o Paulike. . .	The water of Paulike [lit., 'Finish-Together'] is unceasing, sticky and tight . . .
Kekahi nō 'oe o ka'u mea i aloha ai	You are the one that I love,
E kū wiwili ho'omamau nei o ke kulu'aumoe . . .	Restlessly embracing, continually in the late night . . .
Naue aku kaūa o ka wai hu'ai pa'u o Namolokama	We two tremble in the moist, gushing waters of Nāmolokama [a mountain on Hanalei, Kaua'i, lit., 'The Interweaving-Bound-Fast']
'O ia wai kahea noi ka ihu o ka moku,	This water calls out to the prow of the boat
E ka na'auao, e aloha ke 'oe,	Oh wisdom, love indeed to you. (Translation, Lili K. Dorton)

ioned of the Earth Mother, and human beings are produced. (We shall return to these Maori ideas in subsequent chapters.) The Hawaiian creation chants (such as the well-known Kumulipo) are similar, except that the Illuminated Sky (Wakea) and Terrestrial Stratum (Papa) are primordial humans (Malo 1951). Sky (Wakea) lives with his own daughter to sire, first, the taro plant, secondly, the progenitor of chiefs; subsequent children of the highly incestuous original family are the several classes of Hawaiian society; or, in certain versions closer to Maori, the children are the Hawaiian Islands.

Because this is a system of common descent, the semantic relations between the several planes of cosmos and society are not metaphoric only, or merely metonymic in the sense of a physical contiguity. Descent in Polynesian thought is a logic of formal classes: the ancestor is to his descendants as a general class is to its particular instances. The offspring are tokens of the parent type. The system, then, is a veritable ontology, having to do with commonalities and differentiations of substance. Relations logically constructed from it—e.g., heavens are to earth as chiefs to people—are expressions of the essence of things. Hence the relations and deeds of primordial concepts as represented in myth become, for the persons descended of such concepts, the paradigms of their own historical actions. Every Hawaiian union recapitulates the original congress of male heavens and female earth, and what is born of chiefly parents is another god. The genealogical scheme thus serves the *pensée étatique* as "totemism" functions in the *pensée sauvage*. All the necessary operations of classification, transformation, and instantiation are inherently entailed in it. Sex, as Hocart says somewhere, is the sign of sex. Hawaiians can see it everywhere about them because it is already lying there.

Consider the 'hidden meaning' (*kaona*) of the inscription above the entrance to the Honolulu Board of Water Supply:

Uwe ka lani, ola ka honua
'The heavens weep, the earth lives'.

Unlikely that the *haole* ('white men') and Japanese who now dominate the Hawaiian bureaucracy are aware that this anodyne snippet of pastoral poesy refers to a primordial copulation (cf. Elbert 1962). More, the proverb is a condensed symbol of the history and poetry we have just resumed. The male seed of natural and divine origin is absorbed by the woman and transformed into human substance: again, a spiritual hypergamy. Yet in the event, "the heavens weep." This may be the idea in the peace and coolness of sexual intercourse, a neutralization of the hot and raw passion of the male by the female. Still another meaning is on the Hawaiian surface-of-things, since 'the heavenly one' (*ka lani*) is the commonplace epithet of 'the chief.' Which brings us to another art form that readers of *Anti-Oedipe* will not fail to recognize as the central pillar of the political ideology: the genital chants of the Hawaiian aristocracy.

The social distribution of genital chants (*mele ma'i*) probably extended beyond the chiefs proper (*ali'i*) into respectable families of the countryside (Pukui et al. 1972, 1:76–77, 84–85).[14] But the famous surviving examples are hymns of praise to certain royal genitalia. Accompanied by hula, such chants "were the traditional conclusion of a formal presentation of dances honoring the chief" (Barrère et al. 1980:21). Still, for all Hawaiians the genitals are a person's "precious possessions." Covering them with clothing is not explained by reference to modesty or shame, but as the protection of one's valuables. Clearly a secondary formation, the explanation should be taken for what it is worth, which is plenty—and a nice contrast again to the views of the missionaries, who thought people ought to wear clothing as a covering to their "deformity." The earliest recorded chants in the Hawaiian language, collected by Samwell during Cook's voyage, were of the *mele ma'i* type. Here is the shorter (perhaps a fragment) of two obtained by Samwell—

[14] Mrs. Pukui says that genital chants were widely distributed among the people. It is particularly difficult, however, to determine the social distribution, since in name at least, the form was suppressed in the Christian era (from 1820). A modern Hawaiian dancer and student of *mele ma'i* writes:

> Early on Hawaiians learned not to discuss sex openly, particularly in regard to hula, which was soundly denounced by missionaries and other upstanding *haole* (white men) in Honolulu in the 19th century. As Hawaiians became increasingly acculturated, they ceased to discuss *mele ma'i* even among themselves, or at least [they discussed them] only in very private groups. For instance as students in the *hālau* [dance school] we were taught to dance *mele ma'i* but were rarely told what the chant meant or what its function was. Hawaiians did not do away with them altogether, however, they merely changed their

An *ule* [penis], an *ule* to be enjoyed:
Don't stand still, come gently,
That way, all will be well here,
Shoot off your arrow.[15]

Chants of praise (or enticement), as well as proper names, were often bestowed upon the chiefs' precious parts more by way of anticipation than in recognition of mature exploits, since males and females both were so honored at the time of birth. Queen Lili'uokalani's chant sings of "frisky, frolicking genitals that go up and down" (Pukui et al. 1972, 2:85). Her brother King Kalākaua was endowed with Hālala, 'enormous [sexual equipment]' in the celebrated chant, "Your lively *ma'i* ['genitalia']":

> Your lively *ma'i*
> That you are hiding—
> Show the big thing,
> *Hālala*, to the many birds.
> (Elbert and Mahoe 1970:67)

The genital chant still sung and danced in honor of the great Kamehameha (died 1819) is called "The birds are nesting." The song is also notable for its final, attributive phrase, identifying Kamehameha with Kūnui'ākea—the god (image) of human sacrifice:

> Punana ka manu i Hāili la,   The birds are nesting at
> Ka nu'a lehua i mokaulele la   Haili,
> Aia ko ma'i i lehua la ea . . .   The lehua flowers are piled
> He ma'i no Kúnui'ākea.   thick at Mokaulele,
>   There are your genitals in
>   the lehua flavor . . .
>   A genital chant for
>   Kūnui'ākea.
>   (Dorton 1981)[16]

classification to *mele inoa*, 'name chants', or to *mele aloha*, 'love songs' (Dorton 1981; I am particularly indebted to this excellent work).

[15]Samwell recorded the chants phonetically (according to his lights). They were transcribed in modern Hawaiian orthography and translated by Mary Kawena Pukui for J. C. Beaglehole (1967:1234 n). However, *ule*, 'penis' remains in Hawaiian in the published translation.

[16]By internal evidence, this chant was at least modified in Christian times,

Où regne la beauté, la reine est belle. The ideal beauty of the chief is counterpart of his or her ideal potency—and we are speaking, of course, of ideals. The high chief is "divine," as we should say ourselves: huge, fattened, skin lightened by protection from the sun, body glistening with perfumed oil, bedecked in the dazzling feather cape that is the treasure of his kingdom. And why not generate a kingdom on such a fundament? Existing only in the eye of the beholder, beauty is necessarily a social relationship. As a force of attraction that can compel an exchange in testimony to a desire, beauty may even serve as the functional equivalent to a norm of reciprocity. Many Oceanic societies thus employ the aesthetic at the boundaries of the moral: in the relationships beyond the control of kinship right or obligation. The beauty of persons and objects comes into play at the peripherae of constituted groups and the interstices of moral orders: as in supplications of the god or of the trading partner; or in feasts exchanged between tribes of strangers (cf. Guidieri 1973). But in Hawaii, beauty is placed as it were at the center of society, as a main principle of its organization.

Here the beautiful functions as a natural paradigm of the political. Magnetically fixing the gaze of the multitude upon its possessor, the unique beauty of the chief institutes a relation of attraction and coherence that is not only centered or hierarchical, but makes the *subordination of those who behold it an act of love.* The name of the political relationship in Hawaii is *aloha. Aloha,* 'love,' is the people's consciousness of their servitude. It is how they describe their obligations and justify their loyalties to the chief. Reciprocally, the chief should have *aloha* for his people. But it is in several senses a play on the word. The chief should show compassion, *pitié;* but as singularly endowed with a divine beauty, he is the privileged object of a universal affection. Ha-

---

since there is also a play on sounds and dance gestures that involves recitation of the vowels of the alphabet. Nevertheless the association between genital prowess and human sacrifice (also, the divinity of the chief—see text below) remains strong. I am told by a modern hula master that Kūnui'ākea, name of the god of human sacrifice, was also a name of Kamehameha's genitals. The image of the god is fashioned from the *'ohia lehua* tree, the flowers of which stand for 'vagina' in the chant. Lili Dorton writes that the *lehua* flower "is a symbolic vagina because it is a very soft, furry flower, red in color, and rather resembling a powder puff. It falls apart when shaken too much." *Pūnana,* 'bird's nest', is another common term in genital chants, still in use today as jargon for 'vagina'.

waiians refer to their chiefs by numerous variations on a theme of sentimentality, whose refrains seem disingenuous to no one's ears but our own: "the precious one," "the beloved one," "the cherished one."

Also, most commonly, "the heavenly one" (*ka lani*). The specific quality of aristocratic beauty is a brilliance and luminosity that Hawaiians do not fail to connect, in myth, rite, and chant, with the sun. Such beauty is properly called divine, for like the gods themselves, it causes things to be seen. Hence, the connection with the chiefs' sexual potency, which on the human plane has the same creative effect. Here is a text in point from a well-known myth, the story of Kila, son of Mo'ikeha. The hero is about to do battle with his father's younger brother Makali'i. The prize of their contest is the beautiful chiefess Lu'ukia, sequestered in the land of Kahiki where Makali'i is king. Kila will win the battle and take the woman, who was once his father's wife. The passage describes Kila at the moment of his advent at Kahiki:

> At sight of Kila, the crowd began to shout, admiring his beauty. Even the ants were heard to sing in his praise; the birds sang, the pebbles rumbled, the shells cried out, the grass withered, the smoke hung low, the rainbow appeared, the thunder was heard, the dead came to life, the hairless dogs were seen and countless spirits of all kinds were seen. All these things mentioned were the people of Moikeha, who upon the arrival of Kila his son, caused themselves to be seen, in testimony of Kila's high-chief rank (Fornander 1916–19, 4:168).

The cosmos reveals itself to Kila's beauty. Man, nature, and even spirits become visible in his light: which is to say, in the political capacity of subjects. We are probably close to the essence of *mana*, though the power of the Hawaiian concept is such that I hesitate to touch it myself. Enough to notice that the effects of *mana* are mediated by the gaze. The eye is the symbolic site of subjection. Valeri observes that: "The two sentiments that permit the transcendence of the self are, according to Hawaiians, desire and respect. One and the other are called *kau ka maka*, literally, 'to set one's eyes on'" (Valeri: in press). 'To see' (*ike*) in Hawaiian (as in French or English) is 'to understand', but it is also 'to know sexually'. Witness to the order, the world of forms generated by the chief, the eye, then, is the sacrifice of those who violate that order. The left eye of the slain tabu-transgressor is swallowed by Kahoali'i, ceremonial double of the king and living god of his sacrificial rites. Like the sun, chiefs of the highest tabus—those who are called "gods," "fire," "heat," and "raging blazes"—cannot be gazed directly upon without injury. The lowly commoner prostrates before them face to the ground, the position assumed by victims on the platforms of human sacrifice. Such a one is called *makawela*, 'burnt eyes'. But if I go on to recount the symbolic riches of these associations, there will be space for nothing else.[17] Let me instead epitomize the political philosophy by this contrast: When a commoner, having violated the tabu, is destined for sacrifice, his eyes are first put out by the king's executioners; but when the great chief Keoua in historic times resigned himself to the altars of his victorious rival Kamehameha, he first cut off the end of his penis.

If we think merely of "ideology" or "superstructure," we deceive ourselves: this is a political economy of love. Love is the infrastructure (as Godelier might say). The erotic is the pragmatic—in a double sense. From the point of view of the acting subject, commoner as well as chief, sexual conquests are means to a variety of material advantages. This is easy enough to understand, but the second sense, which is the sociological corollary, we have no ready theory of: the structure of the kingdom is the sublimated form of its forces of sexual attraction. Hawaiian society was not a world of determinate kinship groups and prescribed relationships, of presupposed forms and norms, as in the good anthropological tradition of corporate lineages and prescribed marriage rules. Not simply that the system was, technically speaking, complex. It was performative: rather literally a "state of affairs," created by the very acts that signified it.

---

[17] The symbolic structure of the system of human sacrifice in Hawaii has been brilliantly documented and analyzed by Valeri (in press); my own discussion is greatly indebted to this work. The main standard sources on Hawaiian chieftainship are: Malo (1951), S. Kamakau (1961; 1964; MS), Fornander (1916–19; 1969), Handy and Pukui (1972), I'i (1959), K. Kamakau (in Fornander 1916–19, 6:2–45), Rev. Ellis (1828), and Remy (1861). A good summary may be found in Goldman (1970).

The solar associations of chieftainship range from the chiefs' descent from Wakea, personification of the sun at the zenith, to nineteenth-century praise songs, such as 'For You, O glittering Sun' (*Iā 'Oe, e ka La e 'Alohi nei*), written for King Kalākaua. Of course, I am not speaking of a solar cult; it is more a question of the sun as the king than the king as the sun.

From family to state, the arrangements of society were in constant flux, a set of relationships constructed on the shifting sands of love.

Now Marc Bloch taught us to be comparativists, or else we are antiquarians. And one of the advantages of comparison in the strong or linguistic sense—comparison of "genetically" related structures—is that we are permitted to speak of permutations marked by a significant absence. Hawaii is missing the segmentary polity of descent groups known to cognate Polynesian peoples: organization of the land as a pyramid of embedded lineages, with a corresponding hierarchy of ancestral cults, property rights, and chiefly titles, all based on genealogical priority within the group of common descent. Not that these concepts have left no historic traces, or even systematic functions. They organize the earlier generations of great royal cum cosmological genealogies which, beginning in divine sources and proceeding patrilaterally through senior and cadet branches, fix the dynastic relations between the several islands. As a general rule, the oldest and most senior lines are in the western islands, Kaua'i and O'ahu, whence originate also the highest tabus. But then, the historical dynamism of the system is in the east, among Maui and Hawai'i chiefs, who are able to differentiate themselves from local competitors, or even from their own dynastic predecessors, by appropriating ancestry from the ancient western sources of legitimacy. In this genealogical game—favorite arena of politics for the Hawaiian monarchy until well into the nineteenth century—lineage is not so much a structure as it is an argument.

Hawaiians in fact do not trace *descent* so much as *ascent*, selectively choosing their way upward, by a path that notably includes female ancestors, to a connection with some ancient ruling line.[18]

---

[18]The famous Hawaiian chiefly genealogies—some over 900 generations depth—were kept by certain experts in tradition, men and women, and the genealogical adepts were traditionally attached to high chiefs. Nineteenth-century genealogy books (as those deposited in the Bishop Museum and the Archives of Hawaii), some of which can be traced to the first decades of the century, testify to the way the specialized knowledge of remote ancestral sources on the part of the genealogy masters was reconciled with current chiefly interests in ascent to these sources. Line by line—or "side" by "side," as Hawaiians say—the immediate male and female ancestors of the chief are attached to the great cosmological genealogies, usually at some ancestral point within the last 10 or 12 generations.

Recall that men, nature, and the gods revealed themselves to Kila "in testimony to his high-chief rank." Yet Hawaiians also say, "in the womb is the rank of the child determined." The meaning is not matrilineal descent, as an older generation of scholars supposed, but that the rank and tabus transmitted through their respective mothers differentiate the claims of rival chiefs and contending heirs. Hence the quest for the sacred woman in the myth of Kila, but also in numerous stories of legendary kings and in the documented practices of their historic successors (cf. Valeri 1972). Thus, if Polynesian genealogical principles are preserved, it is because descent is acquired by alliance.

Again, Hawaiians say that "every chief acts as a conqueror when he is installed." The reference is not merely to the celebration of a victory over one's predecessors which here, as elsewhere, marks the coronation ceremonies of the divine king. Whether he comes to power by usurpation or inheritance, the chief at his accession redistributes title to all the land districts, large and small, among his immediate kinsmen and henchmen. These people are the chiefs who 'eat the district' (*ali'i 'ai moku/ ahupua'a*). Hawaiians, moreover, prefer the Machiavellian principle of ruling by servants rather than by barons. In redistributing the lands, the ruling chief is disposed to empower lesser chiefs connected to the royal family by its numerous secondary unions, thus counterposing his affines to the collateral kin who are his most dangerous rivals. Here, then, is a main source of the sexual politics. The corollary of the land custom is an aristocratic obsession with conspiracy and intrigue, in which sexual intrigue is a means of choice.[19]

The genealogy books also offer eloquent testimony to the interest of Maui and Hawai'i chiefs in their connections with ancient lines of O'ahu and Kaua'i, particularly the Nanaulu line. The total effect of the shape of royal genealogies when diagramed (e.g., Fornander 1969: end paper) is a structure rather bare of elaboration in the first scores or hundreds of generations (i.e., a restricted set of patrilateral lines including the occasional junior branch), becoming then a reticulate network of relationships through men and women in the most recent generations. Yet all such representations do not do justice to the intricacies of chiefly kinship in latest generations, occasioned by the multiple and inbred unions, primary and secondary, of men and women both.

[19]On land tenure, apart from the standard sources of chieftainship (note 17) see, among others, Handy (1965), Wise (1965), Lyons (1875), and Commissioner of Public Lands (1929:1−12).

The marriage system (I use terms loosely) of Hawaiian chiefs was a lifetime fete of polygynous and polyandrous matings that defies any simple description. Incest and exogamy, hypergamy and hypogamy: every kind of union had its advantages, according to the context of the situation. Nor could Hawaiians fail to be aware of the advantages, since in the end parenthood had to be socially attributed—"altogether savages as we are, we also know how to calculate." Impossible for us also to have any reliable statistics, since our main sources are American missionaries, reveling as it were in Hawaiian depravities. Brother Thurston's notice of a secondary wife of Kalaniopu'u, king of Hawaii in Cook's time, is typical:

> By her own account she has had during her lifetime not less than forty husbands and according to the former custom of high chiefs who were not the principal wives of reigning kings, she usually had several of them at one time (Letters: Kailua, 10 Dec. 1828).

Yet the significance, if not the extent, of those apparently casual liaisons is above suspicion. Out of the nexus of sexual attachments is precipitated the organization of the kingdom.

A certain entropy is thus imparted to the rank system, releasing in turn an outburst (*huahua'i*) of aristocratic sexual energies. Given the labyrinthine intertwining of genealogies occasioned by the continuous intertwining of the chiefs, the system of rank and the tabu moves always toward a most probable state of non-differentiation (cf. Valeri 1972). Everyone could say: *nous aussi, nous avons des aïeux*. But where everyone has such claims of legitimacy, no one can guarantee the legitimacy of his claims. Nor was there any assurance of retaining title to what one already possessed. Except, perhaps, by a series of liaisons that would bring unique distinction to one's descent and the support of others to one's ambitions—in the hope, of course, of furthering their own in the distribution of land and office. We can see now that the erotic prowess celebrated in the birth chants of the Hawaiian elite is not the reflex only of a general association between the chiefship and cosmic fertility. The aristocratic genitalia are truly valuable means of social production.

What was true of the kingdom applied as well to the humbler domestic realm of the people: constant fluctuation of household arrangements and membership, due in good measure to shifting sentimental attachments. No rigid rules of marital residence or prescribed family forms (e.g., patrilocal extended families). A certain incidence of polyandry and polygamy. Above all, a prolonged period of mobility among younger adults devoted to the pursuit of pleasure. Great value was attached to *u'i*, 'vigorous, youthful beauty'. Young women were reluctant to settle down and rear children because of the adverse effects on their figures. It is said this was a main cause of abortion and infanticide, but the incidence of these practices is uncertain. Certain it is that infants were often left for the grandparents to rear while the mother went on her ways. For young men, domestic responsibility entailed the added disadvantage of placing oneself under a chief's land agent (*konohiki*), subject to his demands for labor and produce. Often, then, domestic stability was not realized until a relatively advanced age. Among the people it was called simply *noho pu*, 'living together'; but the difference from earlier, provisional unions—*moe aku, moe mai*, 'sleep there, sleep here'— is not clear-cut. For ordinary people "marriage" was not ritually marked, or very little. Nor did Hawaiians have terms for 'husband' and 'wife' beyond those for 'man' (*kane*) and 'woman' (*wahine*). They did, however, have affinal kin terms. And a man's wife was deemed his *kuleana*, his 'property claim' in her family. So in the end, for the people as for the chiefs, the effect of sex was society: a shifting set of liaisons that gradually became sorted out and weighted down by the practical considerations attached to them.[20]

Moreover, the connection between these two realms, the domestic and the political, civil society and state, was made by the same sexual means that respectively organized each. The com-

---

[20]For insights into the domestic and sexual habits of Hawaiians in the earlier nineteenth century—to be used with due care and sensitivity to the biases in the missionary sources—see Wyllie (1846; cf. Malo 1839). See also Handy and Pukui (1972), Keesing (1936), and Howard (1971) for more recent observations. Another revealing source on Hawaiian sexual practice consists of court records from the 1830s and 1840s, when a law code inspired by Puritan morality was imposed on the kingdom. (Statistical summaries can be found in the Archives of Hawaii—"Courts, Miscellaneous," "Attorney General, Miscellaneous," etc.— and case material also in the District and Supreme Court records.) For example, a tabulation of convictions—apparently from all islands, and including a certain fraction of cases involving whites—for 1838 (Kanoa [attrib] 1839):

mon people, too, had an interest in the erotic exploits of the nobility and ambitions to become the object of their affections. Not
merely *aloha* but sexual attachment, which for the people was an
important avenue of the upward mobility called *'imi haku*, 'to
search for a lord'. Reports from Hawai'i Island tell of a local form
of *jus primae noctis*, which was as much a privilege for the daughter of the people as for the chief:

> Before a girl took a husband, the chief must *wāwāhi*
> ['break open']. If there was a child, that child was reared
> by her family and her husband with pride. This hus-
> band had a 'lord' *haku* to rear. This lord was important
> because he could be a 'backbone' [*iwikuamo'o*, a sup-
> porter and kinsman] in the court of the chief. The chief
> could break open any girl, and the family would like
> that and try to bring it about (Informant statement).

For the people on the land, there was no protection of lineage.
There was no lineage. The local chiefs periodically 'placed'
(*ho'onoho*) and replaced by the powers-that-be upon the districts

Offense	Number of Persons Convicted
"Adultery"	246
"Lewdness"	81
"Theft"	48
"Riot"	32
"Falsewitness"	30
"Seduction"	18
"Mutiny"	15
"Manslaughter"	4

Or again, cases in Kaua'i District Courts, 1 April 1846–1 April 1847:

Offense	Number Tried in District Court
"Fornication"	140
"Stealing"	34
"Working on Sabbath"	21
"Fighting and Brawling"	10
Miscellaneous	16

(Report of H. Sea to Attorney General, AH)

In all such statistics for this period, the offenses variously labeled "adultery,"
"prostitution," "fornication," "pandering" (*weawea*), "seduction," and/or "lewd-
ness" run on the order of four or five times the frequency of crimes against property, and invariably constitute the largest general class of court proceedings.

of the countryside had no necessary or essential kinship to the people there. But at the same time, this system of land redistribution among the elite left no space to alternate local structures of lineage solidarity and collective property—and, least of all, to an alternative authority emanating from the people as the senior line of their own ancestry. By traditional definition, commoners are people who cannot trace their genealogies beyond their grandparents. Nor did they inherit land so much as replace their parents or grandparents in a relation of subordination to the chief who had been put in charge. Over the fairly short-term, even once prominent people (*ko'iko'i*) and *quondam* chiefs living on the land would find themselves bereft of privilege by the successive generations of victorious chiefs imposed upon them. Broadly speaking, it was a society of diminishing returns. Hence the significance of this 'search for a lord'.[21]

The search might begin at birth. Many families in the countryside selected a 'favorite child' (*punahele*), male or female, to rear in effect as a sacred chief within a household of people. It was the equivalent of the attention accorded to the chiefly child, and particularly the complement to the sexual capacities anticipated in birth chants of aristocratic infants. The favorite child among the people was consecrated to family ancestors. The person, clothing, foods, and activities of the favorite were accordingly restricted by tabus, in the same way as a sacred chief. An old text tells of the dedication of the favorite child to a god of the opposite sex: a form of theogamy, enjoining virginity during youth and looking forward to the eventual union with a visible god cum chief which was the explicit purpose of the consecration. The prayer of dedication for a favorite daughter is eloquent regarding the anticipated benefits:

[21] The argument on the absence of corporate lineages in Hawaii, whether among chiefs or common people, is taken in opposition to received notions about the famous *'ohana* (e.g., Handy and Pukui 1972). Among the people, the word *'ohana* refers primarily to egocentric kindred relations, or to local networks of kinsmen under a provincial "big man," but not to sociocentric and corporate lineages properly so-called. The abundant records and testimonies of the great land division (*Mahele*) of 1846–54 deposited in the Archives of Hawaii make it clear that there were no lineage corporations in charge of land segments. The term *'ohana* is virtually absent from these records; nor were the *ahupua'a*, *'ili'aina*, or *mo'oaina* land sections occupied by groups of common descent. I intend to make the full argument and exposition of this question in another publication.

O Border of the West,
The Upper Firmament,
The Lower Firmament,
Here is your treasure.

Offer her to the man who will rule the land,
A husband who rules a land district,
A chiefly husband,
To preserve your [the child's] parents,
To preserve your offspring . . .

Preserve my genitals
For my husband to see . . .

Look you, guardian spirits of the night,
Preserve your child,
Secure for her a chiefly husband who rules the land
(Kekoa 1865)

We can see why Hawaiians are so interested in sex. Sex was everything: rank, power, wealth, land, and the security of all these. Happy society, perhaps, that could make the pursuit of all the good things in life so enjoyable in itself.

III. Performative Structures

Not like ourselves, for whom drudgery and pain are the *a priori* conditions of pleasure. Still, like ourselves in that the society seems sedimented, as if by an Invisible Hand, out of the pragmatic interests of its acting subjects, hence as historical form is continuously being done and undone. Also, then, like the Eskimo, the Tswana, Pul Eliya, or the so-called loosely structured societies of New Guinea. And all these peoples have another characteristic in common: they defy anthropological explication. They are monuments to the failure of the anthropological imagination—and beyond that, to the limitations of Western social thought. We see them through a glass darkly, by *post facto* "statistical models," which must be content to total up the effects of numerous individual choices and then certify the empirical results as a genuine cultural order. We long for the "mechanical models" granted us by people who know how to act according to prescribed relationships, rather than determining their relationships from the way they interact. We are much more comfortable with the Aristotelian logics of "social structure" bequeathed by the scholastic doctors: the corporate groups and juridical norms of a Radcliffe-Brown, neat little boxlike arrangements of noncontradictory categories and unproblematic behaviors, a role for every status and everyone in his place. We are worshipers at the shrines of Terminus, god of boundary stones.

Confronted by peoples who seem to make up the rules as they go along, constituting the social fact as a fiction of their truer interests, we are reminded of ourselves, and begin to speak mysteriously, or dialectically, of antithetical principles, properties, and kinds of causation. We discover ontological differences between structure and practice, system and event, state and process, norm and behavior. The one—system or structure—appears as "ideal," "ideological," or "merely symbolic"; whereas, life-as-lived is real, empirical, and practical. We find it difficult to imagine that at the level of meaning, which is to say of culture, being and action are interchangeable.

More properly, we have difficulty finding the theoretical place of this idea, although we recognize and act on it in our own existence. For us, friendship is a relation of mutual aid. It is presupposed that friends will help each other: the action is prescribed in advance by the relationship. Yet it is also proverbial with us that "a friend in need is a friend indeed." The one who helps you is *really* your friend: the relationship is even more certainly created by the performance, than is the performance guaranteed by the relationship. (In anthropology we hear of prescriptive marriage systems, enjoining unions between certain categories of kinsmen, such as cross-cousins. In my experience, the Fijian is a perfectly prescriptive system of cross-cousin marriage. All Fijians marry their cross-cousins. Not because the people who are so related marry, but because the people who marry are so related—whatever their previous relationship, if any, may have been.) My point is that at the level of meaning there is always a potential reversibility between kinds of action and categories of relationship. Verbs signify just as well and as much as nouns, and the structural order can be worked as well from one direction as the other. All societies probably use some mix of those reciprocal modes of symbolic production. But there are systems with predominantly Radcliffe-Brownian movements: with bounded groups and compelling rules that do prescribe in advance much of the way people act and interact. Call them "prescriptive structures." By relative contrast, the Hawaiian is a "performative structure."

It is continuously making relationships out of practice—especially, I have tried to show, out of sexual practice. Just now I underlined the point by an apparent oxymoron, suggesting that the grammatical subject can stand in predicate relation to the verb. Yet the Hawaiian language is like that. Word order is governed by the principle called "fronting," the advance of the most salient information toward initial position in the sentence, place usually occupied by the verb. The verbs themselves are marked for aspect, or degree of realization, rather than tense proper; and the most frequently used verbs are the so-called statives, denoting what we consider a state or condition rather than an action. Indeed, in this language without inflections the same terms generally function as nouns, verbs, adjectives, or adverbs, depending on position. I am not rehearsing the idea, commonly attributed to Whorf and Sapir, that the categories of grammar determine the categories of thought. The same interchangeability of being and doing is as manifest in social structure as in grammatical structure, and nothing tells us *a priori* that one such domain should be privileged over the other. But taken together, the Hawaiian cultural logic does suggest that the opposition between state and process or substance and action enshrined in our own historical and social science is not pertinent—however much the distinction seems to us a condition of thought itself.

In Hawaiian thought, we have seen, kinsmen are made as well as born. 'Feeding' (*hānai*), the so-called adoption, may as effectively institute parenthood as would birth. The logic is highly productive and meaningfully consistent. *Kama'āina* or 'child of the land' refers to someone "native" to a place. Yet one may equally be a *kama'āina* by action or by prescription: by long-term residence or by birthright. The consistency is that all these relationships of childhood and nativity have a common denominator. They all invoke the common human substance of the people so related. Parents and children are people of the same kind: they are composed of the same thing, whether by the re-production of substance or its common consumption. It follows logically that a person whose food comes from a certain land— '*āina*—is a child—*kama*—of it, a *kama'āina*, just as those who are born to it. (In folk etymology, '*āina*, the 'land', is glossed as the 'feeding-place'. The derivation is historically inaccurate, yet full of historical good sense, since the Polynesian root in question is the familiar **kaainga*, meaning an abode and a group of kinsmen begotten through sexual intercourse—and throughout Polynesia sexual intercourse is 'eating'.)

All this helps explain the seeming paradox of a society that is able to reproduce a received cultural order through the free pursuit of happiness, *le'a*, which is to say (in Hawaiian) by the contingencies of sexual attraction. Seen from the vantage of the libidinous subject, sex is a consuming interest, not only for its own sake, but for its many practical benefits. Yet from the global perspective of society, these subjective ends become means of constituting a definite economic, political, and spiritual order. And although the individual choices seem free, or at least very liberal, the global outcome is by no means culturally aleatory. It expresses in a valid way the customary distinctions and relations between men and women, chiefs and people, gods and mortals; in sum, the traditional cosmic scheme of things. The structure resides precisely in these distinctions and relations, themselves (relatively) invariant, rather than in the shifting arrangements formed and reformed on them. Social system is thus constructed out of passion, structure out of sentiment.

This apparent miracle depends on several interrelated conditions of the mode of symbolic production, the performative mode, of which I emphasize two only. First, that the customary, meaningful values of persons and the objects of their existence inhabit the interests and intentions of personal projects, often as the unreflected premises of action. Everything contractual is not in the contract. And the counterpart of this Durkheimian aphorism are the aphorisms, percepts, and concepts of everyday life, the *habitus* or "structuring structures" so brilliantly described by Bourdieu (1977), profiling thus a greater order in personal interests and actions. It follows from such understandings that a society that runs on the free pursuit of interests is not thereby free of motivated relations between signs (see chapter 5, below). And secondly, being and doing or relationships and conducts, as meanings inhabit the same universe of discourse and are subject to common conceptual operations. We are not adding apples to oranges or counterposing "ideal" to "real" things. The scheme which connects certain acts to certain relationships is itself systematic. Not just by sharing any experience do Hawaiians become kinsmen or fellow "children of the land," only by those experiences that entail the appropriate value of consubstantiality. By a common logic which is virtual to both, action and relation may thus function alternately as signifier and signified to the other.[22]

But if this process of signification is not symbolically *ad hoc*, it is often *post-factum*. We thus return to historical issues, specifically to the historicity of performative structures. The *calcul sauvage* seems to share with its more famous cousin (*la pensée sauvage*) a great capacity to neutralize the events that beset it. Nothing human was truly foreign to the Hawaiians—if not always the other way around. There was always the category *akua*, usually glossed as 'god' or 'divine'. By my reading this, rather than the famous *mana*, functions as a zero semantic category, signifying not so much a determinate content as the remarkability of the experience. At first, Hawaiians liberally applied the term to the persons, ships, and mechanical contrivances of the foreigners. Later, as these were incorporated within Hawaiian society, they became *kama'āina*, 'children of the land'. Everything happened as if nothing happened: as if there could be no history, as there could be no unexpected event, no happening

---

[22] So Peter Huber argues in an analogous way regarding the Anggor of New Guinea:

> Melanesian society has presented a very wry face when viewed as an abstract system of rights and duties, or groups and categories, founded in kinship. If society is thought to be constituted through the enforcement or orderly implementation of such a system, then Melanesian society, I argue, is ritually constituted through the production of events that mobilize people in a certain way. These events are not necessarily characterized by inutility or supernaturalism—they are not ritual in that sense—but by the fact that they are informed by a scheme of symbolic classification. It is because they enact this scheme of classification that they constitute society (Huber 1980:44–45).

not already culturally provided for. The intention of Hawaiian women rushing to the European ships they took to be signs of the god was, "make love, not history"—and *pas de histoires*.

Yet, the implication can hardly be that the Hawaiian is a "cold society." On the contrary, it proved extremely vulnerable to change. This integration of things and persons European, first as divine (*akua*) then as native (*kama'āina*), was an invitation to cultural disaster. The most general and obvious reason: that the foreigners who were so generously accorded an indigenous status had their own reasons of existence, and no obligations to conform to the preconceptions by which Hawaiians thought them. By encompassing contingent events in received structures, perceiving mythical relationships in historical actions, the system appears merely to reproduce itself in a flexible way. But, then, to borrow Pouillon's *bon mot*, "The more it remains the same, the more it changes."

In the end, we must return to dialectics. I did not really mean to ignore the interplay of structure and *praxis*, only to reserve for it a proper theoretical place, viz., as a symbolic process. For all Hawaiian culture is designed to symbolically valorize the force of worldly practice. It then changes precisely because, in admitting the world to full membership in its categories, it admits the probability that the categories will be functionally revalued. The god Lono would no longer be the same concept once Captain Cook was referred to it; nor could the ideas of foreign lands, tabus, or the divine in general be sustained the way they were. And as the given category is revalued in the course of historic reference, so must the relationships between categories change: the structure is transformed (cf. Sahlins 1981).

What Marc Bloch observed of fifteenth-century Europe happened even more dramatically in Hawaii: "although men were not fully aware of the change, the old names which were still on everyone's lips had slowly acquired connotations far removed from their original meaning (1966:90)." One may ask, then, why Marc Bloch, who knew so well that practice was the reason for this process, did not himself succumb to some positivist form of utilitarian reasoning? Was it not because he was studying societies so ready to give familiar names to varying practices that they could not conceal they were dealing with the world by a relative cultural scheme?

2

Other Times, Other Customs: The Anthropology of History

> The nature of institutions is nothing but their coming into being (*nascimento*) at certain times and in certain guises. Whenever the time and guise are thus and so, such and not otherwise are the institutions that come into being.
>
> —Vico, *The New Science*

Western historians have been arguing for a long time over two polar ideas of right historiography. As opposed to an elite history, narrated with an eye singular to the higher politics, others propose a study whose object would be the life of communities. "For the last fourteen hundred years, the only Gauls, apparently, have been kings, ministers, and generals," Voltaire complained, and vowed to write instead a "history of men" (which he found, however, "a collection of crimes, follies, and misfortunes"). The latest "new history" is also of the populist persuasion. Sometimes client of the social sciences, it is concerned with such matters as unconscious structures, collective mentalities, and general economic trends. It tends to be populist in the salience it gives to the practical circumstances of underlying populations. A distinguished historian (Stone 1981:23) invokes Thomas Gray: "Let not . . . grandeur hear with a disdainful smile / The short and simple annals of the poor." The idea is that history is culturally constructed from the bottom-up: as the precipitate, in social institutions and outcomes, of the prevailing inclinations of the people-in-general.[1]

Yet before we congratulate the new history on having finally learned its anthropological (or political) lessons, we should recall that the passage from an elite to a more collective consciousness actually occurred in the history of Western society, as a difference in real-historical practice, and this long before the decline of monarchy in favor of popular democracies and market economies made the mass production of history seem the self-evident truth of our own—should we not say, our bourgeois?—social experience. Jean-Pierre Vernant (1982) brilliantly analyzes the same transformation in the first millennium B.C., in the passage from the sovereignty of Mycenaean god-kings to the humanized institutions of the Greek *polis*. Or is it that we have to do, in society and consciousness both, with a "structure of the long duration": a cyclical alternation between Caesarism and the power of the people, the *gumsa* and *gumlao* of Indo-European history, each social form always pregnant, at least a little bit, with its historic opposite?

Vernant in fact begins by comparing Athenian royal traditions with the divine kings of Scythian legend. In repeated quarrels over the succession, the Athenian princes eventually divide between them the functions—priestly, military, and economic—that were characteristically united in Indo-European kingships of the heroic age. So commences the idea of politics as the mutual accommodation of differences, whose more democratic form will be achieved in the *polis*. But in contrast to the Athenian princes, the divinely favored grandson of the Scythian Zeus is alone accorded royal power by his older brothers, as he alone is able to carry off the prototypical golden objects emblematic of the Dumézilian three functions: the libation cup, the war ax, and the plow (Herodotus, *Hist.* IV, 5–6). Here the sovereign is classically presented, "as a person above and beyond the vari-

---

[1] Stone's chapters on historiography (Part 1) in *The Past and the Present* (1981) afford an excellent introduction to the "new history." Barraclough (1978) on the same subject also refers to Thomas Gray—a custom of English historians in America? The remarks from Voltaire's *Essai sur les moeurs* are noted by LeGoff (1972) in an essay of his own most pertinent to the present discussion; cf. Braudel (1980), Dumoulin and Moisi (1973), Gilbert and Graubard (1972), LeGoff and Nora (1974), Hexter (1972), Ricoeur (1980).

ous functional classes that made up society, since he represented them all; and since all equally found in him the virtues by
which they defined themselves, he no longer belonged to anyone of them" (Vernant 1982:42). At once encompassing and
transcending the society, the divine king is able to mediate its
relations to the cosmos—which thus also responds, in its own
natural order, to his sovereign powers.

In the *polis*, however, an organization constituted by its self-
awareness as a human community, the *arche* (sovereign power)
"came to be everybody's business" (women and slaves, as usual,
excepted). Rotating the authority among the several groups of
citizens, thus making domination and submission alternating
sides of the same relationships, rendering its decisions by public
debate among equals in the public square, hence as open cove-
nants openly arrived at, so elevating speech to preeminence
over all other instruments of power, speech that was no longer
the compelling ritual word pronounced from on high but an argument to be judged as persuasive in the light of wisdom and
knowledge verifiable by all as something called truth, the *polis*,
by these and many other means, subjected social action to the
collective will and made men conscious of their history as human history.

I take up Vernant's thesis as the general point of this essay:
that different cultural orders have their own modes of historical
action, consciousness, and determination—their own historical practice. Other times, other customs, and according to the
otherness of the customs, the distinctive anthropology that is
needed to understand any given human course. For there is no
simply "human" course (*devenir*), as Durkheim said, "but each
society has its own life, its own course, and similar societies are
as comparable in their historicity [or mode of development] as in
their structure" (1905–6:140).[2] This mention of structural types
is perhaps enough to forestall the idea that I am making merely
an idiographic point of historical relativity. Rather I begin with
certain reflections on divine kingship, the type of structure from
which the *polis* took radical departure, in order to examine the
general cultural practice of heroic history.

[2] I have translated freely, especially taking liberties with *devenir*, yet I think
without altering Durkheim's intent.

Heroic History

The idea is from Vico, after Homeric precedents, but as further worked out in the anthropology of archaic kingship by Frazer and Hocart, and tempered in Dumontian concepts of hierarchy.[3] The historical implications follow from the presence of divinity among men, as in the person of the sacred king or the powers of the magical chief. Accordingly, the principle of historical practice becomes synonymous with divine action: the creation of the human and cosmic order by the god.

Of course, I am not suggesting some neolithic form of the great-man theory of history. Nor do I speak of "charisma" simply—unless it be the "routinized charisma" that structurally amplifies a personal effect by transmission along the lines of established relationships. In a version of the Social Contract that still stands as the philosophic Magna Carta of the General Will, Rousseau argued that "each State can have for enemies only other States, and not men; for between things disparate in nature there can be no real relation." Yet ethnography shows that the Maori chief "lives the life of a whole tribe," that "he stands in a certain relation to neighbouring tribes and kinship groups," and that "he gathers the relationship to other tribes in his person" (Johansen 1954:180). The chief's marriages are intertribal alliances; his ceremonial exchanges trade; as injuries to himself are cause for war. Here history is anthropomorphic in principle,

[3]Besides Frazer (1911–15), Hocart (1969 [1927], 1936), and Dumont (1970), the ideas on divine kingship and hierarchy presented here draw especially on recent anthropological studies by Heusch (1962, 1972, 1982), Valeri (in press), Geertz (1980), Tambiah (1976), and Adler (1978, 1982), as well as such earlier classics as Evans-Pritchard (1962), Frankfurt (1948), Dumézil (1948), Meek (1931), Kuper (1947), Krige and Krige (1943); cf. below, chapter 3. I make no taxonomic issue of the differences between "divine kings," "sacred kings," "magical kings," and "priest-kings"—or even between "kings" and "chiefs." With regard to the last, I rather agree with Heusch that the state is a creation of the divine king, instead of the other way around, in which case the principal reason for differentiating divine kingship from divine chiefship loses its force. For a discussion of the taxonomic problems surrounding divine kingship, as well as an excellent analysis of Jukun, see Young (1966). No doubt my decision to go with a broad category of heroic polities, without fine regard for the variations, can be advantageous for present theoretical purposes and over the short run only. I have no illusions about the greater durability or value of the category.

which is to say in structure.[4] Granted that history is much more than the doings of great men, is always and everywhere the life of communities; but precisely in these heroic polities the king is the condition of the possibility of community. "'If I eat,'" says the Kuba man, "'it is the King; if I sleep, it is the King; if I drink, it is the King'" (Vansina 1964:101).[5] In the greater states of Fiji (e.g., Mbau, Thakaundrove), no one can stir abroad in the morning, no community life or work appears, until the sacred drink of kava is offered fo the king or 'human-god' (*kalou tamata*): every day, the king recreates the world (Lester 1941–42:113–14; Sayes 1982).

The general life-conditions of the people are hegemonically ordered, as social form and collective destiny, by the particular dispositions of the powers-that-be. Nor is the process a reflexive "ideology" merely, since the general will is not generally the sovereign interest, except as it is the interest of the sovereign. The sovereignty itself may have its contradictions or even contentions—in other kingships as much as the Indo-European (see chapter 3); it does not function, therefore, without cognizance of collective circumstances. Only that such circumstances are historically realized, as they are globally defined, by an hierarchical encompassment in the projects of kingship. Hence the pertinent historiography cannot be—as in the good Social Science tradition—a simple quantitative assessment of the people's opinions or conditions, based on a statistically random sample, as if one were directly taking the pulse of generative *social tendencies*. Heroic history proceeds more like "Fenimore Cooper Indians"—to use Elman Service's characterization: each man, as they walk

---

[4]Besides, in the Fijian case, quite literally, a chief can be the sister's son to another chiefdom (e.g., *vasu ki Rewa, vasu ki Mbau,* etc.)—thus a relation between things apparently "disparate in nature." The personifications of political forces entailed in Fijian *vasu* (uterine nephew) relationships are discussed below.

[5]The informant cited, however, is one of the "skeptics" in a fascinating debate among Kuba, reported by Vansina (1964:101–2), concerning the divinity of the king. The skeptics take a functionalist view of royalty as a necessary condition of order in a society otherwise segmentary, conceding that the king has powerful magic but denying he has divine powers. Apart from such ideological arguments, the Kuba practice a classic set of rituals by which the king, deprived of his natal kinship relations, is placed above as well as outside the clanic order of the society—at once as a force of nature, a representative of the god, and an incestuous sorcerer.

single-file along the trail, careful to step in the footprints of the one ahead, so as to leave the impression of One Giant Indian.

Thus for over a century after their conversion by Methodist missionaries, Fijians could still refer to Christianity as "the religion of Thakombau" (Derrick 1950:115).[6] Thakombau was the ruling chief of the great Mbau confederacy, the dominant power in the nineteenth-century Fiji. On 30 April 1854, he finally declared for Jehovah, after more than fifteen years of missionary hectoring. Earlier, in mid–1852, the missionaries had counted only 850 "regular worshippers" in the Mbau area (Meth. Miss. Soc.: Fiji Dist. 1852). But directly on Thakombau's conversion, together with certain military successes, "the Holy Ghost was poured out plentifully" in the Mbau dominions, so that by mid–1855 church attendance had increased to 8,870 (Williams and Calvert 1859: 484). This proves that in the mathematics of Fijian history, $8,870 - 850 = 1$. The statistical difference was Thakombau.

On the other hand, the figure of 850 for 1852 by far underestimates the number of Fijians, including Thakombau, who for years had acknowledged the "truth" of the foreigner's god. Even many of the Fijian gods, speaking through priests, had already conceded the supremacy of Jehovah and fled elsewhere, or else indicated they were themselves prepared to become Christians.[7] "Confessing that Christianity was true," Thakombau in 1850 counseled Brother Calvert to have patience, as when he himself turned, "all would follow" (Williams and Calvert 1859:445–46). And this proves that the politics of conversion is no simple expression of conviction.

The repeated reference to "truth" in these archives indicates that the widespread disposition to heed Christianity was a matter of Fijian mythopoetics, if not yet of chiefly politics. For the

---

[6] The usual phrase is *na lotu nei Ratu Cakobau*, in orthodox Fijian spelling. In the present article, I have reverted to an earlier and unorthodox orthography, easier for English speakers to pronounce. When asked once why he did not learn English, Thakombau said it was because he had heard Englishmen speaking Fijian.

[7] On the other hand, when certain Mbau gods resisted Christianity even after Thakombau had converted, the chief assembled their priests and whipped them (Waterhouse 1866:265–66). The earlier relations of Fijian priests/gods to Jehovah may be followed in the journals of Cross (e.g., 24 Oct. 1840), Hunt (18 Feb. 1839; 10 May 1839), Calvert (15 Aug. 1841; 20 Oct. 1841), among others.

Fijian 'true' (*dina*) is a gloss of *mana*, as Hocart (1914) observed, denoting a power of bringing-into-existence, even as an action that fails for want of *mana* is a 'lie' (*lasu*). So the Fijian chief said to the Methodist missionary: "True—everything is true that comes from the white man's country; muskets & gunpowder are true, & your religion must be true" (Schütz 1977:95; cf. Waterhouse 1866:303). The extraordinary European presence was for Fijians a "total" social fact, "religious" at the same time it was "political" and "economic." More exactly, it could be made intelligible only in the terms of a native theory that stood Marx on his head by its insistence that ("in the final analysis") the economic base depended on the spiritual superstructure. In 1838, the paramount chief of Rewa, soon to be Thakombau's great enemy, but never a professing Christian, admits the missionary's point that "the gods of Fiji are not true: they are like the Tongan gods," he says, of whom it has been shown that "they are not gods; those who trusted them have been destroyed, and those who attended to the religion of the foreigners are prosperous" (Cross: 22 Oct. 1838).[8] If the missionaries labored for years in central Fiji without famous success—save most notably among the sick, who supposed by the same theory that the Wesleyans' god made their medicines work—it was not for lack of credence in popular opinion. Rather, the issue turned on the ruling chiefs, especially of Mbau and Rewa, who had been fighting each other since 1843.

Asked why they did not heed God's word, the people of Viwa Island, subject to Mbau, would tell Brother Cross, "'I wait for [my chief] Namosimalua'" (Meth. Miss. Soc.: District Minutes, 1841). So "the common people wait for their Chiefs," as another

---

[8]Paradoxically, then, a theory of determination by the infrastructure will appear true of Fijian history—i.e., the propagation of a new faith (in Jehovah) follows upon the practical demonstration of European power—because of the preexisting concept that such power has its "supernatural" reasons. This raises the interesting question of whether elsewhere also the mechanical sequence of infrastructural change→ superstructural change does not likewise depend on the *a priori* status of practical activity as a cosmological "scheme of things." While such an understanding might deny the usual radical opposition of pragmatics and "ideology," it offers certain obvious advantages, such as an end to simple reflexive-functionalist "explanations" of their relationship and a better comprehension of the interchange between worldly action (*praxis*) and cultural concepts (see chap. 5).

missionary complained, "one Chief waits for another [superior chief], one land waits for another land, thus there is in many areas a stalemate" (Jaggar: 21 Oct. 1839). "If Rewa would take the lead," says a third, "we should soon have one hundred thousand *professed* Christians in Fiji" (Williams and Calvert 1859: 408). But as one chief thus waited for another, the other was waiting for the right moment. Thakombau was not about to change gods in mid-war. And when he finally did change, the same option was precluded for his rival, the Rewa chief: " 'If we all *lotu* [become Christian],' " the latter said, " 'we must give up fighting; as it will not do to pray to the same god, and fight with each other' " (Williams and Calvert 1859:356).

The conversion came only as a tactic of despair.[9] In the twelfth year of war, Mbau was virtually under seige by Rewan and allied forces, even as its European trade was under embargo and its own allies were deserting to the enemy by the clan, village, and chiefdom. Mbau itself was beset by revolt, led by a near relative of the chief. At this juncture, Thakombau found "the true God," and his profession of faith abruptly redefined the terms of battle. Thakombau became the incarnate hope of Christianity in the Fiji

[9]Thakombau's intelligent resistance to missionary preaching is documented throughout Waterhouse's *The King and People of Fiji* (1866). This includes his indifference to the suggestion of a passing Catholic bishop, who told him that the reason the Methodist missionaries had failed to get access to Mbau was that the Virgin Mary was keeping the place for Catholicism: "Whereupon the king told the bishop to leave him and his city to the care of the Virgin, and to come back again when the Virgin had converted them" (*Ibid.*, p. 196).

Two decades earlier, Protestant missionaries in Hawaii were being subjected to similar experiences as their colleagues in Fiji. " 'If he [King Liholiho] embraces the new religion,' " Rev. Ellis was told in 1822, " 'we shall all follow' " (Ellis 1969:41). One day when the missionary Hiram Bingham went to remonstrate with the royally drunk King, "and told him God was not pleased with such conduct," Liholiho replied, " 'I am god myself. What the hell! Get out of my house' " (Hammatt: 6 Jan. 1823). In the ensuing events, which included Liholiho's death, Christianity was taken up as an instrument of rule by the King's foster mother and her brothers, the effective governing group, and as in Fiji it became an overnight sensation (cf. Bingham 1969). Indeed, we seem to be in the presence of a great regularity or law of conversion valid for the Polynesian heroic polities. In New Zealand also there was a quantum statistical leap forward in the conversion process about 1838–39, after a long period of relatively desultory success (notably among Maori slaves). Once again, the lead was taken by the chiefly class (Wright 1959:141 f.).

Islands, as against the "pagan" enemy. If he thus lost some Fijian support, he stood to gain certain windward Christian soldiers—from the Tongan Islands—not to neglect the commitment to his cause of the Lord's English servants. Aided now by missionary intrigue and the decisive military intervention of the Christian King of Tonga, Thakombau was able to rout his enemies in the battle of Kamba in April 1855. He was indeed saved.

The old religion then gave birth to the new. For as Fijians say, "in olden times, the chief was our god," and Christianity owed something to this ancient conception of divinity. Christianity was destined to become "the religion of Thakombau" because it was won in a battle whose causes were as identified with the chief as the reasons men fought lay in their constituted obligations to serve him, the terms and modes of that service (*nggaravi*) being the same as ritual adoration of the god. Moreover, the same sense of divinity orchestrated the course of battle, with a parallel domino-effect on the outcome.

The Fijians fought like Tacitus's Germans: "The chief [*princeps*] fights for victory; the followers [*comites*] for their chief" (*Germ.* XIV).[10] Some weeks before the decisive engagement at Kamba, the paramount chief of Rewa died suddenly of dysentery, without regaining consciousness or passing the charge of war to a successor. Immediately and quasi-totally, the principal Rewan opposition to Bau disintegrated. The surviving notables sued Thakombau for peace, telling also of their willingness to follow Jehovah. It cannot be that they were merely crypto-rationalists who knew how to find good ideological reasons for extricating themselves from an untenable military situation, since all this happened when they were on the threshold of victory. In the following weeks, rebels from Mbau were able to rally certain people of Rewa against Thakombau and Christianity. But Rewa

[10] During the Mbau-Rewa war, when an important chief defected to the enemy, as Thokanauto of Rewa, for example, went over to Mbau, a considerable number of clans and villages subordinate to the chief accordingly changed sides. The change was effected without great embarrassment, since, as Rev. Hunt remarks, "whatever party they fought for, they were fighting for their own chief" (19 Oct. 1845). Derrick likewise paraphrases Tacitus: "As for the common people, their chief's cause was their cause" (1950:78). These defections are a good demonstration of the relation between hierarchical solidarity and "tribal" or "national" consciousness, on which more is said below.

was no longer functioning as a coherent force. And in the ensuing battle of Kamba, the absence of the main Rewan host proved a serious (if not fatal) weakness for Thakombau's remaining adversaries.[11] The real correlation of forces and consequent course of events—with effects still visible in the structure of Fijian politics—had turned on the being of the sacred chief, whose sudden removal dissolved the purpose and articulation of his armies.

This really *is* a history of kings and battles, but only because it is a cultural order that, multiplying the action of the king by the system of society, gives him a disproportionate historical effect. Briefly, I recapitulate certain interrelated tendencies of the Fijian case, on the conjecture that they are paradigmatic of a history in the heroic mode. First, the general force of circumstance, such as the European presence, becomes the specific course of history according to the determinations of the higher politics. The infrastructure is realized as historical form and event in the terms of ruling interests, and according to their conjuncture. Second, this history shows an unusual capacity for sudden change or rupture: a mutation of the cultural course, developing as the rapid popular generalization of an heroic action. Hence the statistical quantum leaps. As a corollary, a history of this structural type produces great men, even geniuses, by transforming the intelligent acts of individuals into fateful outcomes for the society—consider the brilliant results of Thakombau's conversion. Or more generally, where history thus unfolds as the social extension of the heroic person, it is likely to present a curious mixture of tactical geniality and practical irrationality. If Thakombau consistently exemplifies the first, the collapse of Rewa at the death of its chief and on the brink of victory makes an example of irrationality that sorely tries our own native sense

[11] Not only Rewa proper, but many of its 'fighting-lands' (*bati*) or allies were absent from the Kamba battle—Derrick's statement (1950:112) to the opposite effect notwithstanding. Aside from Nakelo and seven warriors from the land called Tonga, I find no historic mention of Rewa's traditional allies in Kamba (e.g., Mburembasanga, Notho, Nuku, etc.). This is consistent with the testimony of modern informants, who also claim only one of Nakelo's twelve or thirteen towns joined Thakombau's enemies in the final battle. Moreover, Calvert, who often visited Kamba while it was occupied by the Mbau rebels, said that the latter (under Ratu Mara) had intended to attack Rewa after defeating Thakombau, for having settled with Mbau upon their chief's death (Journal: 7 April 1855).

of hardheaded surrealism. Still, Chadwick (1926:340–41) found analogous episodes—the capture or death of the enemy king leading to "destruction of the enemy's organisation" and "forthwith to the end of hostilities"—a recurrent feature of the Germanic heroic age, both as poetry and as history. And anthropologists could come up with many exotic events of the same structural form, if at the risk of obliterating the distinction between history and ritual.[12]

Consider the incident famous in Zulu annals where the triumphant army of Shaka's predecessor Dingiswayo suddenly dissolves upon the abduction and assassination of the latter: a complete reversal of fortune that elicits from the missionary-ethnographer unflattering comment on "the innate helplessness of the Bantu people when once deprived of their leader" (Bryant 1929:166). Indeed, the whole Mtêtwa confederacy fashioned by Dingiswayo broke up at his death, making the opening for Shaka, leader of the subordinate Zulu "tribe."[13] The rest, as they say, is history, including the crises of cosmic proportions that attended attempts on Shaka's life, and again at the death of his mother, female complement of the Nguni dual sovereignty (cf. Heusch 1982). The entire Zulu nation was plunged into paroxysms of in-

[12] Hocart makes the possibility of general collapse a structural condition of divine kingship:

> The king has to test the efficacy of his consecration by a combat. Fighting for the throne becomes a regular practice. Oriental wars are largely personal conflicts for sovereignty, like our Hundred Years' War. Patriotism is not the incentive: the people fight merely to support the god who brings welfare. If he is killed they lose all further interest and accept the victor. Persian, Indian, Sinhalese armies dispersed as soon as their leader was killed, although they might be winning (1933:272).

[13] The mutations in organization that followed also testify to an heroic historicity, not only by Shaka's capacity to introduce rapid and general change, but in the attention he gave to hierarchical solidarities while reconstituting the conquest state. Repeating the victories of Dingiswayo, Shaka was careful not to repeat his predecessor's policies of leaving intact the leadership and organization of the conquered tribes. Liquidating the one with the other, and regrouping the remnants of the enemy armies in the Zulu regimental system, Shaka constructed an order that avoided the faults in Dingiswayo's hegemonic ambitions, viz., the confederate system that had divided the interests of the tribes by the existence of their leaders (Bryant 1926; Flynn in Bird 1888; Isaacs 1970; Krige 1936; Wilson 1969).

ternal slaughter, seeking to forestall, by these massive purges of evil, the conjunction of Sky and Earth that would naturally follow the fall of the heavenly ruler.[14]

I purposely associate the cosmological catastrophe with the military debacle on grounds that the two are the same in principle. The disarray of the victorious army bereft of its leader is an enactment, in the modality of history, of the same ritual chaos that sets in at the death of the divine king, well-known to ethnography as the return to an original condition of cosmic disorder. In Hawaii, for example, where the "antistructure" appears not only in characteristic reversals of status—we shall have occasion later (chapter 4) to document these—but in the removal of the heir-apparent from such scenes of tabu pollution. Bereft thus of all leadership, the people give vent to their grief in various forms of self-mutilation, and so die with their king. For ten days the world dissolves; whereupon, the royal successor returns to reinstate the tabus and redivide the lands—i.e., to recreate the differences that make up the natural and cultural order.[15] Yet we

[14]Firsthand accounts of these incidents are given by Fynn (in Bird 1888:81–84, 91–93) and Isaacs (1970:108 f.). Mr. John Kelly has written an excellent M.A. thesis, "Mongol Conquest and Zulu Terror: An analysis of cultural change," with a detailed cultural analysis of the Zulu scheme of heroic dominance (University of Chicago, Department of Anthropology, 1982).

[15]On the death rites of Hawaiian ruling chiefs, see Handy and Pukui (1972: 156–57); Kamakau (1961:104–7); Ellis (1969:175 f.); Stewart (1970 [1830]:216); etc. I put "antistructure" in quotation marks to signify the usual reservations to V. Turner's (1969) concept of *communitas* as an amorphous condition of solidarity, in opposition to structural order (*societas*). It is, of course, not an absence but an inversion of structure, thus a form in its own right, whose alternation with the normal kingship signifies important relations of sovereignty (see chap. 4).

Hawaiian history also testifies to the "actual" collapse (or the incapacity) of an organized, collective response to military threats in the absence of the ruling chief. The British naval commander Broughton provides an example from a revolt of 1796, when a rival chief, profiting from the absence of King Kamehameha, easily seized the greater part of Hawai'i Island. Nor could much resistance be expected, according to Broughton, as there was no one to lead it:

He [the rebel, Namakaeha] now possessed four out of [the Island's] six districts, and was approaching near to Karakakooa [Kealakekua], where there was little chance of resistance, as the people were averse to fighting, having no chief in whom they confided to lead them on; indeed the only person of that rank was Mahooa, who had lost his eye-sight. He wished much to go with us to Wohahow [O'ahu] that he

speak of this as "ritual," while holding apart the homologous collapse of armies as "battle," and by such means merely mark our own distinctions between "make-believe" and "reality," while preserving a sense of history as the kingdom of practical reason. Could we remove the praxological scales from our eyes, it would be seen that all these and other events, ranging from the fratricidal strife of the East African interregnum to the seclusion of the king in Polynesian rites of world-renewal, refer to the same system of hierarchy. But I cannot rehearse here the whole text of *The Golden Bough*.

Suffice it to call attention to certain sociological aspects of the kingship as a cosmic principle of order. I mean the various social forms underlying the generalization of heroic action or the One-Giant-Indian effect. Those I single out—heroic segmentation, hierarchical solidarity, positional succession, division of labor in historic consciousness—are not universal in the heroic societies, but they are probably sufficiently typical.

Old-time students of social structure will appreciate the differences between heroic modes of lineage formation and developmental processes of the classic segmentary-lineage system. The segmentary lineage reproduces itself from the bottom-upward: by natural increase among its minimal groups and fission along the collateral lines of a common ancestry. Societies such as Zulu and Hawaiian, however—or the Nguni and Polynesian chiefdoms generally—present also the reverse evolution. The major "lineage"/territorial divisions develop from the top of the system downward, as the extension of domestic fission in the ruling families. Call it "heroic segmentation." Initiated by the centrifugal dispersion of the royal kindred, typically in anticipation of a struggle over succession, the process entails redistribution of the underlying (or defeated) peoples among members of the ruling aristocracy. The principles of descent are in effect superceded at the higher levels of segmentary order by the privileges of authority. Barnes (1951, 1967) supplies notable examples from the Ngoni: the establishment of "quasi-agnatic" communities around the several royal wives and their respective sons, whose

---

might explain what happened to Tamaahmaah [Kamehameha], but the people, having no other chief, would not permit him (Broughton 1804:69).

rivalry may issue finally in independent kingdoms. Organized by the relations of power among contemporary princes, rather than by ancestral reference, the main political groups are thus constituted as the social projections of heroic ambitions.[16] Parenthetically (and speculatively), might not the whole remarkable expansion of Nguni states since the late eighteenth century, including Zulu, Swazi, and Ndabele, be the historic trace of such heroic processes? The state probably originates as the structural means of some personal project of glory.

We need a notion of "hierarchical solidarity" to go alongside Durkheim's mechanical and organic types. In the heroic societies, the coherence of the members or subgroups is not so much due to their similarity (mechanical solidarity) or to their complementarity (organic solidarity) as to their common submission to the ruling power. The corollary of hierarchical solidarity is a devaluation of tribalism as we know it, since the collectivity is defined by its adherence to a given chief or king rather than by distinctive cultural attributes—even as bonds of kinship and relations to ancestral lands are dissolved by such processes as he-

---

[16] Gifford's description of heroic segmentation in the Tonga Islands were destined to become a celebrated locus of sociological argument among Polynesianists:

> Everything points to the necessity of a line of powerful chiefs as a nucleus about which the lineage groups itself. Without such chiefs it appears to wilt and die and its membership gradually aligns itself with other rising lineages. This process of realignment naturally contravenes the rule of patrilineal descent, which theoretically, and largely in practice, determines lineage membership (Gifford 1929:30).

The arguments have been laid to rest (or should have been, anyhow) by Elizabeth Bott's (1981) careful description of the Tongan organization, together with excellent examples of the segmentation process in question (pp. 41 ff.). One of the lessons of the controversy might be that we should not expect a "lineage consciousness" in the underlying populations of the hierarchical Polynesian societies. Indeed, in Hawaii, where heroic segmentation is taken even further, with the leadership of the districts down to relatively low levels of segmentation redistributed by each ruling chief among his kinsmen at his accession, the local lineage order has been completely eroded. Nor could it be expected that the people would have their own extensive genealogies, hence their own senior lines and collateral relations of solidarity, in opposition to the chiefs constantly being imposed upon them. The more subtle ways that Maori "clans" (*hapū*) are formed by dominant chiefs and as political alliances have been sensitively documented by Schwimmer (1963, 1978).

roic segmentation. Chadwick repeatedly remarks on the absence of "national" sentiment or interest in the European heroic
age; rather, the state was apparently "regarded as little more
than the property of the individual [ruler]" (1926:336). So Benveniste observes that, apart from Western Europe, a term for
society does not appear in the classical vocabulary of Indo-
European institutions. The concept, instead, "is expessed in a
different fashion. In particular one recognizes it under the name
of *realm* [*royaume*]: the limits of society coincide with a certain
power, which is the power of the king" (1969, 2:9). In this light,
the potential for *déracinement* which we have seen in Africa, and
which could be matched for migration and conquest by Ger-
mania, Mongolia, or Polynesia, appears as characteristic of the
heroic age: the counterpart in historicity of a certain hierarchy.[17]

Beyond personal ambition and glory, the battle royals at the
center of these historic maelstroms must also refer to certain
structures. I can show this for the fratricidal strife of Fijian chiefly
families, and the explication would probably hold for Nguni
states, likewise marked by the polygynous alliances of the rulers
to ranking women of strategic clans or neighboring states. Such
alliances make up the larger set of political relations. But in the
event, the sons of a given paramount, as representatives of their
respective mothers' peoples, condense in their own persons the
entire regional system of political interests. An extensive correlation of social forces is realized in and as the interpersonal relations of royal households, especially the rivalries of paternal

---

[17] Chadwick writes of "the instability of heroic society:"

> The military followers of a peace-loving king, unless he was very
> wealthy and generous, were liable to drift away, while the bulk of the
> population counted for nothing. In the absence of any truly national
> organization or national feeling all depended on the personal qualities
> of the leaders. Under Theodric the Ostrogoths were the chief power in
> Europe; but within thirty years of his death they disappear and are not
> heard of again. Under Dušan the Servians seemed destined to absorb
> all that was left of the Greek empire; after his death they failed to offer
> any effective resistance to the Turks. The kingdoms of the Greek
> Heroic Age seem to have succumbed to much less formidable antag-
> onists. So numerous indeed are cases of this kind that one is perhaps
> justified in regarding national disaster as the normal ending of such
> epochs (Chadwick 1926:461–62).

half-brothers—and rides on their outcome. Uneasy then lies the head that wears the kingly crown. The structural weight that aristocratic kinship is forced to bear helps explain the byzantine intrigue, climaxed by cruel scenes of fratricide or parricide, so often told in the annals of heroic history.[18]

And insofar as all the dead generations structurally "weigh like a nightmare on the brain of the living," these struggles may never end. "Yes, 1852," said the Tongan, "that was the year . . . I fought King Tā'ufa'āhau." But, comments the ethnographer, "the actual person who fought King Tā'ufa'āhau was the speaker's great-great-great-grandfather" (Bott 1981:23). We have all heard of the "royal we." Here, as an expression of *positional succession*, is an even more radical "heroic I." Thus a subclan headman of the Luapula Kingdom of Kazembe:

> We came to the country of Mwanshya . . . I killed a puku [antelope] . . . We gave some of the meat to Mwanshya. He asked where the salt came from and he was told. So he sent people who killed me. My mother was angry and went to fetch medicine to send thunderbolts. She destroyed Mwanshya's village . . . Lukoshi then told me to go forward and that he would stay and rule Mwanshya's country. So we came away . . . Lubunda . . . heard about my strength. He came to see us and married my mother. They went away and I remained (Cunnison 1959:234; cf. Cunnison 1951, 1957).

All these events, including the narrator's death, transpired before he was born.[19]

By the heroic I—and various complements such as perpetual kinship—the main relationships of society are at once projected historically and embodied currently in the persons of authority.

[18] On the royal intrigues of the Fijian states of Mbau and Rewa, see Waterhouse (1866), Derrick (1950), or Wilkes (1845, vol. 3); for Lau, Hocart (1929), Reid (1977). For European analogues, see Chadwick (1926:338 ff.).

[19] The "heroic I" is found in Maori, Tonga, Fiji, among Yoruba as well as Luapula, and probably numerous other hierarchical orders. This usage is discussed in Sahlins (1981) as "the kinship I" following Johansen (1954) on Maori. The Maori case is indeed relatively democratic, although the chief is more likely than other people to use the first-person singular in reference to noted ancestors or the clan (*hapu*) as a whole.

Contemporary ancestors, such heroic figures are structuring simply by being, insofar as the existence of other people is defined by theirs. In European talk this is "power," but "power" then is a positional or systematic value, that may work as well by "influence" as by coercion. Moreover, the structure as incarnate in such powers-that-be may thereupon prove immune to what other people actually do. At issue is the historical relation between cultural order and empirical practice—which I illustrate again from Fiji:

Dynastic legends tell of the origin of the ruling line from the union of an immigrant prince with a ranking woman of indigenous people.[20] The chiefs stand henceforth as wife-takers and sisters' sons to the people of the land. As we shall see in the succeeding chapter (3), the Fijian concept of the chief's divinity is a corollary of this founding relationship. For the famous prerogative of the sister's son is to appropriate the sacrifices made to the god of his mother's lineage. The chief is thus entitled to the offerings made to the indigenous gods. He substitutes for the people's gods in this world, becomes their visible form or man-god (*kalou tamata*) (Hocart 1915, 1936). Now, it does not matter, structurally, that certain current marriages between lesser women of chiefly clans and men of the people may run counter to the divine status of the ruling line as wife-takers. Precisely, what ordinary people do is not systematically decisive, in comparison with the higher-order social effects sedimented by aristocratic relationships. And high Fijian chiefs, we have seen, continue to differentially make history by polygynous marriages that amount to systems of intertribal alliance. The structure is not statistical. It is not the expression in institutions of the empirical frequencies of interactions. As the Maori proverb goes, "the great man is not hidden among the many."[21]

[20] Fijian polity is analyzed in greater cultural detail below (chap. 3).

[21] The long-term constitution of relationships by a "founding marriage," perhaps legendary, is of course characteristic of systems of positional succession. And the differential weight attached to aristocratic marriage generally is a principled reason, valid at least for societies of a certain type, why the distinction between prescriptive and preferential marriage rules need not be received by a structuralist analysis. So the rule of generalized exchange, operating *sometimes* among the highest chiefs, seems as critical in the organization of Tongan society as it is minimal in social practice. In any event, in the Polynesian societies, the ordinary people hardly marry at all, ritually speaking, as opposed to a living to-

Writing of the new history, Professor Barraclough (1978:58) tells us that "all generalizations," including such historical judgments as "significant," are "inherently quantitative"—which presumably also goes for what he just said. For heroic history, then, the effective statistical rule would be something like a Principle of the Significant One: the one who counts. This demonstrates, quantitatively, that "significance" is a qualitative value—in the first place (cf. Thompson 1977:254–55).

The complement of such heroic statistics is a political division of labor in cultural and historical consciousness. The time of society is calculated in dynastic genealogies, as collective history resides in royal traditions. In the state rituals and political councils of the elite, the cultural schemes are subject to manipulation and comment by specialists, such as priests and genealogists, attached to the ruling interests. Whereas, in the villages, anthropologists encounter a certain indifference to the historic Great Tradition, coupled with an inclination on the people's part to offer improvised pragmatic responses to questions about "custom," in place of the exotic exegeses on the meaning of things their interlocutors had been trained to consider "the culture." The short and simple annals of the poor.

"There are probably no people possessing an equal amount of intelligence," wrote an early white trader among Zulu, "who are less well-acquainted with their history than the Kaffirs" (Fynn in Bird 1888:104). Judging from Bryant's (1929) success in collecting a detailed Zulu tradition, the assertion must refer to the generality of common folks. Besides, Europeans residing early and late among the equally intelligent Austronesians have run into the same experience, at least in certain quarters. The missionary Hunt said of Fijians that, "they know next to nothing of their past. Their origin and history are both a complete mystery to them" (28 Oct. 1843). Malani of Lakemba (Fiji) was garrulous enough, Hocart found, "but was said to know little because he had been brought up among the common people and not the nobles" (WI:22). Similarly a recent notice of Madagascar relates: "History is not evenly distributed because to have it is a sign of politico-religious power and authority" (Feeley-Harnik 1978:402;

---

gether (*noho pu*) whose duration and outsome are uncertain until children are born and acknowledged.

cf. Fox 1971, on Roti).[22] Examples could be multiplied, but the best would probably remain Cunnison's brilliant analysis of political distinctions in historical consciousness among the Luapula peoples (1951; cf. Cunnison 1957, 1959).

Pocock's well-known article on "The Anthropology of Time-reckoning" (1964) makes the differential historical consciousness an aspect of the formal logic of hierarchy. "The larger co-ordination," Pocock writes, or higher level of social system, "subsumes the less." The kingship thus provides a general time-indication for the diverse incidents of lineage tradition or personal recollection which, taken by themselves, would be, in a strict sense, socially meaningless and temporally mere duration. Just so, in exemplary expressions of hierarchical encompassment, the old-time Hawaiian figures his own biography in terms of the king's activity: "I was born when Kamehameha conquered O'ahu;" "I was old enough to carry stones when Kamehameha

[22] In the (Austronesian) kingdoms of Polynesia, the reservation of historical-genealogical (hence also, cosmogonic) knowledge to the elite was similarly marked. So this early notice on Tonga by the missionary John Thomas:

> We may observe that the knowledge of the gods, their origin, or the origin of things below, were not common subjects which fell within the province of the common people to know, or to be concerned about; their duty being to obey their chiefs, who had been informed by persons of much higher rank than themselves, what was right for them to do, and believe in reference to their sacred things. One of these chiefs of the highest rank, and viewed as a kind of demigod herself, was the late Tamaha [sororal niece of the sacred king, Tui Tonga] who was a most intelligent Lady—a living oracle; it was truly surprising to hear her relate events that have taken place, with the names of chiefs who have governed, with the names of their wives and families for several generations past. It appears that this kind of information was entrusted to members of this and other great families, who were most careful of it, and faithfully communicated it to proper persons to be kept (Thomas, MS).

In the same way, Kamehameha, famous conqueror of Hawaii, selected his brother's daughter to be the repository of chiefly lore and genealogy:

> The system by which she was taught was exceedingly rigourous. Persons were employed by the direction of the king, who acted as teachers and she was confined with them in the closest manner for many hours of the day, with little interruption, for several years (*The Polynesian*, 21 June 1845 [Honolulu]; obituary of Kekauluohi).

built the fish pond at Kiholo"; and the like.[23] Their own lives are
calqued upon the king's—

> Upon the king! Let us our lives, our souls,
> Our debts, our careful wives,
> Our children, and our sins, lay on the King!
>   (*Henry V*, IV, i)

At the extreme, the people verge on "historylessness." In Hawaii, the continuous redistribution of lands among the ruling
chiefs preempts any local lineage formation, reducing genealogical memories among the common people largely to personal rec-
ollections. Having lost control of their own social reproduction,
as Bonte puts it for the analogous situation of Tuareg, the people
are left without an historical appreciation of the main cultural
categories (Bonte and Echard 1976:270 f.). For them, the culture
is mostly "lived"—in practice, and as *habitus*. Their lives are run
on an unconscious mastery of the system, something like Everyman's control of the grammatical categories, together with the
homespun concepts of the good that allow them to improvise
daily activities on the level of the pragmatic and matter-of-fact.
Such unreflexive mastery of percept and precept is what Bourdieu calls *habitus*: "schemes of thought and expression . . . [that]
are the basis for the intentionless invention of regulated im-
provisation" (1977:79).
   The people's code, however, is not altogether so "restricted."
True, Hawaiian kings have genealogies going back 963 generations, associated with cosmic myths and royal legends whose
telling, especially in political argument, is an express manipulation of the cultural categories. Yet the common people for their
part have scores if not hundreds of contemporary kith and kin
about whom they endlessly "talk story"—tell the news. Now,
news is not just anything about anybody; it is likewise a selective determination of what is significant according to canons of
cultural value. If "So-and-so, the youngest son of So-and-so,
married So-and-so—you know the adopted favorite daughter of

---

[23] Excellent examples of this type of autobiographical reflection can be found
in the testimonies of the Boundary Commission of the Hawaiian Kingdom in the
1860s: Department of Land and Natural Resources, Boundary Commission
Books, in the State of Hawaii Archives.

the Kealoha folks—and moved inland to take up farming," then
a whole series of distinctions and relations between land and
sea, agriculture and fishing, junior and senior, birth and adoption—the same sorts of difference that make a difference in royal
rite or myth—are being engaged in the recitation of the quoti-
dian and mundane. Besides, the people's gossip often retails en-
chanted happenings as fabulous as those of myth. It is something of the myth of everyday life.[24] The cultural consciousness
objectified in historical genres among the elite appears, rather,
in the practical activities and current annals of the people: a division of cultural labors corresponding to the heroic mode of historical production.

We need not exaggerate the contrast to ourselves, given that
the general interest of the bourgeois state is the particular interest of its ruling classes, as Marx taught. But capitalist society
does have a distinctive mode of appearance, therefore a definite
anthropological consciousness, pervasive also in the theoretical
dispositions of the Academy. The native "Boo-jwas" theory is
that social outcomes are the cumulative expressions of individual actions, hence behind that of the prevailing state of the
people's wants and opinions, as generated especially out of their
material sufferings. The society is constructed as the institutional sum of its individual practices. The classical locus of this
folklore is, of course, the marketplace, where the relative success of autonomous individual agents, thus the political order of
the economy, is measurable by the quantitative shares respectively obtained in the public boodle at the cost of whom it may
concern. Yet this social process is *experienced* by the participants
as the maximization of their personal satisfactions. And since all
such satisfactions—from listening to the Chicago Symphony to
calling home by long-distance phone—require the reduction of
diverse social conditions and relations to their lowest common
denominator of pecuniary expense, for the purpose of a rational
allocation of one's finite resources, the impression is given that
the whole culture is organized by people's businesslike econo-

---

[24]The relation between ordinary gossip and, say, royal genealogies is happily
illustrated among Luapula peoples by the etymology and fate of the term *ilyashi*,
referring to group "affairs" or "traditions." It comes from plateau Bemba where it
means mere "gossip," yet latterly has been replaced by the English word *meaning*
(Cunnison 1951).

mizing. This impression is doubled by the democratic political process in which Everyman counts as "one" (vote), so representing the governing powers as "the people's cherce." The prevailing quantitative, populist, and materialist presuppositions of our social science can then be no accident—or there is no anthropology.

On the other hand, the different cultural orders studied by anthropology have their own historicities. Even the kinship orders. Ignoring the passage of time and generation, Crow/ Omaha kinship turns contingent events of marriage into perpetual relationships by freezing whole lineages into the familial positions assumed at an initial alliance. Likewise, the elementary marriage systems would reproduce indefinitely the relationships of intermarrying groups; whereas, the complex systems, defined negatively by rules against kin marriages, introduce discontinuity in group alliances and their reformulation generation to generation. The Ilongot act on the sense that they invent their own social lives, each generation as it were rediscovering the Philippines (Rosaldo 1980). But do they not thus refer to a system of complex marriage, combined with optative (cognatic) filiation, which besides generates long-term closure of its moments of kindred and residential dispersion? Only that for the Ilongot, as for the Americans, the structure is reproduced as travestied in the aphorisms of the *habitus*—"we follow our hearts"—and through the unreflected mastery of its percepts. The issue is not the absence of structure, but its inscription in *habitus*, as opposed to its objectification as mythopoetics.[25] Here is a main distinction of structures, crosscutting the others to which I alluded: between those that are practiced primarily through the individ-

[25] The Ilongot historical practice is in so many respects the antithesis of the Maori "mytho-praxis" about to be described that it is necessary to underscore R. Rosaldo's observation that, "Even the most brute of brute facts I found to be culturally mediated . . . Ilongot statements about their past were embodied in cultural forms that highlighted certain facts of life and remained silent about others through their patterned way of selecting, evaluating, and ordering the world they attended to" (1980:17–18). Otherwise the Ilongot ideology might evoke on the ethnographer's part a rabid methodological individualism. Fortunately also, Rosaldo is able to link Ilongot historical consciousness to the system of marriage, a combination of complex and exchange-marriage that unifies each generation while opposing it to adjacent ones, and to show, too, the cycles of kinship repartition and coalescence (cf. 1980:199).

ual subconscious and those that explicitly organize historical action as the projection of mythical relations. I turn to an extended example of the latter, chosen again for the scandal it makes to a received historiography.

Mytho-Praxis

In the "Introduction" to the *Peloponnesian War*, Thucydides tells of his intention to eliminate all elements of the marvelous from his history since, as he modestly explained: "My work is not a piece of writing designed to meet the taste of an immediate public, but was done to last forever." So begins the Western historiography of the Unvarnished Truth or the triumph of *logos* over *mythos* (cf. Vernant 1979:196 f.). Curious, then, that Sir George Grey, in the "Preface" to his *Polynesian Mythology*, tells how he was compelled to gather his great corpus of Maori myth in order to fight a certain Polynesian war. Appointed Governor of New Zealand in the midst of a Maori uprising, Sir George soon discovered that he could not negotiate the critical issues of war and peace with Maori chiefs unless he had a sound knowledge of their poetry and mythology:

> To my surprise . . . I found that these chiefs, either in their speeches to me or in their letters, frequently quoted, in explanation of their views and intentions, fragments of ancient poems and proverbs, or made allusions which rested on an ancient system of mythology; and, although it was clear that the most important parts of their communications were embodied in these figurative forms, the interpreters . . . could . . . rarely (if ever) translate the poems or explain the allusions . . . Clearly, however, I could not, as Governor of the country, permit so close a veil to be drawn between myself and the aged and influential chiefs whom it was my duty to attach to British interests and to the British race . . . Only one thing could, under such circumstances be done, and that was to acquaint myself with the ancient language of the country, to collect its traditional poems and legends, to induce their priests to impart to me their mythology, and to study their proverbs (Grey 1956 [1855]: unpaged front matter).

The documented history of the Polynesian wars thus begins where the landmark history of the Peloponnesian wars left off. And if anthropology then inherits a famous collection of myths from the practicalities of battle, it is because the Maori, who think of the future as behind them, find in a marvelous past the measure of the demands that are made to their current existence (cf. Johansen 1954).

I exemplify by a letter composed in the style of public oratory, in the course of which the author, a chief, sends a threat of war to another chief in the form of a love song (Shortland 1856:189–92). According to the *pākehā* (European) authority to whom the example is due, the threat lies in the refrain, "The hand that was stretched out and returned *tapu* shall become *noa* [i.e., 'free from *tapu'*, 'profane']." The woman in this way tells her previously rejected suitor that if he tries again he will have better success— presumably that what was before untouchable (*tapu*) shall become touchable (*noa*).[26] So the chief is telling his enemy that although last time he came away unscathed, if he dares to return he can expect a warm welcome. Maori will get the allusion since from the beginning of mankind sex has been a battle which women win, turning the death of the man (detumescence) into the life of the people (the child). Maori say, "the genitals of women are killers of men." Behind that, too, is the myth of the origin of death wherein the trickster Maui, in a vain attempt to win immortality for mankind, is crushed to death in the vagina of the ancestress-guardian of the underworld (Best 1976 [1924]: 146 f.; 1925:763–67, 944–48; Goldie 1905; Johansen 1954:228 f.; J. Smith 1974–75).

Clearly, Maori are cunning mythologists, who are able to select from the supple body of traditions those most appropriate to the satisfaction of their current interests, as they conceive them. The distinctiveness of their mytho-praxis is not the existence (or the absence) of such interests, but exactly that they are so conceived. The Maori, as Johansen says, "find themselves in history" (1954:163).[27]

---

[26] Or else the meaning is that the male who before preserved his *tapu* shall next time mix with the woman, and thereby lose it, an interpretation supported by the Maori concept of sexual intercourse as the death of the man (see below).

[27] Maoris . . . describe the past as *nga ra o mua*, "the days in front,"

Although there are extant examples of such mythic discourse from the very rebellion that brought Sir George (then Captain) Grey to New Zealand, I am rather in the same quandary as he in trying to decode them.[28] Perhaps, then, I may be allowed to make use of a similar speech from John White's (1874) reconstruction of the daily life of the Ngapuhi, the tribe that instigated the uprising in question. The speaker, Rou, a man of some standing in the community, although not the highest, had lost a son in battle and is now protesting the decision of the tribal notables that the enemy victims taken in revenge be buried instead of eaten, because of kinship relations between the warring groups. Rou begins by reciting the legend of the origin of the clan, hence the common descent and character of himself and the elders. This leads into a disquisition on the relation of microcosm and macrocosm: "Man is like this world . . . He has a voice: the world has its wind. The world has soil: man has a heart," etc. Rou acknowledges the chiefs' powers over the cosmos, however, and enunciates the principle of heroic generalization: "Man is like the wind. If the wind blows one way, it all blows that way. If one man praises the chief, all men praise him . . . As the wind blows in one way, so men blow in the direction you indicate . . ." But now he sets forth his disagreement, which begins at the origin of the world. He recites the myth of the Children of Rangi (the Heavens)—myth collected by Grey, inciden-

---

and the future as *kei muri*, "behind." They move into the future with their eyes on the past. In deciding how to act in the present, they examine the panorama of history spread before their eyes, and select the model that is most appropriate and helpful from the many presented there. This is not living in the past; it is drawing on the past for guidance, bringing the past into the present and the future (Metge 1976:70).

[28]The speeches made by friendly Maori chiefs during a meeting with the Government in the course of this war are partly preserved in the correspondence of the then governor, Fitzroy. But the speeches, "were so full of allegorical references and responses to ancient Maori customs, that much of them was not understood by the missionaries, who could not render them into English" (Buick 1926:41n; cf. Carleton 1874, 2:78–79). Just so, Best describes the traditional war councils of chiefs, when "the most stirring and eloquent speeches were made, speeches teeming with strange old saws and aphorisms, with numerous allusions to the famed deeds of ancestors and to the classic myths of the Polynesian race" (1902–3:46).

tally, in *Polynesian Mythology*. The story tells of the origin of cannibalism among the divine ancestors, a cannibalism that is also
the institution and possibility of human existence. Tū, ancestor
and patron of man as warrior, defeats his older brothers, the
other sons of Rangi, who are the parents of birds, trees, fish,
wild and cultivated foods. To defeat is to render *noa* (without
tapu) and consumable. Tū is thus able to consume his brothers'
offspring, power he passes on to mankind. "If then the gods eat
each other," Rou argues, "and they were brothers . . . I ask,
why was I not allowed to eat those who killed my child?" Rou
goes on to double this mythical argument with another about
the divine origin of witchcraft, which explains how evil came
into the hearts of men, including his own project of cannibal
vengeance. Assuring the chiefs he will not now go against their
wishes, he nonetheless concludes by citing two proverbs that
signify he will alone and in due time have satisfaction. "You
know the proverb that says, 'The anger of relatives is a fire that
burns fiercely' [i.e., his own anger at his son's death], and another that says, 'the hand alone can get food to spare for its own
body'" (White 1874:185–93).

The Maori past is a vast scheme of life-possibilities, ranging
from ancient myth to recent memory through a series of epochs
parallel in structure and analogous in event, while successively
changing in content from the abstract and universal to the concrete and individual, from the divine to the human and on to the
ancestral group, from the separation of Heaven and Earth to
the delimitation of the clan territories.[29] The kind of transformation between sacred myth and historic legend that Dumézil
(1968) finds operating between different branches of the Indo-
European stock thus appears within the Maori tradition as a
connected succession of stages, with the added consideration
that the movement from the cosmic to the "historic" is consum-
mated by the ultimate expression of the same structure as—real
life. In the cosmic myths are the generic possibilities. Birth,
death, illness, sex, revenge, cannibalism: the elementary experiences are constituted by the deeds of primordial gods/ancestors.

[29]The ideas on the Maori sense of history presented here were especially
stimulated by and are much indebted to Johansen (1954) and to an unpublished
paper by Gregory Schrempp, "The Pattern of Maori Mythology."

But each 'tribe' (*iwi*) also has a humanity specific to itself, arising from the attributes of its particular ancestors and the saga of their migration from Hawaiki, spiritual homeland of the Maori (cf. the examples in Simmons 1976). The order of social structure is then established by the progression through the New Zealand landscape of tribal and clanic ancestors, leaving their respective traces in the local set of geographic features named from their doings, and in the particular set of persons, both human and "natural," descended from their multiple unions with women of the indigenous 'land people' (*tangata whenua*). In this, social structure is the humanized form of cosmic order. The prototype is the primordial search of the divine ancestor Tāne—Tāne, the Fertilizer—for the *uha*, the female element: search that gave rise, in a series of exotic sexual experiments, to various kinds of birds, trees, insects, waters, and rocks, and eventually to mankind through the mating of the god with a woman fashioned from the *mons veneris* of the Earth Mother (Papa). As Tāne did on an elemental scale, thus did the tribal ancestors in New Zealand. So the main cultural relationships devolve through a series of pro- gressively distinctive and delimited forms, corresponding to the devolution in social sphere or segmentary level, from primordial myths to tribal and clan legends, and from clan legends to fam- ily histories, until—as carried forward in the ancestral refer- ences of proverbial sayings, proper names, or the pronoun 'I'— they become the order of present existence. The final form of cosmic myth is current event.

"The life that the ancestors lived forth in history is the same as that active in the living" (Johansen 1954:163). Johansen thus in- troduces a contrast of the Maori to the Western historical sense analogous to Furet's deft critique of *l'histoire événementielle* as necessarily the client of finalist ideologies, there being no other way of making intelligible events conceived as sudden irrup- tions of "the unique and the new into the concatenation of time" (1972:54). For Maori, such events are hardly unique or new but are immediately perceived in the received order of structure, as identical with their original. Hence where Western thought struggles to comprehend the history of contingent events that it makes for itself by invoking underlying forces or structures, such as those of production or *mentalité*, the Maori world un- folds as an eternal return, the recurrent manifestation of the same experiences (cf. Eliade 1954). This collapse of time and happening is mediated for Maori by a third term: *tikanga*, the distinctive action of beings and things that comes of their particular nature. If the present reproduces the past, it is because the denizens of this world are instances of the same kinds of being that came before. This relation of class to individual is the very notion of descent, i.e., of the relation of ancestor to descendant, and as is well-known the whole universe is for Maori a comprehensive kindred of common ancestry. Such being the ontological case, we should be wary, as Johansen cautions, of imputing to Maori our own ideas of the individuality of event and experience: "We find it quite obvious that once an event has happened, it never returns; but this is exactly what happens" (1954:161). Hence the very experiences of the past are the way the present is experienced:

> It was a source of *pure, unadulterated joy* for the old time Maori, to be able to say to an enemy, "I ate your father" or "your ancestor," although the occurrence may have occurred ten generations before his time . . . (Best 1902–3:71; emphasis added)

For Maori, ontogeny "recapitulates" cosmogony. The human sexual act recreates the original union of male Heaven (Rangi) and female Earth (Papa). In particular, the incantations used in conception rites are those that enabled the first parent Tāne to produce human offspring with the Earth-formed-woman (Hine-ahu-one) fashioned from Papa. The physiology of birth becomes the saga of creation (cf. Goldie 1905; Best 1929). The womb is the *pō*. *Pō* in myth is the long night of the world's self-generation, issuing finally in the *ao*, the 'day' or world of humans and gods (*ao marama*). A synonym for the placenta is *whenua*, otherwise 'land' or 'earth', a reference thus to the primordial mother. The umbilicus attaching this earth to the child, product of the divine male seed, is itself called the *iho*, a term also denoting the heart and strength of a tree (H. W. Williams 1975:75). Here again is Tāne, parent and body of trees, who in myth assumed just this position between the Earth and the sacred Heavens. The "self-extolling," the "degeneration-causing" younger brother of the gods, Tāne stood upon his head, pressed against the Earth

Mother, and in an act likened to parricide pushed the Sky Father
from her embrace. By then propping up the Sky with four poles,
Tāne and his divine accomplices—including the warrior Tū,
who performed the necessary (human) sacrifice—make it possible for their human progeny to take possession of the Earth
(cf. Grey 1956 [1855]; Best 1976 [1924]; J. Smith 1974–75; S. Percy
Smith 1913–15; also below, chapter 4). Or again, at a later time
man 'descends' (*heke*, 'migrates') across the waters from the
spiritual homeland of Hawaiki to New Zealand, by means of a
canoe fashioned of a tree, another body of Tāne. Creation, migration, and parturition are so many versions of the same story.
So the father chants to his newborn son:

> It was he [Tāne] who put the poles of heaven above us,
> Then you were born to the world of light (Johansen
>   1954:161).

We thus return directly to history, in fact to the very uprising
that brought Sir George Grey to New Zealand and (to close the
circle) gave us the canonical texts of this mythology. The whole
revolt of 1844–46 was about a certain pole, likewise having to
do with possession of the Earth: the flagstaff flying the British
colors above Kororareka in the Bay of Islands, long the most
populous European settlement. I am not speaking figuratively
(merely). On four separate occasions between July 1844 and
March 1845, the Maori "rebel" Hone Heke and his warriors of
the Ngapuhi tribe cut down that flagpole. And Heke's persistence in downing it was matched only by the British insistence
on resurrecting it. Following the final storming of the pole, British troops, aided by certain Maori "loyalists," fought three major engagements with Heke and his allies—in the first two of
which the colonials were well and truly beaten. But throughout,
for Heke, the flagstaff itself remained the *putake o te riri*, the 'root
cause of the war', in the sense also of *the* strategic objective.[30]

[30]The principal sources of the present discussion of Hone Heke's rebellion are:
Buick (1926), Burrows (1886), Carleton (1874), Cowan (1922), Sinclair (1972),
Wards (1968), W. Williams (1867), and the account given to Maning by an anonymous chief of the Ngapuhi who fought on the British side (Maning 1906:220–
323). The books of J. Rutherford on Heke's war and the Treaty of Waitangi have
not been accessible to me at this writing (but see Rutherford 1961: chap. 8). Nor
(unfortunately) have I been able to consult the abundant archival sources in New
Zealand and England.

"He contends for one object only," reads a contemporary newspaper account, "the non-erection of the flag-staff" (Carleton 1874, 2: Appendix, vi). Nor did Heke condone the interest in plunder that seemed to motivate certain others. " 'Let us fight,' he told his ally Kawiti, 'with the flag-staff alone' " (*Ibid.*, xliv). For the fourth assault, of 11 March 1845, Kawiti and his warriors were deployed to make an attack on the European settlement at Kororareka *as a diversion*, so that Heke could go up the hill and take the flagpole! Their own mission accomplished, Heke and his men thereupon sat on the hillside to watch the fracas in the town below. In May 1845, Heke was discussing with Rev. Burrows the Governor's possible terms for peace: " 'One condition,' he said, 'must be that he [the Governor] does not erect another flagstaff' " (Burrows 1886:30).

For their part, the British, if they did not attach exactly the same finality to the flagstaff, knew how to appreciate its "symbolic" value and to take the appropriate response—of general panic. Nearly every time the pole went down, fresh calls for reinforcements were sent to Australia: to show the Maori, as one dispatch urged, that Britons were willing to protect their women from insult and their flag from "dishonour." But when the Maori insurgents made their attack on Kororareka, the British, after at first beating them off, precipitously abandoned the town, to the utter "mystification" of the Maori, who "had never asked for it, or fought for it," and in their "bewilderment" even hesitated momentarily before they looted it (Carleton 1874, 2:93). About the flagstaff itself, the colonials had always shown a better resolve. The Government considered it an imperious necessity to "show the colours" and provided the flag with greater protection upon each occasion of its replacement, the fourth time surrounding the pole with a stockade and blockhouse.

There may have been some working misunderstanding here, since the Maori seem not at all as interested in the flag as they were in the pole. At the third assault, Heke, having toppled the flagstaff, was content to leave the flag itself in the hands of certain Maori "friendlies" who had been set to guarding it. Yet the blockhouse ultimately must have confirmed the rebels' interpretation, for the whole construction now plainly resembled a Maori *tūāhu*: a fenced altar within which were erected one or several poles, such as constituted the sacred precincts of Maori settlements and embodied their ancient claims to tribal lands.

Essentially, then, the British would agree with the Maori view. In September of '45 the Governor sent a letter to Heke outlining the British terms of peace, which were: first, that the 1840 Treaty of Waitangi yielding "sovereignty" to the Queen be respected; and second, "the British colours to be sacred" (Buick 1926:207). Indeed in April 1845, when 470 British troops sailed into Kororareka to reestablish "the Queen's sovereignty," their first act upon landing was to hoist the Union Jack on the beach.

Likewise when the ancestors of the Tūhoe and Ngatiawa peoples landed at the Bay of Plenty, "the first serious task performed by the immigrants was the making and sanctifying of a *tuahu*, or sacred place" (Best 1925:724). Best describes this sacred precinct, also called a *pouahu* or 'post-mound', as a post or tree set in a low mound. The installation is mimetic of the god Tāne's fructification of the Earth Mother, from which issued mankind, or else of Tāne's primordial separation of Heaven and Earth— Tāne, of course, being a tree. In the ancestral *tūāhu* of the Tūhoe, a physical emblem (*mauri*) was placed, representing the prestige and stability of the tribal group. Descriptions from other areas have an old canoe-end (again Tāne) as the central post of the shrine, and the emblem kept near or in the post was the people's god, likewise housed in its 'canoe' (*waka*) or special container (Skinner 1911:76; Hiroa 1977:480–81). Given this association between the *tūāhu* and the ancestral land claim, one can understand why Hone Heke always said that the British flagstaff meant their possession of the land—else why did they persist in re-erecting it? On the other hand, contemporary chronicles are virtually unanimous in saying that Heke was put up to his attacks on the flagpole by outside agitators, notably the local American consul. Only Rev. Burrows (1886:6) writes that the flag above Kororareka was pointed out to Heke as "a *tohu*," a 'sign' that "their country had gone from them." Otherwise, we are supposed to believe that Heke and other chiefs were being told by certain interested white men that the Maori could put an end to British domination by cutting down the flagpole. One may judge the message as understood by Heke, however, from his own discussion of it:

> I said, "what meaning is there in the flagstaff?" The white people told me, "the *mana* of the Queen is in the flag, there are three tribes [*iwi*] in it." I said, "God made

this land for us, and all our children" (Carleton 1874, 2, Appendix C:xlvii-xlvii).

The "three tribes" are probably the English, Scots, and Irish.[31] In any event, the Maori had already manifested their own interpretation of similar poles in 1836, when a French man-o'-war and two merchant vessels anchored at the Bay of Islands and set up small flags about the harbor for surveying purposes. The local Maori attacked these erections of the "Oui-Ouis"—so the French tribe was known—as they had immediately concluded "that the country was being taken possession of" (Carleton 1874, 2:29).[32]

There are traditional Maori rituals, practiced within or outside the sacred precincts (tūāhu), which involve the use of poles set in mounds analogous to the manipulations performed by Heke on the flagstaff set upon the hill. A negative, female pole of death (toko mate) called 'Great Mound (or Mons Veneris) of Papa (Earth)' is overthrown, leaving erect a 'Tūāhu of the Heavens' or male pole of life (toko ora), all with appropriate incantations signifying the expulsion of undesirable effects (cf. Best 1925:1072–

---

[31] Alternatively, Heke was referring to the British, French, and Americans, all three varieties of pāhekā being pertinent to this period of Maori history; or even to the soldiers, sailors, and settlers, the main divisions of local Europeans during the rebellion, also considered by Maori as distinct ancestral kinds. The Anonymous of Ngapuhi speaks thus of British soldiers and sailors at the first battle with the Maori rebels:

What a fine-looking people these soldiers are! Fine, tall, handsome people; they all look like chiefs; and their advance is like the advance of a flight of curlew in the air, so orderly and straight. And along with the soldiers came the sailors; they are of a different family, and not at all related to the soldiers, but they are a brave people, and they came to seek revenge for the relations they had lost in the fight at Kororareka. They had different clothes from the soldiers, and short guns, and long heavy sword[s]; they were a people who talked and laughed more than the soldiers, and they flourished their guns about as they advanced, and ate tobacco (Maning 1906:248).

[32] Conceivably, these poles were taken as *tapu* signs (*rahui*), which was also a certain Maori opinion of the flagpole at Kororareka, at least while the customs duties were still in effect (before September 1844). Even so, the pole would have essentially the same significance as those of the *tūāhu* and other poles (see below).

74).[33] But in the myth of Manaia, as rendered in his own *Polyne-sian Mythology*, Sir George Grey could have found the most exact interpretant of Hone Heke's apparent flagpole fetish. The myth rehearses a common Maori motif of contention over land between successive parties of immigrants from Hawaiki. By a *ruse*, the people of the *second* canoe are able to prove that the local *tūāhu* is theirs, or else that theirs is the older one—"Then they looked at the poles of the *tūāhu*; the poles of the Arawa's *tūāhu* were raw [i.e., still green]; those of the Tainui were cooked by fire in order to speed up their drying" (H. W. Williams 1975:444). In the face of such arguments, the original settlers can do nothing, and are forced to leave their lands, go elsewhere.[34]

The mytho-practical force of the argument is that the sacred precinct, in recreating at the level of community Tāne's original separation of Heaven and Earth, recreates the act which allowed mankind to inherit the Earth. Such separation of Heaven (Rangi) and Earth (Papa) or darkness (*pō*) and light (*ao*) is, as Johansen says, "the proper substance of creation, what makes the world fit to live in for a Maori" (1958:85). The fence or corner uprights of the *tūāhu* are the *toko*, term used in the Tāne myth to designate the poles propping up the Sky-Father, and meaning as a verb 'to support', 'to push to a distance', and 'to divorce'. *Toko*

---

[33]The existence of a negative (or "dark") pole in the *tūāhu*, by opposition to the positive (or "light") pole, is generally related to the function of preservation by the absorption or neutralization of malevolent effects—thus the female aspect of the negative pole, with analogies to the role of living women in *tapu* transformations. The chief's hair clippings, for example, might be put in the *tūāhu*, protecting both chief and community against careless exposure of such dangerous substance. Hence the village latrine—notably, the bar on which one squats, separating life (before) and death (behind)—may also be known as a *tūāhu*, being the site of famous rituals.

[34]Cf. Shortland 1882:69–70. The twist in Grey's Manaia story is that the original settlers had neglected to construct a *tūāhu*, so that when the newcomers were able to point out the sacred place they had built, Manaia was forced to acknowledge their claims to everything else, including the houses and clearings he and his own people had made (Grey 1956:179–80). Best's Ngati-awa informant provides still another version, perhaps the most pertinent to the present discussion. Pio, who took pride in his descent from the indigenous people of the land (*tangata whenua*), was careful to point out to Best that the *tūāhu* of the immigrants from Hawaiki was really the sacred place (*pouahu*) of the original people, thereby condensing in a phrase the usurpation by aristocratic and violent foreigners (Best 1925:724, 1045).

may be used for the central pole or posts, too; alternately the term is *pou*, which as a verb denotes 'to fix; to render immovable' (H. W. Williams 1975:297, 434; Tregear 1969:528–29). It follows that the establishment of a *tūāhu* or *tapu* house of the god amounts to the separation of Heaven and Earth on the terrestrial plane itself—leaving the better part of that plane free (*noa*) for human occupation. Hence it is said that, "the chief of any family who discovered and took possession of any unoccupied land"— the *tūāhu*, as we have seen, being the sign of such possession— "obtained what was called the *mana* of the land" (Shortland 1882:89).[35]

Hone Heke's war was already many generations old before it began. He once tried to explain to the Governor that his own unruliness also was "no new thing" but inherited from his ancestors; a prominent Maori adversary indeed confirmed that it had been going on for five generations (Buick 1926:42, 198). The war had immediate precedent, however, in the career of a famous Ngapuhi chief of the previous generation, Hongi Hika, whose conquests, alliances, and person Hone Heke sought to assume. Heke's career followed a traditional mode of usurpation, or at least of upward mobility, by the warrior-chief of demonstrated *mana*, including even Heke's marriage to Hongi Hika's daughter. This respect for precedent extended to Heke's tactical choices of battle sites, taken in the first instance with a view toward the historic associations with Hongi. In the event, the tribal alliances and enmities of the last generation were engaged in the opposition of rebel and pro-British forces during Heke's uprising, albeit many of these relationships of the early nineteenth century were but recent residues of ancient memories of revenge.[36]

[35] Considering the general and productive value of the Tāne myth, it is not surprising that the ritual erection of poles, in the interest of the preservation of some group or individual, is also found in numerous contexts outside the *tūāhu*. The pole at the right-hand side of the entrance to a Maori fortification might house the *mauri* of the place; called *pou reinga*, it apparently connected the fort with Hawaiki (= Reinga; cf. Skinner 1911:76; H. W. Williams 1975:297). Tūhoe might set up a pole as the personal *mauri* of a child, analogous to the practice elsewhere of planting the branch used in "baptismal" (*tohi*) rites (Best 1976:365).

[36] Hone Heke was certainly a *parvenu* in generational terms, and within the Ngapuhi "tribe" probably also in genealogical terms. It was on such grounds (among others) that Tamati Waka Nene—himself apparently a Ngapuhi chief of

A Ngapuhi chief who fought on the British side has left an en-
chanted account of the war, full of the mythopoetic deep structures of Maori politics, as well as fabulous tales of battle of the
kind Thucydides taught us to ignore (Anonymous of Ngapuhi
in Maning 1906:220–323; White 1855:144–46, 175–76). Such ig-
norance was indeed one of the problems the British had, according to this account: they were splendid fighters, but they just
didn't know a thing about omens. However, one could perhaps
take a clue from the received Western historiography and, making a virtue of the limits of time as well as theory, resolve all this
mytho-praxis to the basic utilities of the economic conjuncture.
The mystical activity must have really been practical—or was it
that the practical activity was really mystical?

   Between 1840, when the British took over New Zealand, and
1844, the northern part of the country experienced a serious de-

---

the blood (cf. Wilkes 1845, 2:383–84)—rallied the Maori opposition against
Heke (Burrows 1886:5, 14–15; Davis 1876:80; Shortland 1856:264; Carleton 1874:
passim; Rutherford 1961:78). With regard to his famous precursor Hongi Hika,
Heke's career is indeed classic, not only in terms of his marriage to Hongi's
daughter, but also by the fact that Heke was Hongi's sister's son, or at least a
classificatory sister's son, as I judge from Carleton's somewhat unclear remarks
(1874, 2:13–14n). It might be noted that Hongi had sons, who inherited his
property, at least two of whom were alive during Heke's rebellion (Carleton
1874, 2:61–62; Davis 1876:56). On the other hand, there is no doubt that Heke
assumed Hongi's place or even person, in Maori eyes, hence he also assumed
certain of Hongi's enemies: "They came to help Walker [Tamati Waka Nene] in
search of revenge against Hongi Ika, for Heke and Hongi are the same" (Anonymous of Ngapuhi, in Maning 1906:241, cf. p. 232). Heke chose to make his first
stand against the British where Hongi is supposed to have uttered his dying
words, *kia toa! kia toa!*, "Be brave! Be brave!" At this place, Mawhe, Heke built a
fort named Te Kahika, 'The Ancestor'.
   The system of alliances and enmities developed during Hongi's time, many of
which go back for generations before that, became in turn a *trace structure* (as it
might be called) in Heke's revolt (cf. Smith 1910; Buick 1926:100n; Wright 1959;
Maning 1906). This structure was inherited with all its faults, or geographical
divisions cum oppositions within Ngapuhi, since it is clear that the Ngapuhi
"tribe" was put together in large measure by Hongi (cf. Binney 1968:58n;
Carleton 1874, 1:65–68, 2:41–43). Dialectically and selectively, the trace structure was brought to bear in 1844–46 by the conflict between Waka and Heke.
Whereas Waka, for his part, and on a traditional Maori model, invoked biographi-
cal ties with the *pākehā* ("Europeans") in explanation of his alliance with the
Government (Maning 1906; Davis 1876:18–19, 34 f.; White 1887–90, 5:210–11;
Shortland 1856:232–34) .

cline in European trade, depriving the Maori of foreign goods to which they had become accustomed. The depression was due in part to *pākehā* depopulation in favor of the new capital at Auckland, in part due to port duties imposed by the new Colonial Government. Still, a simple economic explanation of the 1844 rebellion would be problematic, since many of the Maori loyalists were suffering (if that is the word) as much as Hone Heke's insurgents. The loyalists were led by men of aristocratic lineage opposed in Maori principle to Heke's pretensions, and notably included clans and tribes that had been victims of Heke's predecessor Hongi. But if the structure of the conjuncture cannot be determined directly from material interests, Heke's tilting at the flagstaff does seem logically appropriate to the economic crisis. Or at least, this Maori response to the colonial situation was as mythological as the pragmatics of the European presence were metaphysical. For the Maori, the material crisis was the revelatory sign of something more intangible and enigmatic: of what had happened in 1840 when the chiefs, agreeing to the Treaty of Waitangi, gave up what the British were pleased to call "the sovereignty." [37]

> We all tried to find out the reason why the Governor was so anxious to get us to make these marks. Some of us thought the Governor wanted to bewitch all the chiefs, but our pakeha friends laughed at this, and told us that the people of Europe did not know how to bewitch people. Some told us one thing, some another.
> . . . We did not know what to think, but were all anxious [the Governor] might come to us soon; for we were afraid that all his blankets, and tobacco, and other things would be gone before he came to our part of the country, and that he would have nothing left to pay us for making our marks on his paper . . . and when we met the Governor, the speaker of Maori [i.e., the interpreter] told us that if we put our names, or even made any sort of mark on that paper, the Governor would then protect us, and prevent us from being robbed of our cultivated

---

[37] The view taken here is close to that of Sinclair, who speaks of the economic depression of 1840–44 as the catalytic, although not decisive, circumstance of the war, by virtue of the revelations it afforded the Maori about the colonial situation (1972:65–66).

land, and our timber land, and everything else which belonged to us. . . . The speaker of Maori then went on to tell us certain things, but the meaning of what he said was so closely concealed we never have found it out. One thing we understood well, however, for he told us plainly that if we wrote on the Governor's paper, one of the consequences would be that great numbers of pakeha would come to this country to trade with us, that we should have abundance of valuable goods. . . . We were very glad to hear this (Anonymous of Ngapuhi, in Maning 1906:223–25).

For sheer mystification, the curious hieroglyphs the Maori chiefs appended to the Treaty of Waitangi could be equaled only by its several provisions. Her Majesty's Government had been moved to intervene by the extensive project of land acquisition announced by the New Zealand Company. Initially, the Government meant to forestall the Company and protect remaining Maori lands. (There was also the potential menace of the French, who were in the process of annexing Tahiti.) Hence the Treaty was urgently pressed (together with the usual gifts) upon the chiefs as an economic good thing, the assurance of their future prosperity. On the other hand, the combination it offered of yielding the sovereignty to the Queen and keeping the land to themselves would be perfectly unintelligible to Maori: "The speaker of Maori then went on to tell us certain things, but the meaning of what he said was so closely concealed we never have found it out." Just before the Ngapuhi chiefs signed at Waitangi, the Reverend Mr. Colenso respectfully intervened to ask the Governor (Hobson) if he thought the Maori understood the terms. " 'I have spoken to some of the chiefs concerning it,' "Colenso said, " 'who had no idea whatever as to the purport of the treaty' " (Buick 1936:155).[38]

---

[38] The hieroglyphic signatures on the Treaty are usually said to be attempts of the chiefs to imitate their facial tattoos (for a facsimile of the Treaty signatures, see Buick 1936: facing 352). Hone Heke was the first to so sign the Treaty of Waitangi. Whether on the previous day he had also strongly supported the Treaty or vehemently attacked it is a vexed documentary issue (cf. Buick 1936:140n).

Charles Wilkes, commander of the U.S. Exploring Expedition, was at the Bay of Islands two months after the signing of the Treaty. His remarks on the under-

The Maori text would be enough to keep its own secrets. In Article 1, the "sovereignty" the chiefs agree to surrender is glossed by an adjunctive (or concretive) form of the English loanword for 'govern/governor', *kawanatanga*, concept of which the Maori as yet had little or no direct experience. But in Article 2, the Maori are solemnly guaranteed the *rangatiratanga*, the 'chiefship'—or, if you will, the 'sovereignty'—"of their lands, their settlements and all their property" (Buick 1936:360–62).[39] And while the English missionaries, Henry Williams especially, were pleased to think they had on numerous occasions satisfactorily explained the Treaty to the Maori, it was precisely the missionaries' deceptions in this regard that Hone Heke brought up when they remonstrated with him about the flagstaff. "Heke did

---

standing of it by the Maori chiefs in general and the important Ngapuhi chief Pomare in particular are serving of American interests, no doubt, but the content does not seem any less Maori in character:

> So far as the chiefs understand the agreement, they think they have not alienated any of their rights to the soil, but consider it only as a personal grant, not transferable. In the interview I had with Pomare, I was desirous of knowing the impression it had made on him. I found he was not under the impression that he had given up his authority, or any portion of his land permanently; the latter he said he could not do, as it belonged to all his tribe. Whenever this subject was brought up, after answering questions, he invariably spoke of the figure he would make in the scarlet uniform and epaulettes, that Queen Victoria was to send him, and "then what a handsome man he would be!" (Wilkes 1845, 2:376).

[39] After these lines had been penned, I was happy to find good anthropological authority for them:

> There are two versions of [the Treaty], one written by Captain Hobson in English and another, substantially ambiguous one, written by Rev. Henry Williams in Maori. The English version said the Maoris were to cede their 'sovereignty'. The Maori version said they were to cede their 'kawanatanga', a word coined for the purpose of the treaty and meaningless except in the context of western constitutional law of which the Maori signers were ignorant. The treaty, in English, guaranteed to the Maoris the 'possession' of their land; in Maori this word was rendered as 'rangatiratanga' which may, indeed, mean possession but which may equally well mean 'chiefship'. A Maori would be hard put, in 1840, to tell the difference between what he gave up (kawanatanga) and retained (rangatiratanga) (Schwimmer 1966:107).

not allow this opportunity to pass without alluding to the Treaty of Waitangi, and of having been deceived by the Archdeacon [Williams] and others in inducing so many chiefs to sign it, when they [Williams et al.] must have known that they (the chiefs) were signing away their lands, etc." (Burrows 1886:9; cf. p. 32). Problem was that the distinction between political supremacy and the occupation of (or "title to") the land was not pertinent to Maori. So long as a chief and his people maintained residence on their ancestral land, and the willingness to defend it, no other chief could rule there. Beyond all Western ideas of property or sovereignty, the land is "the inorganic body of the clan community" (to adopt Marx's phrase). It is the objectified *mana* of the kinship group. Maori and Western concepts on this score are incommensurable. Still, Firth must be right when he says that "the concept of *mana* in connection with land is . . . most nearly akin to the idea of sovereignty" (1959:392; cf. White 1855:190–91). For when Heke determined that the Treaty of Waitangi was proposing some new sacred arrangements of property, he concluded that it must mean for Maori the loss of the *mana*—as occurs in conquest, dispossession, and enslavement. The British were putting up their own *tūāhu*.

In this respect the economic deprivations that followed upon the Treaty were symptomatic merely of a larger issue: the meaning of the British presence; or the fate of the Maori. Maori said that the Government claimed to be a parent, but only showed itself to be "'soldiers, barracks, constables and gaols'" (Sinclair 1972:31). Debate continued among Maori chiefs about what the treaty had signified. Various metaphysical speculations were improvised. The best known, by one Nopera Panakareau, ran to the effect that, "The shadow of the land goes to Queen Victoria, but the substance remains to us." That he said in May 1840. By the following January, Nopera had reversed the terms: "The substance of the land goes to the Europeans, the shadow only will be our portion" (cited in Wards 1968: front matter). Whatever the Treaty meant, says the Anonymous of Ngapuhi, "this one thing at least was true, we had less tobacco and fewer blankets and other European goods than formerly and we saw that the first Governor had not spoken the truth, for he told us that we should have a great deal more" (Maning 1906:230–31). The whaling and trading ships had nearly stopped coming, and the *pākehā* were leaving the northern districts. The Government had acted in mysterious and deceptive ways. Or was it not that these adverse effects had made Maori aware that the true issue in the Treaty was the *mana*? In this respect, Heke's work on the flagpole was a demystification. It was a reminder that the same had happened before, when the chiefs first came to this New Zealand from Hawaiki, and built their sacred sites (*tūāhu*) on the land, and took control from the original 'people of the land' (*tangata whenua*).

One myth is thus decoded by another (just as Lévi-Strauss says). For the Treaty of Waitangi was a myth, even in European terms. In one of the most scholarly accounts going of Heke's rebellion—albeit written from a *pākehā* vantage—Ian Wards (1968:171) has to admit that, "the Treaty *was* a device to blind and amuse ignorant savages," as contemporary criticism had said. Without undue expense, "quickly and quietly," the Crown had got possession of New Zealand. And if the Treaty, in ostensibly providing for the welfare of the Maori, was not an outright deception, since such a purpose could hardly be reconciled with the massive colonization by Her Majesty's white subjects already underway, it was at the least a contradiction, since the Government had no means to secure Maori interests and soon abandoned the intention. Moreover, the Colonial Office well knew in advance that the difference between sovereignty and property would not be received by the Maori. This was clearly stated in preliminary drafts of the instructions to Captain Hobson for negotiating the Treaty. All the drafts indicate, "that it was not believed that the Maoris understood the distinction between sovereignty and property rights" (Wards 1968:28). But no statement to this effect is to be found in the instructions as issued, "clearly because it was not politic to make such a public admission" (*Ibid.*, p. 29). The Treaty had been negotiated in bad faith.

Or in other words, the essential unrealities as well as the impracticalities of the situation had been laid on by the British. Attacking the flagpole, Heke showed he was able to penetrate, become conscious of, and objectify the meanings the *pākehā* were prepared to conceal sometimes even from themselves. If the response still seems to us displaced or "symbolic," we should not forget that the decisive issue, as Wards also admits, was equally abstract: Heke "was suffering the inevitable pangs of one who

sees, or senses, the eclipse of his own way of life by another"
(*Ibid.*, p. 145).[40]

A Structural, Historical Anthropology

In an oft-cited remark from the Preface to *Search for a Method*
(1968), Sartre asks, "Do we have today the means to constitute a
structural, historical anthropology?" Yes, I have tried to suggest
here, *le jour est arrivé*. Practice clearly has gone beyond the theoretical differences that are supposed to divide anthropology and
history. Anthropologists rise from the abstract structure to the
explication of the concrete event. Historians devalue the unique
event in favor of underlying recurrent structures. And also para-
doxically, anthropologists are as often diachronic in outlook as
historians nowadays are synchronic. Nor is the issue, or this essay, merely about the value of collaboration. The problem now is
to explode the concept of history by the anthropological experience of culture. The heretofore obscure histories of remote islands deserve a place alongside the self-contemplation of the
European past—or the history of "civilizations"—for their own
remarkable contributions to an historical understanding. We
thus multiply our conceptions of history by the diversity of structures. Suddenly, there are all kinds of new things to consider.

[40]Since this paper was first delivered and published, I have made a brief visit to
New Zealand, where I learned that the famous flagpole above Kororareka
—now Russell—was attacked twice in 1982–83 by Maori protest groups. In the
second attempt, of 27 February 1983, two gelignite charges were attached to the
copper sheathing of the flagstaff. Two slogans were painted on the concrete plat-
form below: one read in Maori, "We will fight to the death;" the other, in English, "The treaty is dead" (*New Zealand Herald*, 28 Feb. 1983). Thanks to Dr.
Bruce Sutton, I was also able to see that flagpoles remain prominent features of
modern Maori *marae* (ceremonial cum community precincts). Dr. Sutton also
sent me a photo of one example in which the flagpole is the continuation of the
vertical bar of a crucifix—cf. the remarks in the text on the god in or near the
tūāhu pole.

3

The Stranger-King; or,
Dumézil among the Fijians

I begin with certain historical and ritual incidents which, taken together, amount to a Polynesian philosophy of social life. The great classicist Georges Dumézil suggests that the ideas of political sovereignty in this philosophy are similar to structures he has found in ancient Indo-European civilizations. I will go on to make the comparison. The comparison brings out a characteristic of sovereign power not necessarily stressed by Dumézil, although certainly present in his own and other famous studies of "archaic" kingship. The kingship makes its appearance from outside the society. Initially a stranger and something of a terror, the king is absorbed and domesticated by the indigenous people, a process that passes by way of his symbolic death and consequent rebirth as a local god.

History has been known to reenact this cosmic drama. Consider what happened to Captain Cook. For the people of Hawaii Cook had been a myth before he was an event, since the myth was the frame by which his appearance was interpreted.[1] Cook

This chapter is dedicated to the memory of Pierre Clastres.

[1] Recorded Hawaiian myths of the return of the god Lono, with whom Captain Cook was identified, date from the second and third decades of the nineteenth century at the earliest, forty to fifty years after Cook's voyage (see chap. 4, note below). There is debate about the antiquity of such myths, and about the traditional form of the annual Makahiki or New Year ceremony to which they refer. Clearly, certain aspects of the myths in their late form have been elaborated to account for Cook's advent. On the other hand, the myths make allusions

thus descended upon the Islands from Kahiki, invisible and celestial realms beyond the horizon, the legendary source of great
gods, ancient kings, and cultural good things. A natural reproductive space, Kahiki was also the original cultural time. So the
Hawaiians received Cook as a reappearance of their Year God,
Lono, known especially as the patron of agricultural fertility.
This did not prevent them from killing him on 14 February 1779.[2]
But no sooner dead, Cook was installed as a divine predecessor
by Hawaiian ruling chiefs.

The incidents attending Captain Wallis's arrival at Tahiti in
1767 suggest another aspect of the same Polynesian theory: the
capture of the god/chief is mediated by the gift of woman. The
Tahitians came off to the *Dolphin*, first European ship to anchor
there, and threw banana stalks upon her decks. The plants were
signs of their own persons. Called 'man-long bananas' (*ta'atu o
mei'a roa*), they were used to supplement the victims in great
chiefly rituals of human sacrifice. A few days later, making a
feint of enticing the British with a display of their naked women,
Tahitian warriors showered the decks of the *Dolphin* with vol-
leys of rocks. And just as the *mana* of the sacrificed Cook de-
volved upon Hawaiian kings as a sign of their legitimacy, so the
pennant Wallis left on the beach of Matavai was woven into the
sacred loin cloth (*maro 'ura*), insignia of Tahitian royalty (Wallis
in Kerr 1824:120–241; Robertson 1948; Henry 1928:11; cf. Oliver
1974:1215–16 et passim).

---

to—indeed, incorporate relations and incidents from—the epic legends of
Cook's royal predecessors in the capacity of Lono from Hawai'i island, notably
Lono-i-ka-makahiki and Ka-'I-i-mamao, and probably also La'amaikahiki of
Kaua'i and O'ahu (cf. Beckwith 1972). The authenticity and antiquity of this epic
corpus is much less debatable, and in structure as well as detail the legends em-
body the same theory as is represented in the Makahiki rites, as well as in the
later Cook-Lono myths. Beyond that, the New Year ceremony associated with
the November rising of the Pleiades, of which the Hawaiian Makahiki Festival is
a local version, is pan-Polynesian, even Austronesian (cf. Makemson 1941).
Likewise the Orpheus-Eurydice and Demeter-Persephone motifs, which speak
to the cosmological drama of seasonal life and death enacted in the Makahiki,
are found elsewhere in Hawaiian and Polynesian myth (Handy 1927:81–82).
From all this, one may judiciously conclude that Cook's appearance in January
1778 and again in November 1779 had specific mythical and ceremonial precedents, probably quite like the versions recorded around 1820–30.
    [2]The principal published and archival sources on Cook's voyage are cited in
the text and notes of chapter 4, below.

At about the same date, according to local genealogical traditions, a similar scene was being staged thousands of miles to the west: the Fijians of the Lau Islands were installing the first of their present dynasty of ruling chiefs. The event was analogous to the treatment of Cook or Wallis because at his own accession the Fijian chief is symbolically poisoned, and in this way captured and domesticated as a god of the indigenous people. The poison is in the sacred offering, the drink made from the kava plant that consecrates the chief. Kava is the preeminent offering of the ancient *lewe ni vanua*, 'members of the land', to the ruling chief, always himself a foreigner by origin. Myth tells that kava first grew from the dead body of a child or young chief of the native people—in the Tongan version, very much like the Lauan, the child had originally been sacrificed for the chief's food. The stranger-king thus consumes the land and appropriates its reproductive powers, but only to suffer thereby his own appropriation (Hocart 1929:67 ff.; Sahlins 1983).

To borrow Pierre Clastres's phrase, it is "society against the state." These Polynesian incidents suggest there is something true and important in Clastres's controversial thesis of populist resentment (1977). Granted, Clastres formulated the idea by reference to the modest developments of chiefship in lowland South America, and there is much to criticize in the notion that the people could reject in advance, by "intuition" and "premonition," the kind of political society they had never experienced. Still, the Tiv of West Africa, reflecting on their own comparable political circumstances, say that 'men come to power through devouring the substance of others' (P. Bohannan, cited in Balandier 1967:72). In the same vein, one of the most respectful salutations a lowly Fijian commoner can offer a ranking chief is '"Eat me"'! (Waterhouse 1866:338). It is thus not surprising that the negation of power Clastres asserts for tribal South America is echoed even in the divinity with which the Polynesians—in the same way as the classical Indo-Europeans—did hedge their kings. "The chiefs of Hawaii were termed gods, because of the death of a subject," observes a native sage (Kaawa, MS). But, says another, "Some of the ancient kings had a wholesome fear of the people" (Malo 1951:195).

Clastres also happened to develop his argument in the context of a different native philosophy of power: the quaint Western concept that domination is a spontaneous expression of the nature of society, and beyond that, of the nature of man. This was not always the average scholarly opinion. The origin of the state in conquest, theory well known from the works of Gumplowicz and Oppenheimer, was at least faithful to ancient European doctrine—the legend of Romulus, for example—in that it could comprehend power only on the condition that it originated beyond society and was violently imposed upon the general will. But this native conception of power as foreign to society has latterly given way to a variety of others—Marxist, biological, the social contract—alike in their understanding of political authority as an internal growth, springing from the essence of human social relations or dispositions.

I do not offer a competing historical theory, since it should be clear that I am not talking about what "actually happened." Yet what I am talking about—indigenous schemes of cosmological proportions—may be even more significant historically. The fate of Captain Cook suggests that such schemes are the true organization of historical practice, if not true memories of primordial events. On the other hand, it is possible that fashionable social-science discourses on the origin of inequality are also, in certain respects, versions of the myths they purport to explain.

The latest sociobiology, for example, merely internalizes as human nature the opposition between power and culture characteristic of the received folklore. These *ad hoc* claims of a continuity between dominant apes and one or another current species of political despotism seem truly, as Clifford Geertz says, "a mixture of common sense and common nonsense."[3] For the affinity we commonly sense between power and nature is itself a social construction, passing by way of their mutual opposition to civil society. Power and nature are alike as what is beyond and apart from the norms of ordinary culture. Bent on a privileged appropriation of words and things as hierarchical values, rather than as reciprocal means of human communication, power is the negation of community, and so is ideologically banished to the kingdom of natural forces. Since this is where our sociobiological colleagues find it, they suppose it to be the birthplace.[4]

---

[3] "A Wary Reasoning: Humanities, Analogies and Social theory," lecture presented at the University of Chicago, 15 December 1979.

[4] Balandier (1967: 125) quotes P. Valery: "The political acts upon men in a manner which evokes 'natural causes'; they submit to it as they submit to the *caprices*

My main purpose will be to examine, in a loose typological frame, certain Polynesian analogues of the same theory. I say "analogues" because the conception of divine kings we find in Hawaii or Fiji also happens to preside over the subterranean history of our own democracies—whence also emerges periodically the king's cosmic antithesis, "the laughing people." Still the comparison might hold little interest were it not for another claim that can be made for it. I hope to show, necessarily in a summary way, that the anthropological concept of "structure" is not most usefully set forth in a Saussurean mode, as a static set of symbolic oppositions and correspondences. In its global and most powerful representation, structure is processual: a dynamic development of the cultural categories and their relationships amounting to a world system of generation and regeneration. As a program of the cultural life process, the system has an internal (structural) diachrony, of its nature temporal and changing. Structure is the cultural life of the elementary forms. Yet precisely as this diachrony is structural and repetitive, it enters into a dialogue with historical time, as a cosmological project of encompassing the contingent event.

The political dimensions of the structure in question, the ideology of external domination and social usurpation, are well known to anthropological studies of archaic states and protostates. The famous works of Sir James Frazer and A. M. Hocart on divine kingship document a worldwide distribution of the same basic scheme of power, from the Fiji Islands and the Americas through India and the classical world (Frazer 1905, 1911–15; Hocart 1969 [1927], 1970 [1936]). Luc de Heusch (1958, 1962, 1972) has brilliantly synthesized its description from many parts of Africa. Heusch calls upon the studies of Dumézil for certain descriptive concepts, and Dumézil for his part finds fundamental aspects of Roman sovereignty repeated in Polynesia, Dahomey, and pre-hispanic Mexico, as well as ancient Ireland, India, Persia, and Scandinavia. "It is not even among the Indo-Europeans," Dumézil writes, "that these facts are most clear or complete." To study them from "the point of view of general sociology," it would be better to look at the Polynesians or the In-

---

of the sky, the sea, the terrestrial crust." The analogy, Balandier comments, "suggests the distance at which power places itself—outside and above society."

dians of Northwest America, and the best commentary on the accession of the ancient Hindu king Prthu "is perhaps furnished by scenes which, only recently, marked the succession of the sovereign in the Fiji Islands" (Dumézil 1949:41–42).[5]

To take the viewpoint of a general sociology: in all the afore-mentioned civilizations, basically composed of kith and kin, of diverse lineages and clans, the ruler as above society is also con-sidered beyond it. As he is beyond it morally, so he is from the beyond, and his advent is a kind of terrible epiphany. It is a re-markably common fact that the great chiefs and kings of political society are not *of* the people they rule. By the local theories of origin they are strangers, just as the draconic feats by which they come to power are foreign to the conduct of "real people" or true "sons of the land," as various Polynesians express it. The stranger-kings, we shall see, are eventually encompassed by the indigenous people, to the extent that their sovereignty is always problematical and their lives are often at risk. But it is just such conditions that motivate a naturalistic theory of domination. By his own nature outside the homebred culture of the society, the king appears within it as a force of nature. He erupts upon a pas-toral scene of peaceful husbandry and relative equality which the nostalgia of a later time may well recall as a golden age. Typi-cally, then, these rulers do not even spring from the same clay as the aboriginal people: they are from the heavens or—in the very common case—they are of distinct ethnic stock. In either event, royalty is the foreigner.

Fijians often complain that their ruling chief is a *kai tani*, a 'dif-ferent person' or 'stranger' in the land; or else, he is a *vulagi*, a 'guest', a term that Hocart also analyzes as 'heavenly god'. " 'The chiefs . . . came from overseas'," Hocart was told by a Lauan, " 'it is so in all countries of Fiji'" (Hocart 1929:129). Here, in very condensed form, is a typical Fijian myth of the origin of the cur-rent ruling clan (*mataqali*):

[5]Dumézil is probably referring to the Fijian "coronation ceremonies" de-scribed and analyzed by Hocart in *Kingship* (1969 [1927]). (See also Dumézil 1948, 1949, 1968, 1977, among his many works on Indo-European societies.) On the problem of the classification of "divine kings," "priest-kings," "magical kings," etc., see note 3 of chapter 2. In the Polynesian (including Fijian) systems, an active ruler on the order of a magical king and a sacerdotal divine king are complementary parts of the same (diarchic) kingship (cf. Valeri 1982).

A handsome, fair-skinned stranger, victim of an accident at sea, is befriended by a shark who carries him ashore on the south coast of Viti Levu. The stranger wanders into the interior where he is taken in by a local chieftain, whose daughter he eventually marries. From this union springs the line of Noikoro ruling chiefs, the narrator of the story being the tenth descendant on that line. He and his clansmen are called 'The Sharks' (Na Qio) (Brewster MS).

It is all as in the Hawaiian proverb: "A chief is a shark that travels on land" (Handy and Pukui 1972:199). Luc de Heusch quotes Saint Just to the effect that "between the people and the king there can be no natural relation." Yet the idea was not entirely revolutionary. Many peoples had long before concluded that power is not inherent in humanity. It can only come from elsewhere than the community and relationships of humankind. In this classic sense, power is a barbarian.

It is typically founded on an act of barbarism—murder, incest, or both. Heusch calls this "the exploit," a feat mythically associated with the ancestor of the dynasty, and frequently reenacted at the installation of each successor. The very negation of kinship behavior, this original violence is the complement of Clastres's thesis—as also of the theses of illustrious predecessors, who likewise made much of the conflicting principles of State and Civil Society, *Gemeinschaft* and *Gesellschaft* or *Civitas* and *Societas*. Power reveals and defines itself as the rupture of the people's own moral order, precisely as the greatest of crimes against kinship: fratricide, parricide, the union of mother and son, father and daughter, or brother and sister.

Speaking still from the most general point of view, it is not significant that the exploit may be "merely symbolic," since it is symbolic even when it is "real." By certain versions of the legend, Romulus killed Remus for stepping over the furrow he had traced in (Mother) earth to mark the walls of the future Rome. The East African king acts out the same homicidal/sexual associations when, having won a fratricidal war of succession, he mates with his half-sister. Zeus did no better to his father Cronos and his sister Hera, but then he had Cronos's own example to follow. The Hawaiian dynasty of sacred chiefs began with the legendary incest of a father and daughter; it effectively ended in historic times with the sacrifice of King Kiwala'o by his (classificatory) brother Kamehameha, who thereupon married his victim's daughter.[6] And as Oedipus, whether myth or complex, has again the same structure, perhaps no more need be said about the power of signs to function as signs of power.

It is more important to notice that power is not represented here as an intrinsic social condition. It is a usurpation, in the double sense of a forceful seizure of sovereignty and a sovereign denial of the prevailing moral order. Rather than a normal succession, *usurpation itself is the principle of legitimacy*. Hocart shows that the coronation rituals of the king or paramount chief celebrate a victory over his predecessor. If he has not actually sacrificed the late ruler, the heir to the Hawaiian kingship, or some one of his henchmen, is suspected of having poisoned him. There follows the scene of ritual chaos (described in chapter 2), when the world dissolves or is in significant respects inverted, until the new king returns to reinstate the tabus, i.e., the social order.

Such mythical exploits and social disruptions are common to the beginnings of dynasties and to successive investitures of divine kings. We can summarily interpret the significance something like this: to be able to put the society in order, the king must first reproduce an original disorder. Having committed his monstrous acts against society, proving he is stronger than it, the ruler proceeds to bring system out of chaos. Recapitulating the initial constitution of social life, the accession of the king is thus a recreation of the universe. The king makes his advent as a god. The symbolism of the installation rituals is cosmological. Hence the Frazerian equation between the life of the king, the well-being of society, and the concordance of cosmic forces.

[6]The legendary progenitors of the Hawaiian chiefs were Wakea and Hoohokuokalani, his own daughter by Papa. The story is a humanized counterpart of the Maori myth in which the god Tane generates mankind by mating with a woman fashioned from the *mons veneris* of Papa or Earth, Tane's mother (see chap. 2). Hawaiian and Maori legends generally contrast in this way, as mythic and epic versions respectively of the same themes (cf. Dumézil 1949, 1968, 1977). Within this general contrast, however, both tend to pass into historical genres in discourse about the most recent heroes, while maintaining the categorical relations of ancient myth.

Social scientists often see in all this a mystification of power, framed in'the interests of the rulers. Yet as a "dominant ideology" it is at least equivocal, since as in the instance of Captain Cook or anthropological analogues of the priest of Nemi, it may also authorize the people to "sit upon the ground and tell sad tales of the death of kings." But to speak of an interested ideology in the first place is to sadly impoverish the description of these facts. The rationalization of power is not at issue so much as the representation of a general scheme of social life: a total "structure of reproduction," including the complementary and antithetical relations between king and people, god and man, male and female, foreign and native, war and peace, heavens and earth.

The political appears here as an aspect of the cosmological: the expression as human battle of transformations between life and death that are universal. Yet the political is not merely a reflex of the natural, as Frazer thought. Nor is it the other way round, the death (or pseudo-death) of the king a political catharsis in the trappings of a cosmic ideology, as functionalist theory has it. Again, the system is not adequately characterized by familiar structuralist notions of a transposition between the parallel codes of culture and nature. If the Polynesian scheme is unlike the so-called totemism, as Lévi-Strauss (1963) says, because of the genealogical continuity (or consubstantiality) between "supernatural," "natural," and human beings, then it is a universal system of differential homologies rather than of homologous differences. The scheme stresses the several descent relations between "natural" ancestral phenomena and social persons or groups, while by the same means differentiating them—hence the residual resemblances to "totemism." It follows that the logical relations between the several planes of cosmos and culture are not metaphoric merely, or even simply metonymic. The relations are synechdochic: an ancestral system of formal classes (see chapter 1). Proportions such as king: people:: heavens: earth are propositions about the nature of things, a veritable ontology.

Let us take seriously Dumézil's suggestion that the installation rituals of the Fijian chief are a clue to the system of the Indo-Europeans. Frazer had already set certain terms of comparison. The legends of the Latin kings from Romulus to the

second Tarquin, as the Greeks from Tantalus and Pelops to Agamemnon, show consistent similarities in the philosophy of polity. The king is an outsider, often an immigrant warrior prince
whose father is a god or a king of his native land. But, exiled by
his own love of power or banished for a murder, the hero is unable to succeed there. Instead, he takes power in another place,
and *through a woman*: princess of the native people whom he
gains by a miraculous exploit involving feats of strength, ruse,
rape, athletic prowess, and/or the murder of his predecessor.
The heroic son-in-law from a foreign land demonstrates his divine gifts, wins the daughter, and inherits half or more of the
kingdom (cf. Préaux 1962). Before it was a fairy tale, it was the
theory of society.

So before Romulus, at the beginnings of the Romans in Italy,
came Aeneas the Trojan, whose landing was opposed by armed
natives under King Latinus. Livy (*Hist. Rome* I, 1) gives two versions of what follows, one warlike and the other peaceable, but
both ending with Aeneas receiving Lavinia, daughter of King
Latinus, and the unification of foreigners and natives as one
people under the immigrant king. By the telling of Dionysius of
Halicarnassus, the original treaty was a compact of the respective gods. The indigenous Latins gave land to the Trojans in return for aid in war. Each party contributing thus of its essential
nature, together they are able to make a viable whole. But as the
nature of the Latins is reproductive wealth, on the marital plane
the founding exchange is asymmetrical: the aborigines are wife-
givers. Setting the example, the two kings

> united the excellence of the two races, the native and
> the foreign, by ties of marriage. Latinus gave his daugh-
> ter Lavinia to Aeneas. Thereupon the rest also con-
> ceived the same desire as their kings; and combining in
> a very brief time their customs, laws and religious cere-
> monies, forming ties through intermarriages and be-
> coming mingled together in the wars they jointly waged,
> and calling themselves by the common name of Latins,
> after the king of the Aborigines, they adhered so firmly
> to their past that no lapse of time has yet severed them
> from one another (Dion. Halic. *Rom. Antiq.* I, 60).

On the other hand, Latinus's gift of the woman Lavinia entailed a refusal of local endogamy and involved the combined

peoples in a war with the Rutulians. The Rutulians were inspired to rebel by the rejected suitor of Lavinia, Tyrrhenus (of Dionysius's story, i.e., Turnus of the *Aeneid*). Tyrrhenus was a nephew of the wife of Latinus, Amita, whose own name thus suggests that a frustrated father's-sister's-daughter marriage is at issue. Since father's-sister's-daughter marriage is a form of reciprocal exchange, the wife-takers of one generation becoming the wife-givers of the next, the entire episode encodes a transformation from an indigenous reciprocity between king and people to an hierarchical flow of women in favor of the stranger-king.

Consider also the adoption of the aboriginal name "Latins" as the appellation of the now unified people. This is likewise common Fijian usage. At the several structural levels from the 'clan' (*mataqali*) to the village, the land (*vanua*), and the confederated chiefdom (*matanitū*), the group as a whole is designated by the name of its indigenous and subordinate segment: such is the origin of "Tubou," capital village of Lau (itself the term for the hinterland islands of the chiefdom), or of "Cakaudrove" and "Verata"; the same again is found in the ceremonial titles of ruling chiefs ("Burebasaga" in Rewa, "Matanikutu" in Naitāsiri, etc.). A kind of inverse marking rule which makes the inferior social term nevertheless the generic concept of the totality, this classification expresses literally the encompassment of the king and the contradictions of his sovereignty. The land "belongs" to the 'true people' (*tamata dina*) of the place, as they truly belong to it, relationships perfectly captured in the Fijian term *i taukei*, which may be alternately translated as the 'owners' and the 'indigenous occupants'.

To return to the Latins, Romulus, child of the sacred woman (vestal) of Alba and the war-god Mars, would go on to found Rome on the model of the original Trojan invasion. Numitor, the Alban king, maternal grandfather of Romulus and Remus, takes care to send off with these two his own rebellious subjects. The twins themselves had an "unsociable love of rule" (Dion. Halic., *Rom. Antiq.* I, 85), and when they divided their party in two with the intention of stimulating rivalry, it led to famous discord, with results fatal to Remus. This failure of dualism—noncomplementary at that—is a motivation of the tripartite and hierarchical structure that eventually characterizes the Rome founded by Romulus.

Raised as a rustic herdsman, leader of a youthful robber band, slayer of his own brother, Romulus establishes the city by a ruse: an improvised agricultural festival that attracts the indigenous Sabines of the countryside (indeed, the mountains), whose daughters he carries off. In the ensuing war the Romans are nearly beaten: through the betrayal of the woman, Tarpeia, whose love of riches allows the Sabines to take the citadel. (Riches, of course, are the economic counterpart of the powers of growth and agricultural fertility, hence indicative, as Dumézil observes, of the female side.) By the miraculous intervention of Jupiter, Romulus stays the rout and effects a stalemate, upon which the Sabine women, daughters to one army and wives to the other, intervene to effect a reconciliation. Plutarch (*Lives*, Romulus) signifies the synthetic term produced from their conjunction by a more powerful combinatory logic than the complementary exchange that had united the Trojans and Latins. The Romans adopt the armor, i.e., the military techniques, of the indigenous Sabines; the Sabines take over the Roman names for months, i.e., the ceremonial/agricultural calendar, of the invading warriors. But above all, the Romans now gain the means of their own reproduction in the Sabine women and their dowries, and all live happily ever after in the Eternal City.

There will be further structural permutations necessary to guarantee this immortality. But they are best discussed after bringing into comparison certain of those scenes, alluded to by Dumézil, which "only recently marked the succession of the sovereign in the Fiji Islands." Dumézil had in mind Hocart's description of the Lauan and Bauan installation ceremonies (*veibuli*), and I similarly rely on these and notices of comparable rites from eastern Fiji. The investiture of the Tui Nayau as ruler of Lau (Sau ni Vanua) is now our best source, thanks to the attention to traditional forms at the most recent performance, in July 1969. It will be the focus of the ensuing discussion.[7]

[7]Descriptions of the Lau and Bau installation ceremonies—the latter pertaining to the war-king, Vūnivalu—are found in Hocart (1929). Further texts on the Bau rites include: Hocart (HF) and Tippett (1973:91 ff.). Hocart (1952) also supplies information on Vanua Levu installations, and for several other areas in his Fijian field notes (FN). On Moala, see Sahlins (1962:386–88). Records of the 1969 investiture of the Lau paramount (Tui Nayau/Sau ni Vanua), including official programs, photographs, and a bilingual report in *Na Tovata* are deposited in the

I pass over the preliminary installation of the chief as Tui Nayau at Nayau Island, though its significance will be taken into account. The ensuing investiture of the Tui Nayau as paramount of Lau consciously follows the legend of an original odyssey, which brought the ancestral holder of the title into power at Lakeba, ruling island of the Lau Group. The chief thus makes his appearance at Lakeba from the sea, as a stranger to the land. Disembarking at the capital village of Tubou, he is led first to the chiefly house (*vale levu*) and next day to the central ceremonial ground (*rārā*) of the island. At both stages of this progression, the pretender is led along a path of barkcloth by local chieftains of the land.[8] In Lau, this barkcloth is prescriptively a type considered foreign by origin, Tongan barkcloth. Later, at the kava ceremony constituting the main ritual of investiture, a native chieftain will bind a piece of white Fijian tapa about the paramount's arm. The sequence of barkcloths, together with the sequence of movements to the central ceremonial ground, recapitulate the correlated legendary passages of the Tui Nayau from foreign to domestic, sea to land, and periphery to center. The Fijian barkcloth that in the end captures the chief represents his capture of the land: upon installation, he is said to hold the 'barkcloth of the land' (*masi ni vanua*).

The barkcloth thus has deeper significance. In general ritual usage, barkcloth serves as "the path of the god." Hanging from the rafters at the rear, sacred end of the ancient temple, it is the

David Seidler Collection, Turnbull Library (Wellington). By far the most useful account was generously supplied to me by Mr. Stephen Hooper of Cambridge University from his own field notes, recorded in 1980 from participants in the 1969 ceremonies. I warmly thank Mr. Hooper for his invaluable collegial help— without which this analysis would be much poorer.

[8] In photographs of what appears to be the second stage of these ceremonies, the movement from the chief's house to the ceremonial ground, the chief is also being escorted by elderly women, while two rows of other women sit alongside the barkcloth on which the group is proceeding. This is only one of numerous ritual details signifying the birth (= "appearance") of the chief by women of the land. Again, the presence and shouts of assembled warriors at the chief's disembarkation the night before imply the capture of the immigrant sea-king by the indigenous land people. Below, I give other salient details of the rituals which make such points in different ways. I mention these here to give an indication of how much I simplify and selectively highlight the symbolic riches of the Lauan installation ceremonies.

avenue by which the god descends to enter the priest. The priest, for his part, is a representative of—in certain locales, he is the *malosivo*, the original and superseded chief of—the indigenous people, those the Fijians call 'owners' (*i taukei*) or 'the land' (*na vanua*), in contrast to immigrants such as the chief who comes by sea. Since the stranger-king is himself a triumphant warrior and cannibal, which is to say a god descended upon the land, the installation represents a transposition of sacred temple ceremonies in another key. In Lau, as in Moala, the leaders of ancient priestly groups (*mataqali*) play the central roles of escorting the pretender upon the ceremonial ground and officiating at the installation kava. And this Tui Nayau whom they usher to the throne of Lau is the successor of parricides. Legend tells of the origin of the title in bloody exploits: the slaughter of a younger brother by the son of the elder, followed by an equally cruel revenge by the son of the younger on both the murderer and his father.[9]

[9]Various versions of the Lau chiefly legends may be found in Reid (1977), Thompson (1940:162), Hocart (1929:passim), Dranivia (MS.), Swayne (MS.), and Hocart (FN:2765 f., 2792 f., 3155 f., 3207 f.). The more mythically told advent of the original chiefly line (Tui Lakeba) is recounted by Fison (1904:49–58), in a story that has the same structure as the Lau legends, if told in a more fabulous genre.

The eventual victory of a junior chiefly line over the senior is a standard feature of the Lau royal traditions, as it is in many (all?) areas of Fiji. Also typical is the repetition of the drama of usurpation at several different stages of the chiefly saga, right down to recent times. Certain of these struggles usher into power new descent stocks (*yavusa*), thus a succession of dynasties; others entail changes in the line of royal succession within the ruling 'clan' (*mataqali*). Superseded chiefly stocks (*malosivo*) appear in the present organization of Lakeba as leaders of indigenous 'land' groups, often with priestly functions. The deposition of a senior line by a cadet frequently represents the domestication of the chiefship: the replacement of a more terrible ruler, inclined to eat his own people, by one disposed rather to feed them (e.g., Pokini and Qilaiso in the Lakeba tradition). Hocart (1936) has taken note of this displacement of human sacrifice and cannibalism to external relations of the society as a structural feature. Finally, successive legendary usurpations may also signify shifts in the political value of different chiefly marriage patterns at different stages of the social formation. The original stranger-princes are linked by marriage to native 'owners': they are wife-takers and sister's sons to the indigenous people (*vasu i taukei*). But later displacements of the rule to other stocks or to junior lines are often predicated on advantageous external alliances. Those who now come to power are thus the sister's sons or 'great nephews' (*vasu levu*) of powerful *outside* chiefdoms. So while the Lau chiefs were originally *vasu* to the land people of Lau, later chiefs

There is still more to the barkcloth. The barkcloth which provides access for the god/chief and signifies his sovereignty is the preeminent feminine valuable (*i yau*) in Fiji. It is the highest product of woman's labor, and as such a principal good of ceremonial exchange (*sōlevu*). The chief's accession is mediated by the object that saliently signifies women. The same is repeated, we shall see, at the epiphanal climax, when the ruler drinks "the kava of the land." If the chief then detains "the barkcloth of the land," it is because he has appropriated the island's reproductive powers.

Just as the ancient Indo-European king is the magical son-in-law, so the Fijian ruler is the sacred nephew, descended from the sister's son of the indigenous people (*vasu i taukei*). This founding relationship—mentioned already in the story of the chiefly sharks of Noikoro—is general in Fijian myth and genealogy. The original transfer of power to the immigrant prince is signified by the surrender of a native woman of rank. Similarly, when a Fijian group is defeated in war, they make submission by presenting to their conqueror a basket of earth (the land) and daughters of their own chiefs. The line of conquering chiefs becomes the sister's sons of the conquered people.

"All the chiefly clans of Fiji," writes Rokowaqa, brilliant ethnographer of his own people, "they are of female ancestry" (*Ko ira kece na mataqali Turaga e Viti, era sa vu yalewa*). Hence they are the 'hand of the feast' (*liga ni magiti*), i.e., feast givers to the people, for it was the ancestress who cooked food (*baleta nona dau vakasaqa kakana na vu yalewa*). The gender opposition *in this context* is to the indigenous subjects: they are of the male line, 'hand of the club' (*liga ni wau*), i.e., the chief's guardian-warriors (Rokowaqa n.d.:63; cf. Hocart 1929:236). Thus the usage that long puzzled Hocart, that the Fijian nobility are styled 'child chiefs' (*gone turaga*), while the native owners of the land are the 'elders' (*qase*). The relation is one of offspring to ancestor, as established by the gift of the woman. Notice, however, that it carries another message, since the chiefly immigrants could have been conceived, even by Fijian idiom, as wife-takers to the people's wife-givers, or "the side of the man" to the native "side

---

were successively *vasu* to Cakaudrove, Bau, and Tonga. The trend continues: the present heir-apparent would be *vasu* to Rewa.

of the woman." Everything happens as if the people's own standpoint is the archimedean point of the cultural universe.

But then, in Fijian terms, the people will have to say, "The chief is our god" (Hocart 1970 [1936]:61; 1912:447; Rabuka 1911: 156). For as we have seen already (chapter 2), the paradigmatic ritual privilege of the sister's son is to seize the offerings made to the god of his mother's brother's people (Hocart 1915). The uterine nephew thus takes the role of the god: the one who consumes the offerings. He is 'sacred blood' (*drā tabu*) as Moalans say. If the ruling chief is the usurper of the land through the acquisition of an indigenous princess, it follows that his lineage usurps the place of the people's god. In cosmic terms, the dynastic ancestor marries the earth, and his descendants (e.g., in Bau) appear among the people as 'human gods' (*kalou tamata*).

Hence the distinctive duality of the godhead in traditional Fiji, consisting on one hand of the ancient invisible gods of the land and, on the other, their visible instantiations in living chiefs. The pantheon is not a direct reflection of the temporal power, as in a segmentary ancestral cult. For the great gods that governed the fate of the collectivity, the principal war gods in particular, were not direct-lineage ancestors of the reigning chiefs. Spirits rather of the original chiefs and/or sources (*vū*) of the indigenous lineages, the major gods belonged to the native land people or deposed rulers, who accordingly were their priests. During the cult, the indigenous deities became manifest by entering (*curuma*) the priest. But otherwise and continuously, they were visibly present in the ruling chief, who as uterine nephew of their worshipers had superseded them in this world. Naming the gods of the several village temples, the Tokatoka paramount said to Hocart, "all these are my names."

Nor did the chief's divinity signify merely an occasional and ritual privilege. Documents from the earlier part of the nineteenth century tell that before Christianity the enormous quantities of foods and goods brought for ceremonial exchange (*solevu*) from other lands were presented not to the persons but to the gods of the recipients (Hunt Journals: 11 Feb. 1840; Lyth Tongan and Feejeean Reminiscences, 1:84–86). Nearly everything we call "trade" and "tribute" was at that time sacrifice. If the goods, then, fell to the ranking chief of the group, it was exactly by his divine right as sister's son, right established through the initial transfer of the woman. One is reminded of Hocart's dictum: "There is no religion in Fiji, only a system that in Europe has split up into religion and business" (1970 [1936]:256).

Also relevant is Brother Hazlewood's observation, "their gods are cannibals, just like themselves," since the initial acquisition of the woman by the stranger-king is a social mode of consumption (Erskine 1967 [1853]:247). Like many other peoples, Fijians equate sexual possession with consumption of the woman.[10] Divine and ferocious cannibal from outside, the chief eats the land in the transposed and benign form of marriage.[11] Just as Romulus founded his kingdom by the capture of the Sabine women, so the Fijian ruler, likewise terrible warrior of divine descent, acquires his domain by taking the land's female (reproductive) virtues. And to the god/chief, then, falls the people's offering of first fruits, *i sevu*—a term that does also for the ceremonial prestation of kava (*i sevusevu*).

Notice that in all these genealogies, myths, and rites, Indo-European or Polynesian, we have to do with cultural categories, abstract but fundamental conceptions, represented in persons. The alleged actions of these persons display the right relations between the categories, a process of their combination and organization. Anthropologists call this a "structure," but the term should not be taken for a synchronic scheme of contrasts and correspondences—e.g., the chief is to the people as foreign is to native, the sea is to the land, the wife-takers to the wife-givers, and so on. Just as time and sequence are essential to telling the myth or performing the rite, so too the structure is a generative development of the categories and their relationships. In the event, new and synthetic terms are produced, and elementary categories change their values.

[10] Buell Quain's Vanua Levu male informants told him they salivate when they see a beautiful woman (Quain 1948:322n).

[11] Indeed, it is only polite form for a subject people, when presenting a feast to the chief, to offer to include themselves in it—"the men are the feast":

A little basket [the feast] lies here in the presence of you-two [the chief], and a weak branch of a stump [the kava root] which I put down in the presence of you-two. There is nothing to eat with it. Be gracious; if it is not enough we are its supplement. The men are the feast (Hocart, HF, being a formula of presentation to the paramount chief of Namata, Viti Levu).

Abstractly, the life of society is generated through the combination of opposed yet complementary qualities, each incomplete without the other. Hence the privileged role of the metaphor of male and female. The immigrant sovereign is a ferocious male: virile young warrior and penetrator from the outside. Great creator and pro-creator, he is often associated with the sun and the heavens (see chapter 1). The indigenous people are, *at the initial moment*, "the side of the woman." They are associated with the powers of earth and underworld, with growth and the peaceful acts of agriculture. So, as the Sabines, they are associated with wealth (*opes*); or, most generally, with that which nurtures the godly seed and transforms it into social substance. But we can already see in this the seeds of social contradiction. The underworld is the site of death as well as telluric source of life's sustenance, and male power can have no issue or effect until it is encompassed by the woman. Hence the ambiguous power of the woman. That Fijian barkcloth, woman's good, which provides the path for the god also functions in everyday life as a loincloth, concealing—culturalizing—the primary site of male power. There is a contradiction latent in the chief's appropriation of "the barkcloth of the land." As Hocart puts it, barkcloth is used to "catch" the spirit (1929:237).

Speaking to Indo-European conceptions, Dumézil names the opposed forces in play *celeritas* and *gravitas*, and these Latin terms perfectly fit in the Fijian case. *Celeritas* refers to the youthful, active, disorderly, magical, and creative violence of conquering princes; *gravitas*, to the venerable, staid, judicious, priestly, peaceful, and productive dispositions of an established people. In the initial moment of their combination *celeritas* prevails over *gravitas*, as the invaders capture the reproductive powers of the land to found their kingdom. But the same creative violence that institutes society would be dangerously unfit to constitute it. The combination of two terms produces a third, a sovereign power, itself a dual combination of the war function and the peace function, king and priest, will and law.

This duality of sovereignty is a condition of the "general sociology" of all such kingdoms, Polynesian as much as the ancient Indo-European. The sovereign is able to rule society, which is to say to mediate between its antithetical parts, insofar as the sovereign power itself partakes of the nature of the opposition, combines in itself the elementary antithesis. The Fijian chief is both invading male and, as sister's son, the female side of the native lineage. Notorious cannibal on the one hand, whose anger (*cudru*) is always feared, he is on the other hand immobilized: he "just sits," Fijians say—i.e., in the house as a woman—"and things are brought to him." In fact, the warrior functions of the ruling chief devolve as soon as possible upon a youthful heir, a son whose roving, killing, and womanizing prowess is a cultural prescription. Or else, or in addition, the *gravitas* and *celeritas* powers of sovereignty are divided between senior and junior lines of chiefly descent. But it is not so much the organization of the diarchy to which I call attention. More than a duality, this determination of the sovereignty is an *ambiguity* that is never resolved. It becomes an historical destiny.

It appears as a complementary and cyclical opposition of the two natures of kingship. Above and beyond society and thus counterposed to it, the king also incorporates the society and thus represents the general welfare. Hence certain permutations between the *celeritas* and *gravitas* modes of kingship, as in the Roman royal traditions, where the two forms exchange with each other in a long-term, diachronic structure. Indeed, Romulus initially shares power with the Sabine King Tatius. And although he presumably kills Tatius, he himself disappears without issue, saving his own apotheosis, and is succeeded by the judicious Sabine, Numa. The disappearance and apotheosis already indicate certain of the contradictions. Romulus (by one version) is the victim of the sacrifice he himself offers at the altar of Mars. Mysteriously taken up to heaven at the moment of sacrifice, he becomes the god Quirinus, who is in fact the god not of kings but of the populace. We shall see in a moment that the original Polynesian chief is likewise his own sacrificial victim and the lost god of his people. In any event, Numa, Romulus's Sabine successor, weans Rome from war and founds the priesthood and the cult, means of civic order. Numa's reforms represent the more general popular interest which he, as member of the indigenous people, is disposed to incarnate. Thereafter, the Latin kingship will alternate between *celeritas* and *gravitas*, magical war kings and religious peace kings.

But this alternation between the opposed poles of State and Society is only one of the many other cycles of its type, set on various temporal dimensions. In a cycle of shorter duration, each year the reign of the sovereign Jupiter is interrupted by a popular Saturnalia when all order is put in abeyance.[12] In the Saturnalia, the Lupercalia, their carnival successors and analogous annual festivals of traditional kingdoms elsewhere, a further permutation of the original structure appears. At this time of cosmic and social rebirth, *celeritas* and *gravitas* exchange places: the people become the party of disorder, and the celebration of their community is a so-called ritual of rebellion (Gluckman 1963). A festival of the lower orders, it is the celebration, then, of the "material bodily lower stratum," as Bakhtin (1968) calls it—precisely what we still call "earthy." Inversion combines with subversion, and even perversion, in a scene of general license, revelry, and the interchange of social roles. Master and slave become equals, perhaps reverse their positions. The king is put to flight (*regifugium*) or ritually slain. In the anthropologically famous case of the Swazi *incwala* ceremonies, his capital is pillaged and he is branded with sacred insults as the enemy of the people. In parts of Europe and Polynesia, as well as Africa and the Near East, the reigning monarch is replaced by a mock king or superseded god of the people, who regains the queen of the land and presides over the revelries.[13]

At the Hawaiian annual ceremony of this type, the Makahiki ('Year'), the lost god cum legendary king returns to take posses-

[12] And should we not notice the longer historical duration in which monarchy is superseded by republic, to be replaced in turn by a totalitarian imperialism— or even the repetition of the cycle in modern European history?

[13] Recall the remarkable tripartite comparison Frazer operates in the second edition of *The Golden Bough* between the Hebrew festival of Purim, the Babylonian festival of Sacaea, and the Passion of Christ. The juxtaposition of Matthew 27:26–31 with Dio Chrysostom on the mock king of Sacaea dramatizes the point-for-point resemblance—minus the appropriation of the woman in the Christian version:

> Then released he [Pilate] Barnabas unto them: and when he had scourged Jesus, he delivered him to be crucified. Then the soldiers of the governor took Jesus into the common hall, and gathered unto him the whole band of soldiers. And they stripped him and put on him a scarlet robe. And when they had plaited a crown of thorns, they put it upon his head and a reed in his right hand: and they bowed the knee before him, and took the reed, and smote him on the head, and after that they had mocked him, they took the robe off from him, and put his own raiment on him, and led him away to crucify him.

sion of the land. Circuiting the island to collect the offerings of the people, he leaves in his train scenes of mock battle and popular celebration. At the end of the god's progress, the Hawaiians perform a version of the Fijian installation ceremonies. The reigning king comes in from the sea to be met by attendants of the returned popular god hurling spears, one of which is caused to symbolically reach its mark. Thus killed by the god, the king enters the temple to sacrifice to him and welcome him to "the land of us-two." Yet the death of the king is also the moment of his reascension, and in the end it is the god who is sacrificed. Just as the provisional king of carnival must eventually suffer execution, the image of the returned god is soon after dismantled, bound, and hidden away—a rite watched over by the ceremonial double (or human god) of the king, one of whose titles is "Death is Near." Thereupon, the real usurper, the constituted king, resumes his normal business of human sacrifice (Valeri: in press).

The ritual makes another curious juncture with European history: in the death of Captain Cook, whom Hawaiians had identified as their lost god/king, Lono. The next chapter will document the event in detail; here we may be content with a brief synopsis. Cook's first visit, to Kaua'i Island in January 1778, fell within the traditional months of the New Year rite (Makahiki). He returned to the Islands late in the same year, very near the recommencement of the Makahiki ceremonies. Arriving now off northern Maui, Cook proceeded to make a grand circumnaviga-

---

Compare this treatment of the "King of the Jews" with the king of the Sacaea (by Frazer's rendering of Dio Chrysostum):

> They take one of the prisoners condemned to death and seat him upon the king's throne, and give him the king's raiment, and let him lord it and drink and run riot and use the king's concubines during these days, and no man prevents him from doing just what he likes. But afterwards they strip and scourge and crucify him (Frazer 1900, 3:187).

Frazer's insertion of the Crucifixion in this context of renewal ceremonies came under considerable attack; in the third edition of *The Golden Bough* (1911–15) he professed the interpretation uncertain and relegated it to an appendix (cf. Dorson 1968:285–86). It is noteworthy for present purposes, however, that the Sacaea scene he once thought so like the Crucifixion appears in the one-volume edition (of 1922) in direct connection with the Makihiki festival of Hawaii, as a ritual of the same type (Frazer 1963 [1922]:328–29).

tion of Hawai'i Island in the prescribed clockwise direction of
Lono's yearly procession, to land at the temple in Kealakekua
Bay where Lono begins and ends his own circuit. The British
captain took his leave in early February 1779, almost precisely on
the day the Makahiki ceremonies definitively close. But on his
way out to Kahiki, the *Resolution* sprung a mast, and Cook committed the ritual fault of returning unexpectedly and unintelligi-
bly. The Great Navigator was now *hors catégorie*, a dangerous
condition as Leach and Douglas have taught us, and within a
few days he was really dead—though certain priests of Lono did
afterward ask when he would come back. It was a ritual demise:
hundreds of Hawaiians, many of them chiefs, pressed in upon
the fallen god to have a part in his death (cf. Sahlins 1981). But
then, a lot of kings of traditional states have met a similar fate.
Hocart quotes a Lauan nobleman: "few high chiefs were not
killed" (1929:158).[14]

> What infinite heart's ease
> Must kings neglect that private men enjoy! . . .
> What kind of god art thou, who suffer'st more
> Of mortal griefs than do thy worshippers?
>   (Shakespeare, *Henry V*)

Sovereignty never shakes the ambiguities of its locus. For the
Fijian ruler, all this might have been present at the moment of

[14] In Lau, these chiefly deaths were not the result of people's wars—a concept
that is absent from Fijian legend and recorded history (Derrick 1950:48)—but
the effects of heroic rivalries in royal families. Led by their own senior lines, the
clans or villages of the people, however, might take the part of royal rebels. We
shall see (below, p. 95 f.) that subject clans had determinate and limited obligations to ruling chiefs; if pressed beyond those, they could revise their loyalties.
In another publication I will show how the transcendent ambitions and un-
customary exactations of the famous Cakobau (Thakombau) in the great Fijian
wars of the nineteenth century, by inciting general resentment and desertions to
enemy chiefs, almost brought him down. In Hawaii likewise, regicide was an
aristocratic vice, at least in recorded history and protohistory, although the district of Ka'ū is known for legends of assassinations of "bad kings" by the populace (see above, p. 75). From all this, it follows that heroic historic action is not
absolute (cf. chap. 2). Taken without regard for customary relations, it puts the
king (although not the kingship) at risk. It may be said of the opposition of
"State" and "Society" discussed here that it sets an ultimate—if structurally and
historically relative—limit to heroic pretensions and innovations: i.e., a negative
determination "beyond which one cannot go."

his installation, when Society took some pains to protect itself against the State. Indeed, at the rituals of the installation, the chief is invested with the 'rule' or 'authority' (*lewā*) over the land, but the land itself is not conveyed to him. The soil (*qele*) is specifically identified with the indigenous 'owners' (*i taukei*), a bond that cannot be abrogated. Hence the widespread assertion that traditionally (or before the Lands Commission) the chiefly clan was landless, except for what it had received in provisional title from the native owners, i.e., as marriage portion from the original people or by bequest as their sister's son (Hocart 1929: 97, 98; 1950:88; HF:441; Council of Chiefs 1881:55). The ruling chief has no corner on the means of production. Accordingly, he cannot compel his native subjects to servile tasks, such as providing or cooking his daily food, which are obligations rather of his own household, his own line, or of conquered people (*nona tamata ga, qali kaisi sara*). Yet even more dramatic conditions are imposed on the sovereignty at the time of the ruler's accession. Hocart observes that the Fijian chief is ritually reborn on this occasion; that is, as a domestic god. If so, someone must have killed him as a dangerous outsider.

He is indeed killed by the indigenous people at the very moment of his consecration, by the offering of kava that conveys the land to his authority (*lewā*). Grown from the leprous body of a sacrificed child of the native people, the kava the chief drinks poisons him. Versions of the Tongan and Rotuman myths of the origin of kava, widely related in eastern Fiji, are here ritually recapitulated.[15] Sacred product of the people's agriculture, the in-

[15] Tongan myths of the origins of kava are extensively analyzed by Bott (1972) and Leach (1972). On Rotuma see Churchward (1938–39) and Gardiner (1898). The version recorded by Hocart for Lau is quite similar to the Tongan legends, as might be expected from known historic and prehistoric contacts. There is in Hocart's unpublished writings a statement, somewhat puzzling however, that the child of the land from whose body the kava plant grew was a young man rather than the daughter of the people as in Tonga—transformation paralleled by the use of male kava-servers in Fiji, female in Tonga. Hocart's field notes of the myth (FN: 3220–22) leave the sex unspecified, the reference being merely to a 'child' (*luve*) of a couple who lived in the interior bush (*lekutu*). But the original manuscript of his Lau ethnography (WI) identifies the child as a son. In the Cakaudrove-Natewa myth reproduced in Hocart's Northern States (1952:127), the victim and source of kava is not only male, but a young chief of the land (status of Natewa as *bati* or land-ally relative to Cakaudrove) at the zenith of his manhood. The stranger-king is thus poisoned by the original chief of the people.

stallation kava is brought forth in Lau by a representative of the
native owners (*mataqali* Taqalevu), who proceeds to separate the
main root in no ordinary way but by the violent thrusts of a
sharp implement (probably, in the old time, a spear). Thus killed,
the root (child of the land) is then passed to young men (warriors) of royal descent who, under the direction of a priest of the
land, prepare and serve the ruler's cup. (Rokowaqa [n.d.:40],
writing of Bauan custom, says the *tū yaqona* or cupbearer on this
occasion should be a *vasu i taukei e loma ni koro*, 'sister's son of the
native owners in the center of the village'.) Traditionally, remark, the kava root was chewed to make the infusion: the sacrificed child of the people is cannibalized by the young chiefs. The
water of the kava, however, has a different symbolic provenance.
The classic Cakaudrove kava chant, performed at the Lau installation rites, refers to it as sacred rain water from the heavens
(Hocart 1929:64–65). This male and chiefly water (semen) mixes
with the product of the land (female) in the womb of a kava bowl
whose feet are called 'breasts' (*sucu*), and from the front of
which, tied to the upper part of an inverted triangle, a sacred
cord stretches out toward the chief. The cord is decorated with
small white cowries, not only a sign of chieftainship but by
name, *buli leka*, a continuation of the metaphor of birth—*buli*, 'to
form', refers in Fijian procreation theory to the conceptual action of the male in the body of the woman.

The sacrificed child of the people will thus give birth to the
chief. But only after the chief, ferocious outside cannibal who
consumes the cannibalized victim, has himself been sacrificed

---

I am inclined to believe that this transformation of the Tonga-Rotuma myths is
authentically Fijian, but the evidence is not conclusive, since the Cakaudrove-
Natewa story bears suspicious traces of the Passion of Christ. As briefly described below (in the present text), the full interpretation of the myth requires
consideration of the ritual of kava-serving, with which the identification of the
kava cum child of the land as original (male) chief would be consistent. For other
eastern Fijian variants of the kava myth—which, however, do not definitely resolve this question—see Wallis (1851:347–48), Waterhouse (1866:340), Hocart
(1952:99).

The displacement of the protagonists' homeland—if not also the scene of the
events—to the east, usually Tonga, in the Fijian myths, is likewise consistent
with Fijian political theory. It seems no simple case of myth (or kava) diffusion,
since strong motivation can be found in the Fijian system for the association between a foreign chiefship and the origin of kava-drinking.

by it. For when the ruler drinks the sacred offering, he is in the state of intoxication Fijians call 'dead from' (*mateni*) or 'dead from kava' (*mate ni yaqona*), to recover from which is explicitly 'to live' (*bula*).[16] This accounts for the second cup the chief is alone accorded, the cup of fresh water. The god is immediately revived, brought again to life—in a transformed state.

Having moved from the sea to the land, the foreign to the indigenous, the chief is now encompassed by the people. True, the axis of his divinity rotates from the earthly plane to a position above: gifts of mats brought by people of the land make up his elevated seat upon the ceremonial ground.[17] But at the same time, he has been domesticated and humanized, brought from the periphery of society to the center. This metamorphosis is the essential power of woman: transformation of a natural force, at once creative and destructive, into cultural substance. Subsequent rites of the installation will carry through the metaphor of the chief's birth and initiation, at all stages under the ceremonial aegis of the native people. Henceforth, the chief and his lineage will be 'people of the center of the village' (*kai lomanikoro*). Here the ruler "just sits." Marked off by his sacred tabus—which as Freud (n.d.; following Frazer) observed is as much to protect the people against the Polynesian chief as vice versa—he is condemned to a quasi-isolation.

So do *celeritas* and *gravitas* change places as the structure unfolds. If the chief is brought to the center of the society, where he "just sits" in all his state, the ancient inhabitants become his war dogs (*kolī*, the metaphor is known in Fiji). They are his *bati*, term that signifies at once the 'border' and the 'warrior'. It also means the 'tooth [that bites the cannibal victim]'. For instead of eating the people, the chief must now send for human sacrifices from outside and share them with the people. At the conclusion of the Bau investiture, the Vūnivalu rewards the indigenous chieftain who installed him with the gift of a cannibal victim (Hocart

[16] There is further motivation of the same in the kava taken immediately after the chief's by the herald, a representative of the land. This drinking is 'to kick', *rabeta*, the chief's kava. *Raberabe*, the same reduplicated, means 'a sickness, the result of kicking accidentally against a *drau-ni-kau*' (Capell 1973:168). The herald here takes the effects on himself: *drau-ni-kau* is the common name for 'sorcery'. On the association of kava and poison in Tonga see Bott (1972).

[17] At Cakaudrove, the mats of the chief's sitting-place are laid down by members of a true land group (*vanua sara*; Hocart 1952:93–94).

1929:70).[18] Taken in war from beyond the land (*vanua*), in the privileged instance from traditional enemies and foreign chiefs, such victims are in effect of the nature of the ruling chief himself—terrible outside gods. The chief, poisoned and reborn as a domestic god, must now give feast to the people *on bodies of his own kind.* Having consecrated the victims in raw form, the chief distributes a certain portion of the cooked bodies to native owners, particularly to priests and other chieftains of indigenous lineages, thus sharing with them the divine benefits. This helps explain certain nineteenth-century reports of the unusual treatments accorded the most honored or most hated enemies, including parodies of chiefly installation ceremonies (e.g., Endicott 1923:59–60; Diapea 1928:19–20; Clunie 1977). Hence also the beautiful chant recorded by the English missionary Thomas Williams, wherein the corpse is made to say, as he is dragged to the place of sacrifice by triumphant warriors and mocking women,

Yari au malua,	Drag me gently,
Yari au malua,	Drag me gently,
Koi au na saro ni nomu	I am the champion of your
vanua.	land.

(Williams and Calvert 1859:163).[19]

Cooked men have been given by the ruling chief in return for raw women of the land.[20] Lévi-Strauss did not invent these ex-

---

[18]The Levuka people who install the Vunivalu of Bau (as Tui Levuka) are "true sea people." But in the installation, they play the role of the indigenous "land" side, as they are indeed the original occupants or owners (*i taukei*) of Bau Island (Tippett 1973:91 f.).

[19]Lyth recorded another chant referring to the cannibal victim in the same vein:

Sa bobo na matana,	The eyes are closed,
Sa yadra na lomana.	The mind is awake.
Sa vei ko qaqa?	Where is the hero?
Sa laki yara.	Gone to be dragged (to the oven).
Sa vei ko datuvu?	Where is the coward?
Sa laki tukutuku.	Gone to tell the news.

(Lyth, Reminiscences: 326).

[20]"Cooked men" is here used diacritically. Dead male enemies constitute the privileged as well as the unmarked sense of *bakola* (or *bokola*), 'cannibal victim'.

change equivalencies; Fijians themselves so represent them (Hocart 1929:129). For the chief had already been obliged to make the same transaction with his own person. At the final rites of the Lauan installation, after certain ceremonies of purification, the ruler is once more escorted along a path of barkcloth. But this time by warriors of the most distant and indigenous village of the island, who are singing the traditional chant of victory. Is it the victory of the newly crowned king? The song these warriors sing as the chief passes between their lines is the same they chant over the body of a cannibal victim.

I conclude by taking notice of a final structural permutation. We have seen that the conjunction of chief and people, sea and land, generates a synthetic term, the sovereign power: itself male and female, a combination of *celeritas* and *gravitas*. This permutation gives the system a vertical dimension, the chief above as well as within, but it also motivates its horizontal expansion to include a necessary third term. The fully constituted global structure is a tripartite pyramidal scheme, composed of the same three functions Dumézil determines for Indo-European civilizations, if not exactly in the same arrangement. The totality also develops by the dialectic process Dumézil sometimes adopts to describe it (e.g., 1949:76).

The Fijian ruling chief, once transformed into a local god, inhibits his cannibalistic disposition with respect to the native owners, instead procuring victims from the outside whose distribution is reward for the people's offerings to him—raw women and the raw first-things of agriculture. The displacement of strife and cannibalism to an extramural field of Mars calls forth a third category, analogous to the third Roman tribe of militant Etruscans. In Fiji, these people are likewise 'foreign' by opposition to the 'land' (*vanua*), now composed of chief and people, with whom, however, the foreigners are united in a 'government' (*matanitū*) of higher order. The foreign warriors are of two general classes: allied villages or lands beyond the chiefdom borders (*bati* [*balavu*]), who retain a certain autonomy; and the more fully integrated 'sea people proper' (*kai wai dina*) living within the ruling chief's own land. True sea people are the most prominent assassins; they are the notorious 'dangerous men' (*tamata*

Historical accounts make it clear that, at least in the early nineteenth century, women and children were also eaten.

rerevaki). The Levuka people of Lau, the Butoni of Koro and Cakaudrove, and the Lasakau fishers of Bau are famous examples—the last being fishers of turtle by ceremonial occupation, but fishers of men when the chief has need for human sacrifices.[21] Always of outside origin and condition, considered 'different people' (*kai tani*) even when long established within the chiefdom, such warriors are attached to the paramount's service by founding gift of a royal daughter. As the ruling chief is initially sacred nephew to the native cultivators, so his foreign assassins are in origin sacred nephew to him.[22]

The whole thus makes up an elaborate cycle of the exchange of raw women for cooked men, marked at certain points, however, by transformations which preserve the distinctions between categories and their hierarchical relationship. For at the birth rituals of the royal child, both the mother—the raw woman the chief had obtained from the native people—and her offspring are symbolically cooked.[23] If this enculturates them, in-

---

[21] *Dau ni ika, dau ni tamata*, 'fishers of fish, fishers of men': the phrasing is again Fijian (Hocart 1952:120–21).

[22] I specifically refer to these initial transactions of marriage as 'founding relations' in order to avoid the implication that the flow of women continues empirically in the same direction, in the way of an elementary system of asymmetric marriage (MBD marriage). The founding marriages are charters of the relationships between the triad of basic categories (indigenous land people, chiefs, and foreign warriors or fishers). So when Hocart asked the people of Wailevu, for example, if they ever married women from a certain line of chiefs, they remarked, "He is seeking confirmation of the border [*bati*, land ally] relationship [*i vakadinadina ni bati*]" (Hocart, HF). But marriges in this direction may or may not be repeated regularly, depending on the political situation. On the other hand, once established, the rights and obligations of the relationship can be activated in another modality, i.e., through transactions in whale teeth especially. I should also note that the present discussion is confined to the essentials of the chiefdom formation, its basic categories. Within any of the three mentioned, especially the native owners, there is a further and elaborate division of statuses (*i tūtū*) and functions (*i tavi*), discussion of which would carry us beyond the objectives of this paper.

[23] The "cooking" of the royal child—and also of the mother—is my interpretation of certain episodes of eastern Fijian birth rites pertaining to noble offspring. Especially notable is the *tavu deke*, 'roasting small fry', of Bau, and an analogous ceremony reported for southern Lau (Toganivalu, MS; Thompson 1940:84–85). The *tavu deke* is a feast marking an unusual ritual bathing of the child. On the second or fourth day of life, the royal infant is held in the steam issuing from a bowl of water that had been heated with fired stones. Essentially, that is the way food or bodies get cooked in an underground oven. Further, Jarré (1946) records

corporates them from the natural-spiritual world, it also means that the daughter passed on by the chief to his foreign killers is reduced to human dimensions. In exchange, the foreign warriors bring the chief raw bodies; or, if they fail to fill the ceremonial quotas, they must seek victims from their own kinsmen (in other communities), on pain of making up the deficiency with their own persons. The victims are also identified with the chief as sacrifier; but again, these offerings are cooked and reduced in spiritual value before they are shared with the indigenous cultivators—whose gift of a raw woman had initiated the entire cycle (see Figure 3:1). The transformations between raw and cooked, natural and cultural, thus sustain the hierarchical as well as the intermediate position of the chief: above and between his land people and his sea people, his cultivators and his fishers (or sailors), his domestic subjects and his foreign allies, his internal guardians and his external assassins.

More: the exchange of raw women against cooked men is paradigmatic of the entire chiefdom economy. Fijians make an extensive classification of material things parallel to the basic dualism of native land people and immigrant sea people. Plant food, flesh food, liquids, utensils, domestic furnishings, and personal ornaments are likewise differentiated into land things and sea things: complementary products whose combination is indispensable to a complete cultural existence (Rokowaqa n.d.: 37–39). The same, then, can be said of the ruling chief who, at once or alternately land and sea himself, functions as supreme mediator of the material interchange and great generator of the cultural totality. An immigrant by origin, he is a sea person relative to the people of the land, hence purveyor of sea and foreign goods in exchange for indigenous land products. On the other hand, relative to his immigrant assassins, the 'true sea people', the chief represents the 'land' (vanua), and transfers to his sea allies the agricultural and craft products of the native owners. In

---

of Kadavu birth ceremonies that after a summary bath—the tavu deke?—the child is anointed with oil perfumed by sandalwood and malawaci (Streblus anthropophagorum). Malawaci, as the Latin name suggests, is a plant closely associated with cannibalism: its leaves are used to wrap the body for baking, then are eaten along with it (Capell 1973:133). Besides all this, a smoldering fire is kept burning near the mother and infant for ten days in the rear, sacred section of the house of confinement, and the doors of the house are tightly shut. The atmosphere is described by Toganivalu as excessively warm.

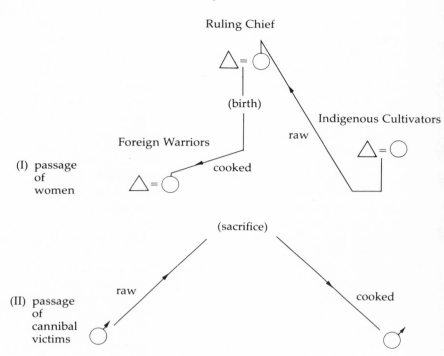

Figure 3:1   Raw women/cooked men: founding relations of the
Matanitu ('Government').

combination with the alternative land/sea status of the sovereign, a simple rule guarantees this continuous reduction of the
triadic scheme to binary exchange: that no one can consume the
special products of his own labor (his *salu*) in the presence of
members of the opposite category. The rule, moreover, becomes
general because the ruling chief is virtual in the transactions between any two groups of the polity even if he is not actually
present (as giver and receiver), since the relationship between
the parties is transitively determined by their respective relationships to the chief.

All this means that the total scheme, in its true mode of movement, is more than any given and static set of contrasts. Here I
make my general point about theoretical practice. A structural
analysis would not be worthy of the name were it content with
some extended table of parallel binary oppositions, or even with

the proportions of the classic A:B::C:D form derived from such a table. There is a great ethnographic industry in these Saussurean proportions. Yet consider the Fijian proposition, men: women::culture:nature::chiefs:people. The statement is valid, but only as a simplified reduction or particular moment of the global structure, taken from a specific local context or perspective. It cannot be a sufficient description of the structure, since it is always falsifiable by similar proportions, also valid but propounded from a different vantage point, in which all the categories change their signs. So it is likewise true for Fiji that men: women::nature:culture::people:chiefs. I believed that such local reversals of value are general conditions of structure, not sufficiently taken into account, for example, in popular studies of the status of women.[24]

It is also commonly concluded that many of the key cultural categories are "ambiguous," "contradictory," or "logically unstable." The conclusion leads to the further observation that the categories can be disambiguated by referring them to different contexts. Yet such conceptions of structure, i.e., as a set of contextualized propositions laid out seriatim, will neither exhaust the logic nor specify it. All these context-bound formulations are merely contingent representations of the cultural scheme: provisional cross-sections of it, taken from some interested standpoint (whether of observer or participant). The logic of the whole lies in the generative development of the categories, by which alone may be motivated all static and partial expressions of it. Only by the internal diachrony of structure can we comprehend 'ambiguity' in such logical forms as synthesis, or the contextual determination of values as a determinate valorization of contexts. Such is the cultural life of the elementary forms.

[24] "In Fiji two contradictory statements are not necessarily inconsistent. They appear to us contradictory, because we do not understand the shades of meaning, and because we do not know, without much experience, the point of view from which each is made" (Hocart 1952:61).

4

Captain James Cook;
or The Dying God

Concerning the Death of Captain Cook:

> . . . what I have here said I do not Aver to be the Real
> Truth in Every particul although in General it may be
> pretty Nigh the Matter. I have carefully Assorted such
> Relations as had the greatest appearance of Truth. But
> indeed they were so Exceedingly perplexed in their Ac-
> counts that it was a hard matter to Colect Certainty, in
> particular cases, or indeed to write any Account at all.
>
> > Log book of Alex: Home, R. N., of
> > Buskenburn, Berwickshire, while
> > with Captain Cook on his Last
> > Voyage

I. "A chain of events which could
no more be foreseen than prevented"
(William Ellis, Surgeon's second mate, HMS *Discovery*)

It was the most generous welcome ever accorded any European
voyage of discovery in this ocean.[1] "Anchored·in 17^{fms} black
sand," reads a midshipman's log, "amidst an Innumerable Num-

---

[1] This essay is related to my previous work, "L'apothéose du capitaine Cook," in
La fonction symbolique, Michel Izard and Pierre Smith, eds. (Paris: Gallimard,
1979), but the ideas of Cook's presence and death in Hawaii, and of the nature of

ber of Canoes, the people in which were singing & rejoicing all the way" (Riou, Log: 17 Jan. 1779). They were singing! Nor in all his experience had Captain Cook ever seen so many Polynesians assembled as were here in Kealakekua Bay. Besides the innumerable canoes, Hawaiians were clambering over the *Resolution* and *Discovery*, lining the beaches, and swimming in the water "like shoals of fish." Perhaps there were 10,000, or five times as many people as normally lived here. And not a weapon to be seen among them, Cook remarked. Instead, the canoes were laden with pigs, sweet potatoes, breadfruit, sugar cane: everything the island produced. Also the women "seemed remarkably anxious to engage themselves to our people" (Ellis 1782, 1:86). A priest came on board and wrapped Captain Cook in the red tapa-cloth decoration of a temple image, then made the offering of a sacrificial pig. On shore, the priest led the Great Navigator by the hand to the temple of Hikiau. Hearing the herald's cry "O Lono," the people on their passage flew to their houses or prostrated face to ground. Lono is the god associated with natural growth and human reproduction who annually returns to the Islands with the fertilizing rains of winter; he is also an ancient king come in search of his sacred bride. In January 1779, at the temple, Captain Cook was put through the customary rites of welcome to Lono. As the priest Koa'a and Lt. King held his arms outstretched and the appropriate sacrifices were made, Cook indeed became the image of Lono, a duplicate of the crosspiece icon (constructed of wood staves) which is the appearance of the god. It was a ceremony of the Makihiki, the great Hawaiian New Year Festival. Sir James Frazer described the Makihiki in *The Golden Bough*: in part 3, The Dying God.[2]

Cook's death at Hawaiian hands just a few weeks later could

---

the Hawaiian New Year Festival (Makahiki) have been substantially altered by subsequent research. The text presented here is essentially that of the Frazer lecture, University of Liverpool, 1982.

[2] An exhaustive discussion of the sources, published and unpublished, of Cook's third voyage can be found in Beaglehole (1967:clxxi–ccxvii). The present essay is based on my own consultation of these sources in London (British Museum and Public Records Office), Sydney (Library of New South Wales), Canberra (National Library of Australia), Wellington, N.Z. (Alexander Turnbull Library), and Honolulu (Archives of Hawaii, Bishop Museum Library, and Sinclair Library, University of Hawaii). The citations of particular journals or logs will be confined here to direct quotation, for the most part.

thus be described as the ritual sequel: the historical metaphor of a mythical reality. Nor were the myths Hawaiian only. There was the complementary British folklore characterized by Cook's biographer J. C. Beaglehole as "the English search for a 'King'." Early on Sunday morning, 14 February 1779, Captain Cook went ashore with a party of marines to take the Hawaiian king, Kalaniopu'u, hostage against the return of the *Discovery's* cutter, stolen the night before in a bold maneuver—of which, however, the amiable old ruler was innocent. At the decisive moment, Cook and Kalaniopu'u, the God and the King, will confront each other as cosmic adversaries. Permit me thus an anthropological reading of the historical texts. For in all the confused Tolstoian narratives of the affray—among which the judicious Beaglehole refuses at times to choose—the one recurrent certainty is a dramatic structure with the properties of a ritual transformation. During the passage inland to find the king, thence seaward with his royal hostage, Cook is metamorphosed from a being of veneration to an object of hostility. When he came ashore, the common people as usual dispersed before him and prostrated face to the earth; but in the end he was himself precipitated face down in the water by a chief's weapon, an iron trade dagger, to be rushed upon by a mob exulting over him, and seeming to add to their own honors by the part they could claim in his death: "snatching the daggers from each other," reads Mr. Burney's account, "out of eagerness to have their share in killing him" (Journal: 14 Feb. 1779). In the final ritual inversion, Cook's body would be offered in sacrifice by the Hawaiian King.

Cook was transformed from the divine beneficiary of the sacrifice to its victim—a change never really radical in Polynesian thought, and in their royal combats always possible (Valeri: in press). Every phase of the transformation had its own kind of offering: the shifting material signs of Cook's trajectory in cosmic value. In the beginning, as he went "to find the King," pigs were pressed upon him; and as he waited for Kalaniopu'u to waken, more offerings of red tapa cloth—proving that the English captain was still the image of the Hawaiian god. The King came away willingly and was walking by Cook's hand to the waiting ship's boat when he was stopped by his favored wife Kaneikapolei and two chiefs, pleading and demanding that he not go on. By all accounts, British as well as Hawaiian, they told him such stories of the death of kings as to force him to sit upon the ground, where he now appeared—according to Lt. Phillips's report—"dejected and frightened" (in Beaglehole 1967:535).

Nothing to this point had evoked the King's suspicions, and likewise it was only now, Phillips recounts, that "we first began to suspect that they were not very well dispos'd towards us" (*Ibid.*). The transition comes suddenly, at the moment the King is made to perceive Cook as his mortal enemy. This is the structural crisis, when all the social relations begin to change their signs. Accordingly, the material exchanges now convey a certain ambiguity, like those Maori sacrifices that pollute the gods in the act of placating them. An old man offers a coconut, chanting so persistently that the exasperated Cook cannot make him lay off. A supplication begging the release of the King? Lt. Phillips considered that "the artful rascal of a priest" was carrying on to divert attention from the fact that his countrymen, gathering to the number of two or three thousand, were now arming to defend their King. About this time, report comes that an important chief has been killed by the British blockading the southern end of the Bay. The King is seen still on the ground, "with the strongest marks of terror on his countenance" (Cook and King 1784, 3:44), but he soon disappears from the scene. Events have gone beyond the power of anyone to control them. "Ye natives" are manifesting that disposition the English call "insolence." The final homage to Cook is tendered in missiles that include stones and clubs among the pieces of breadfruit and coconut. Each side thus responding violently to the perceived threats of the other, they soon reach "the fatal impact."[3]

[3]The only account of Cook's death that we have from one of the party on shore with him is that of Lt. Molesworth Phillips, as transmitted in Mr. Clerke's journal. Actually, Phillips was wounded and knocked down before Cook fell and did not see the end itself. Beaglehole (1967:cxlviii–clvii; 1974:670–72) sifts through the numerous descriptions of the event rehearsed in the private and public journals, including what was seen from the ships' boats offshore. Generally, I follow his thoughtful rendering, which relies especially on Phillips and Messrs. Clerke and King (cf. Kennedy 1978). But I tend to emphasize "symbolic" details in these and other sources which Beaglehole rather ignores. Also, Beaglehole gives very limited credence to information from Hawaiians, direct or indirect, earlier or later; but as we shall see, I have found these data more useful, as well as consistent with certain of the more reliable European journalists, espe-

But just who done it? In historical texts dating from this day to fifty-odd years later, some eight or ten different men are identified as "the man who killed Captain Cook," referring usually to the one who first stabbed him with the iron dagger. Many of the alleged assailants are named—Pahea, Nuha, Pihole, Pohewa, etc. Often they are distinguished by rank, kinship affiliation, and other social indexes: important clues, since as I hope to show, the key to the mystery is elementary categories (my dear Watson).[4]

Death of Cook: death of Lono. The event was absolutely unique, and it was repeated every year. For the event (any event) unfolds simultaneously on two levels: as individual action and as collective representation; or better, as the *relation* between certain life histories and a history that is, over and above these, the existence of societies. To paraphrase Clifford Geertz, the event is a unique actualization of a general phenomenon (1961:153–54). Hence on the one hand, historical contingency and the particularities of individual action; and on the other hand, those recurrent dimensions of the event in which we recognize some cultural order. The paradox for an historical "science" is that the

---

cially for identification of key Hawaiian personnel and the concepts necessary to interpret the fatal deed. Of course, many uncertainties must remain, perhaps the most important being the exact moment in the sequence when the news of the death of the Hawaiian chief Kalimu at British hands reached the beach at Ka'awaloa, where Cook was confronting Kalaniopu'u.

[4]Cook's alleged assailants are identified in contemporary accounts of the expedition as: a certain Nuha, by Samwell (in Beaglehole 1967:1202; 1957:23–24, 41–42), by the astronomer Bayly (Journal PRO-Adm 55/21: 21 Feb. 1779), and by Edgar (Journal PRO-Adm 55/21:14 Feb. 1779); and/or a certain Kalanimano-o-Kaho'owaha-a-Heulu, by Samwell again, as well as by later Hawaiian authors (Remy 1861:34–35; Kamakau 1961:86, 103). Samwell and Bayly had their information from Hawaiian friends. Other contemporary journalists mention an anonymous chief (or chiefs); see Messrs. King (Beaglehole 1967:557), Trevenen (Marginal Notes), and Ellis (1782, 2:109). Appearing in the records of later European voyagers: Pohewa, encountered by Colnett at Kaua'i (Journal: Feb. 1788); Pahea (and others?) encountered by members of the Vancouver expedition in 1793 and 1794—Puget (BM MS: 27 Jan. 1794; PRO-Adm 55/17:27 Jan. 1794), Bell (1929:86), Vancouver (1801, 5:55), and Menzies (Journal: 3 Mar. 1793); a certain Pihole, known to Dimsdell in Hawai'i Island in 1792 (Barber MS.); a commoner named Ka-ai-moku-a-Kauhi, mentioned by Rev. R. Bloxam in 1825 (MS.); and the anonymous commoners referred to by Mariner (Martin 1817, 2:67) and Dampier (1971:65).

contingent circumstances—such as the accidents of biography or geography—are *necessary conditions*. If Cook hadn't done this or that, then . . . Then what? Conversely, the historian will always be tempted to find the one decisive act on some*one*'s part that set off the whole chain of happenings. For Beaglehole, it was when Cook, worn out from his global adventures, lost control and fired the first shot. And this way of thinking even holds the promise that history can be rescued from its "idiographic" plight by *real science*. For example, according to the diagnosis recently made by a distinguished English physician, Cook during this third voyage was showing all the symptoms of a parasitic infection of the intestine (Watt 1979). Worms done him in. Really, there is something faintly heroic in the idea: a medicine man's homage to the place Cook has assumed in Western folklore as a constituting being, responsible for the shape of the world as we know it—as if the Hawaiians, then, could have done no more than respond to his determining presence, in the ways predictable by some naïve psychology. Still, if the tide had been higher and the boats closer in, Cook would have gotten clean away, whatever his intestinal condition, and despite that— another decisive factor—he couldn't swim.

Even to understand what did happen, it would be insufficient to note that certain people acted in certain ways, unless we also knew what that signified. The contingent becomes fully historical only as it is meaningful: only as the personal act or the ecological effect takes on a systematic or positional value in a cultural scheme. An historical presence is a cultural existence. So the specific effect of Cook's individuality was mediated by the cultural category (or categories) which he represented as a *logical* individual. Implied, then, are categorical relations to others. Frazer could have included the Hawaiians among those Polynesians he found able to testify that the king's enemy is a stranger. And if, that day, the Hawaiian people proved so sensitive about the life of their King, was it not because, as Frazer also argued, the divine king lived the life of the people?

Also, the life of the cosmos. My own argument about the death of Cook will begin with the creation, with the famous Hawaiian chant 'Beginning-[in-]Deep-Darkness', Kumulipo (Beckwith 1972). It is the birth chant of Ka-'I-i-mamao, father of the King of Cook's time, and Hawaiians read it alternately as the story of the universe or the biography of the King: the royal child is thus "the cosmos described" (Luomala in Beckwith 1972: xiii). According to late Hawaiian tradition, the Kumulipo chant was intoned by the priest in the temple ceremonies by which Cook was welcomed as Lono. The tradition cannot be confirmed historically. Its truth perhaps lies in the metaphoric relation between Cook and the royal subject of the creation chant. For this man, Ka-'I-i-mamao, was Cook's latest Hawaiian predecessor in the capacity of Lono: deprived of his rule, his life, and his wife by political rivals.

II. *Nānā i ke Kumu*: Look to the Source

The Kumulipo is connected to Cook in another way. The chant sets the origin of the universe at the autumnal rising of the Pleiades at sunset: celestial event that anticipates the beginning of the Hawaiian ritual year, the annual return of Lono—and by eight days in November 1778, the appearance off Maui of Captain Cook. Conversely, the Hawaiian New Year ceremony, the Makahiki, has the sense of an eternal return: the rebirth of the world in the change of seasons, as effected or conceived by Lono. Yet neither Lono nor any other determinate Hawaiian god had presided over the initial creation. In the Kumulipo, as in certain cosmogonic myths of the Maori, the world of natural things is born of primordial notions that are principles themselves of reproduction (cf. chapter 2). The divine first appears abstractly, as generative-spirit-in-itself. Only after the seven epochs of the *pō*, the long night of the world's self-generation, are the gods as such born—as siblings to mankind. God and man appear together, and in fraternal strife over the means of their reproduction: their own older sister. Begun in the eighth epoch of creation, this struggle makes the transition to the succeeding ages of the *ao*, the 'day' or world known to man. Indeed the struggle is presented as the condition of the possibility of human life in a world in which the life-giving powers are divine. The end of the eighth chant thus celebrates a victory: "Man spread about now, man was here now; / It was day [*ao*]." And this victory gained over the god is again analogous to the triumph achieved annually over Lono at the New Year, which effects the seasonal transition, as Hawaiians note, from the time of long nights (*pō*) to the time of long days (*ao*) (see Kepelino 1932).

The older sister of god and man, La'ila'i, is the firstborn to all the eras of previous creation. By Hawaiian theory, as firstborn La'ila'i is the legitimate heir to creation; while as woman she is uniquely able to transform divine into human life. The issue in her brothers' struggle to possess her is accordingly cosmological in scope and political in form. Described in certain genealogies as twins, the first two brothers are named simply in the chant as "Ki'i, a man" and "Kane, a god." But since Ki'i means 'image' and Kane means 'man', everything has already been said: the first god is 'man' and the first man is 'god'. So in the chant, the statuses of god and man are reversed by La'ila'i's actions. She "sit sideways," meaning she takes a second husband, Ki'i, and her children by the man Ki'i are born before her children by the god Kane. Thus the descendants of the man are senior:

> There was whispering, lip-smacking and clucking,
> Smacking, tut-tutting, head shaking,
> Sulking, sullenness, silence.
> Kane kept silence, refused to speak,
> Sullen, angry, resentful
> With the woman for her progeny . . .
> She slept with Ki'i.
> Kane suspected the first-born, became jealous,
> Suspected Ki'i and La'ila'i of a secret union [?] . . .
> Kane was angry and jealous because he slept last with her,
> His descendants would hence belong to the younger line,
> The children of the elder would be lord,
> First through La'ila'i, first through Ki'i,
> Child of the two born in the heavens there
> Came forth.
>
> (Beckwith 1972:106).

In the succeeding generations, the victory of the human line is secured by the repeated marriages of the sons of men to the daughters of gods, to the extent that the descent of the divine Kane is totally absorbed by the heirs of Ki'i (Kamokuiki Genealogy). It is the paradigmatic model of the Hawaiian politics of usurpation. But the story also evokes a more general Polynesian idea of the human condition: that men are sometimes (or even often) compelled to secure their own existence by inflicting a defeat upon the god, appropriating thus the female power—the bearing earth.

If I am allowed to lift a page from *The Golden Bough*: each year the sylvan landscapes of old New Zealand provided "the scene of a strange and recurring tragedy." In a small sweet-potato garden set apart for the god, a Maori priest enacted a sacred marriage that would be worthy of his legendary colleague of the grove of Nemi. Accompanying his movements with a chant that included the phrase, "Be pregnant, be pregnant," the priest planted the first hillocks (*puke*, also 'mons veneris') of the year's crop (Kapiti 1913; Johansen 1958). The priest plays the part of the god Rongo (-marae-roa, =Ha., Lono), he who originally brought the sweet potato in his penis from the spiritual homeland, to impregnate his wife (Pani, the field). During the period of growth, no stranger will be suffered to disturb the garden. But at the harvest, Rongo's possession is contested by another god, Tū (-matauenga)—ancestor of man "as tapu warrior"—in a battle sometimes memorialized as the origin of war itself. Using an unworked branch of the *mapou* tree—should we not thus say, a bough broken from a sacred tree?—a second priest, representing Tū, removes, binds up, and then reburies the first sweet-potato tubers. He so kills Rongo, the god, parent and body of the sweet potato, or else puts him to sleep, so that man may harvest the crop to his own use. Colenso's brilliant Maori informant goes to the essentials of the charter myth:

> Rongo-marae-roa [Rongo as the sweet potato] with his people were slain by Tu-matauenga [Tū as warrior]. . . . Tu-matauenga also baked in an oven and ate his elder brother Rongo-marae-roa so that he was wholly devoured as food. Now the plain interpretation, or meaning of these names in common words, is, that Rongo-marae-roa is the *kumara* [sweet potato], and that Tu-matauenga is man (Colenso 1882:36).

Recall that in Polynesian thought, as distinguished from the so-called totemism, all men are related to all things by common descent. The corollary would be that, rather than the ancestral or kindred species being tabu, Polynesian social life is a uni-

versal project of *cannibalisme généralisé*, or even of endocan-
nibalism, since the people are genealogically related to their own
"natural" means of subsistence. The problem was not as acute
for Hawaiians as for the Maori; but still the Hawaiian staple,
taro, is the older brother of mankind, as indeed all useful plants
and animals are immanent forms of the divine ancestors—so
many *kino lau* or 'myriad bodies' of the gods. Moreover, to make
root crops accessible to man by cooking is precisely to destroy
what is divine in them: their autonomous power, in the raw state,
to reproduce. (Hence the ritual value of the raw-cooked distinction in Hawaii as elsewhere in Polynesia, especially New Zealand.) Yet the aggressive transformation of divine life into human substance describes the mode of production as well as
consumption—even as the term for 'work' (Ha., *hana*) does service for 'ritual'. Fishing, cultivating, constructing a canoe, or,
for that matter, fathering a child are so many ways that men actively appropriate "a life from the god."
 Men thus approach the divine with a curious combination of
submission and hubris whose final object is to transfer to themselves the life that the gods originally possess, continue to em-
body, and alone can impart. It is a complex relation of supplication and expropriation, successively bringing the sacred to, and
banishing it from, the human domain. Man, then, lives by a
kind of periodic deicide. Or, the god is separated from the objects of human existence by acts of piety that in social life would
be tantamount to theft and violence—not to speak of cannibalism. "Be thou undermost, / While I am uppermost," goes
a Maori incantation to the god accompanying the offering of
cooked food; for as cooked food destroys tabu, the propitiation
is at the same time a kind of pollution—i.e., of the god (Shortland 1882:62; cf. Smith 1974–75). The aggressive relation to divine beings helps explain why contact with the sacred is extremely dangerous to those who are not themselves in a tabu
state. Precisely, then, these Polynesians prefer to wrest their existence from the god under the sign and protection of a divine
adversary. They put on Tū (Kū), god of warriors. Thus did men
learn how to oppose the divine in its productive and peaceful
aspect of Rongo (Lono). In their ultimate relations to the universe, including the relations of production and reproduction,
men are warriors.
 It will lend some conviction to this comparative excursion to

note that Captain Cook appears in Maori traditions as "Rongo-Tute" (Rongo-Cook), the precise cognate of his historical appearance in Hawaii. Indeed, the Hawaiians had a sweet-potato ritual of the same general structure as the Maori cycle. It was used in the "fields of Kamapua'a," name of the pig-god said by some to be a form of Lono, whose rooting in the earth is a well-known symbol of virile action. While the crops were growing, the garden was tabu, so that the pig could do his inseminating work. No one was allowed to throw stones into the garden, thrust a stick into it, or walk upon it—curious prohibitions, except that they amount to protection against human attack. If the garden thus belonged to Lono, at the harvest the first god invoked was Kū-kuila, 'Kū-the-striver' (Kamakau 1976:25 f.).

But much more significantly—universally and cosmically—the Hawaiians recapitulated the agricultural cycle of the Maori, down to fine details, in their great New Year ceremonies called Makahiki (cf Sahlins: in press). Each year the critical battle between Tū (Kū) and Rongo (Lono) unfolded in a complex set of rites extending over four lunar months. Except that in Hawaii it is the king, the warrior *par excellence*, who enters the lists against Lono: the king whose gift of victory comes precisely from his feather-god, 'Kū, Snatcher-of-the-Island' (Kū-ka-ili-moku). At the risk of oversimplification, one could say that what pertains to man-in-general in New Zealand is epitomized by the king in Hawai'i. This is the Hawaiian permutation of the Polynesian system: a hypertrophic evolution of hierarchy (rather in the Dumontian sense) or divine kingship (in the Frazerian). The life of the king encompasses the existence of humanity—capacity in which the king seeks to incorporate Lono.

So when the legends of Cook's Hawaiian predecessors in the capacity of Lono are put in chronological order, they likewise illustrate the principle of hierarchy by transposing the primordial struggle of man and god into latter-day wars of dynastic succession—in which the Lono figure becomes the vanquished king.[5]

[5]The relevant legends of Lono-the-god, in earlier sources, include Freycinet (1978:73), Byron (1826:19–22), Ellis (1969 [1842]:134–35), Kotzebue (1830, 2:160–69), Bingham (1969 [1855]:32); Bloxam MS.; Hawaiian Ethnographic Notes (MS, Bishop Mus., 648 f.). On Lono-i-ka-maka-hiki, the earlier Hawaiian Lono-king, see Fornander (1916–19, 4:256–363) and Kamakau (1961:47–63). On Ka-'I-i-mamao, the latest Lono king: Byron (1826:4–6), Fornander (1969:129–35), Beckwith (1972).

Beside the original god, the principal Lonos before Cook were the legendary King Lono-at-the-Makahiki (Lonoikamakahiki) and the protohistorical Ka-'I-i-mamao, for whom the Kumulipo creation chant was composed. Indeed, their several stories are so many versions of the contest between the god, the man, and the woman that had attended the origin of humanity in the creation chant. The discourse of these traditions, however, changes from the mythical to the political as the era of the divine victim in question, the Lono figure, approaches the historical. So the late King Ka-'I-i-mamao loses his wife by abduction to his father's sister's son, leading to the further exchange of insults among the rival kinsmen, and finally to the battle in which the King is (according to the version) deposed and banished, killed or commits suicide. Analogously, the previous King Lono-at-the-Makahiki had deserted or killed his wife because of the amorous advances of a social inferior whose own name, He'a-o-ke-koa, 'Blood-offering of the warrior,' is a reference to the distinctive function of kingship and the diacritic act of usurpation—human sacrifice.

Prerogative of the king, human sacrifice is what puts the god at a distance and allows mankind to inherit the earth. It is a life for a life. As we saw (chapter 2) in the prototypical sacrifice of Maori tradition, a minor deity called Kaupeka ('Offering') was slain by Tū, ancestor of warrior-man, for materials to make the props of heaven; the Sky-Father (Rangi) was thus fixed in a separated state, allowing the gods and their human progeny to abide in the Earth-Mother (Papa). So the temples consecrated in Hawaii by human sacrifice, separating the "sacred" (heavenly) from the "secular" (earthly) or tabu (*kapu*) from *noa*, would liberate the rest of the terrestrial plane for mankind. Something like that happens during the New Year ritual, as played out in the relation between Lono and the King.

This season of Lono's passage, period of winter rains, is the transition from "the dying time of the year" to the time when "bearing things become fruitful." Such is Lono's beneficial effect. The conjunction with the productive god is made possible by keeping the military god in abeyance: the normal temple rites under Kū are suspended. But when Lono is gone, the king reconsecrates the main Kū temples by means of human sacrifices. He then tours the Island reopening the fishing and agricultural shrines—agricultural shrines of Lono. The king has been able to

assume or to put on Lono. Yet in order for the king to thus transfer to the people the fruitful benefits of Lono's passage, the god
himself must be deprived of them. The god will be the first sacrifice of the New Year (cf. Valeri: in press).[6]

The king gains a victory, and the people their livelihood. There
is a special *aloha* between the people and Lono, who is in certain
myths the original god, and whose annual return is the occasion
of general joy. The ritual moment of conjunction with the god is
especially celebrated by the people, if the moment of final separation belongs to the king. The joy, then, is part of the argument
I make that the image of Lono is annually born of a union between the god and the women of the people, just as in certain
myths Lono descends from the heavens to mate with a beautiful
woman of Hawaii. So when Cook descended on Kealakekua Bay
during the Makahiki season, the young women according to
Samwell were spending most of their time singing and dancing—evidently, in a certain marked way, since he collected two
very lascivious hula chants in point (see chapter 1). For the New
Year was the great period of hula, even as the patron of the
dance, the goddess Laka, is described in ancient chant as Lono's
sister-wife. As in analogous rites of the Marquesans and other
Polynesians (Handy 1927), the dance would arouse the god: a
kind of cosmic copulation between the earthly women and the
divine progenitor.

If I am right, the Makahiki image that results from this sacred
marriage is thus the offspring of a union socially symmetrical
and inverse from the one that ritually produces the king. Recall
that on the death of an Hawaiian king, the social order dissolves
into outrageous scenes of tabu violation. These scenes are notably marked by public fornication between chiefly women and
commoner men, sexual relations otherwise strictly prohibited.
The symbolic effect is the heir to the throne, who had been kept
apart from the public license for ten days and now returns to
restore order (the tabus) in ceremonies of installation that (ide-

---

[6]The principal traditional sources for the description of the Makahiki cycle are
Malo (1951), K. Kamakau in Fornander (1916–19, vol. 6), I'i (1959), and Kepelino
(1977). See also Corney (1896) and Lisiansky (1814). Valeri has assembled an exhaustive account (in press). The correspondences that are noted in the present
text between Makahiki lunar dates and the European dates of Cook's sojourn
(1778–79) were computerized for the author by William Fay and Jocelyn Linnekin.

ally) imitate the rites of a noble birth. Hence the king is the metaphoric offspring of a sacred woman by a man socially inferior; whereas, the image of Lono is born of an hypergamous union between a divine male and the women of the people. In the deep night before the image is first seen, there is a Makahiki ceremony called 'splashing-water' (hi'uwai). Kepelino tells of sacred chiefs being carried to the water where the people in their finery are bathing; in the excitement created by the beauty of their attire, "one person was attracted to another, and the result," says this convert to Catholicism, "was by no means good" (1932:96). At dawn, when the people emerged from their amorous sport, there standing on the beach was the image of Lono.

White tapa cloth and skins of the ka'upu bird hang from the horizontal bar of the tall crosspiece image. The ka'upu is almost certainly the albatross, a migratory bird that appears in the western Hawaiian chain—the white Lanyon albatross at Ni'ihau Island—to breed and lay eggs in October-November, or the beginning of the Makahiki season. The legend of the early King Lono-at-the-Makahiki consists of repeated journeys between Hawai'i and the western islands—in a canoe, according to one telling, whose mast is hung with the skins of ka'upu birds (Kamakau 1961:52–53). Discovering his wife's liaison with a young warrior, Lono quarrels with her and kills her. Overcome with remorse, the grieving king travels about the islands boxing with the people, finally to wander demented and impoverished in the wilds of the western island, Kaua'i. Voyage in the direction of death, privation, and the state of nature: such is the condition of Lono during the triumph of warrior-man, which is the better part of each year. For the other part, the Makahiki season, the god returns in his own triumphant procession—the prelude, however, to another banishment, initiated by his boxing with the people.

The yearly tabu of Lono, which includes a prescriptive peace, is proclaimed when the image is seen on the beach. "Peace" means the suspension of human occupation as well as contention, since the god now marries or takes possession of the land— hence "possession" that itself means dominion as well as sexual appropriation. The principal image of 'Lono-the-parent' (Lono-makua), accompanied by certain gods of sport, now circles the entire island in a sunwise direction, to return after twenty-three days to the temple of origin. This is a "right-circuit," keeping the land on the right; and a right-circuit, the Hawaiian sage tells us, "signified a retention . . . of the kingdom" (Kamakau 1976:5). At the border of each district, food and property were offered to the god, collected the same way that "tributes" are levied by the ruling chief. But after they make the offerings that thus acknowledge the god's dominion, the people of each district engage in ritual combats with the crowd in Lono's train. The local people seem to gain the victory, since the god's tabu is lifted: the fertilized land may now be entered. And even as the people then begin the celebrations that will go on for days, the image of Lono is carried from the district facing backward: "so that," it is explained, "the 'wife' can be seen" (I'i 1959:72).

The apparent paradoxes of this sovereign right-hand triumph of Lono, during which the god cedes district after district, are resolved at the end of the circuit through a global showdown with the king. In a ritual battle with the god, the king resumes all local battles and achieves the final victory, winning life for the people and the sovereignty for himself. Structural climax of the Makahiki, this combat is called *kāli'i*. *Kāli'i* means 'to strike the king', and 'to act—or to be made—the king'. All these things happen at once. Struck by a partisan of the god, the king regains his kingship.

It is the sixteenth day of the first Hawaiian month. The image of Lono, returned from its progress, stands on the shore before the temple, defended by a great body of armed warriors. The king, also accompanied by a warrior host, but preceded by an expert in parrying spears, comes in by canoe from the sea (a reminder of the origin of the dynasty in Kahiki). Two spears are aimed at the king. The first is deflected by his warrior-defender, but the second, carried on the run, is caused to touch the king. A symbolic death—which is also the beginning of the king's victory. The tabu on him is lifted, and his warriors charge ashore to engage the defenders of Lono in mock combat. Similarly, in a famous mythical allusion to the *kāli'i* test, the hero chants:

> The points of the spears of Kamalama passed very near to
>   my navel;
> Perchance it is the sign of land possession.
>
>   (Fornander 1916–19, 5:20)

The reference would be to traditional rituals of cutting the navel cord at noble births, conferring the child's sacred dignities; or else to traditions of royal installations of the same form. By the test of the spears, the king dies as an outsider, to be reborn as the king.

The transformation is achieved through, and *as*, the encompassment of Lono. Appropriating the peaceful, productive indigenous god, the conqueror becomes ruler on the condition of his domestication. He assumes the attributes of his divine predecessor, to appear thus as the people's benefactor. Valeri (in press) shows that in the ceremonial course of the coming year, the king is symbolically transposed toward the Lono pole of Hawaiian divinity; the annual cycle tames the warrior-king in the same way as (e.g.) the Fijian installation rites (chapter 3). It need only be noticed that the renewal of kingship at the climax of the Makahiki coincides with the rebirth of nature. For in the ideal ritual calendar, the *kali'i* battle follows the autumnal appearance of the Pleiades by thirty-three days—thus precisely, in the late eighteenth century, 21 December, the winter solstice. The king returns to power with the sun.[7]

Whereas, over the next two days, Lono plays the part of the sacrifice. The Makahiki effigy is dismantled and hidden away in a rite watched over by the king's "living god," Kahoali'i or 'The-Companion-of-the-King', the one who is also known as 'Death-is-Near' (Koke-ka-make). Close kinsman of the king as his ceremonial double, Kahoali'i swallows the eye of the victim in ceremonies of human sacrifice (condensed symbolic trace of the cannibalistic "stranger-king"). The "living god," moreover, passes the night prior to the dismemberment of Lono in a temporary house called "the net house of Kahoali'i," set up before

[7]The correspondence between the winter solstice and the *kāli'i* rite of the Makahiki is arrived at as follows: ideally, the second ceremony of 'breaking the coconut' (Malo 1951:142), when the priests assemble at the temple to spot the rising of the Pleiades (I'i 1959:72), coincides with the full moon (Hua tabu) of the twelfth lunar month (Welehu). In the latter eighteen century, the Pleiades appear at sunset on 18 November (cf. Makemson 1940). Ten days later (28 November), the Lono effigy sets off on its circuit, which lasts twenty-three days, thus bringing the god back for the climactic battle with the king on 21 December, the solstice (= Hawaiian 16 Makali'i; Malo 1951:150). The correspondence is "ideal" and only rarely achieved, since it depends on the coincidence of the full moon and the crepuscular rising of the Pleiades.

the temple structure where the image sleeps. In the myth pertinent to these rites, the trickster hero—whose father has the
same name (Kūka'ohi'alaka) as the Kū-image of the temple—
uses a certain "net of Maoloha" to encircle a house, entrapping
the goddess Haumea; whereas, Haumea (or Papa) is also a version of La'ila'i, the archetypal fertile woman, and the net used
to entangle her had belonged to one Makali'i, 'Pleiades'. Just so,
the succeeding Makahiki ceremony, following upon the putting
away of the god, is called "the net of Maoloha," and represents
the gains in fertility accruing to the people from the victory over
Lono. A large, loose-mesh net, filled with all kinds of food, is
shaken at a priest's command. Fallen to earth, and to man's lot,
the food is the augury of the coming year. The fertility of nature
thus taken by humanity, a tribute-canoe of offerings to Lono is
set adrift for Kahiki, homeland of the gods. The New Year draws
to a close. At the next full moon, a man (a tabu transgressor) will
be caught by Kahoali'i and sacrificed. Soon after the houses and
standing images of the temple will be rebuilt: consecrated—with
more human sacrifices—to the rites of Kū and the projects of
the king.[8]

III. History, or Mytho-Praxis

Christmas night 1778 on the *Discovery*, beating eastward off
northern Hawai'i, was celebrated by the crew "according to
ancient usage from time immemorial" with a general drunken
brawl (Samwell in Beaglehole 1967:1155). Terrified by "such a
Scene of Uproar & Confusion," an Hawaiian on board had to be
rescued by one of the "gentlemen." Sir James Frazer would have

---

[8]I should note that this is hardly the first time the auditors of the Frazer lecture have been invited to contemplate such ritual exchanges of sovereignty. The
whole Makahiki cycle of Hawaii is strongly reminiscent of the investiture ceremonies of the Shilluk king made famous by Evans-Pritchard's 1948 Frazer lecture: the series of battles between the new king and the effigy representing the
founder of the dynasty, wherein also the king finally carries off the woman married by means of the cattle of his ancestral predecessor. Indeed, by a strange
transformation, the Frazer lecture itself, with its customary rites of homage to
and attack upon the immortal academic ancestor, seems to have become a recurrent and iconic representation of the magisterial theory that first inspired it.

been delighted by this world-historical convergence of ye satur-
nalian customs of ye natives: British and Polynesians at the same
moment celebrating with mock battle and collective revel the advent of the year and of a martyred prince of peace. By the Hawaiian calendar, Christmas 1778 was the fifth day of the twelfth
lunar month, or midway through the tumultuous tour of Lono,
on a right-circuit about the Island.

Cook was making the same circuit as the Makahiki image, at
just the same time. Arriving at Maui some eight days before the
Pleiades, the *Resolution* and *Discovery* came off northwest Hawai'i on 2 December 1778; whereupon Cook embarked upon a
protracted right-circumnavigation of the Island, anchoring on 17
January next at Kealakekua on the west coast—to the joyous reception of 10,000 exulting Hawaiians. At Kealakekua or 'The-
Path-[of-] the-God', the image of Lono usually begins and ends
its own circuit. So here at Hikiau temple Cook became the icon
of that icon: anointed with masticated coconut and fed by the
priest, while Lt. King and another held his arms outstretched
and the acolytes intoned the customary chants. This ritual feeding of the god (*hānaipū*) is performed several times during Lono's
progress, at the domestic shrines of the king and high priests
(cf. Sahlins 1981). True, King Kalaniopu'u had not yet arrived,
but there was sufficient testimony to the powers he represented.
Cook, for example, "suffered himself to be directed" by the
priest in kissing and prostrating before the central image of the
temple, figure of the god Kū. In every way Cook acquiesced in
the status the Hawaiians would give him. Except that the circuit
of this Lono had extended some thirteen days beyond the Year
God's usual course. Yet it was still Makahiki time.

We need not suppose that all Hawaiians were convinced that
Captain Cook was Lono; or, more precisely, that his being Lono
meant the same to everyone. With regard to the ordinary women
cohabiting with the sailors on board the ships, Antigonus's remark on his own deification might have been more appropriate:
"That's not my valet's opinion of me." On the other hand, the
priests of Kealakekua assigned a so-called tabu-man to constantly attend Cook, heralding his comings and goings with the
cry "Lono," so that the people could prostrate themselves. This
shows that whatever the people in general were thinking, the
Hawaiian powers-that-be had the unique capacity to publicly

objectify their own interpretation. They could bring structure to bear on matters of opinion, and by rendering to Cook the tributes of Lono, they also practically engaged the people in this religion of which they were the legitimate prophets. "Equality in condition," as Lt. King noticed, "is not the happiness of this island" (Beaglehole 1967:605). Neither was it their theory of history.

The difference of opinion on which history would pivot appeared *within* the ruling class, between certain priests of Lono living near the main temple (Hikiau), where the British also established an astronomical observatory, and the warrior chiefs living with King Kalaniopu'u at Ka'awaloa, on the northern arm of the Bay. Associated with Kū in their capacity as warriors, the King and his chiefs entertained ambivalent relations with Cook/Lono and his priests that seem altogether consistent with the cosmological antitheses of the Makahiki season. And the more the priests reified their conception of Cook as the divine Lono, the more dangerous his relationship to the chiefs. It would end as in the rite of *kāli'i*, with nothing for the defenders of the dismantled god to do but worship his memory and anticipate his return. Hence the famous question asked by the two priests— one was the "tabu-man"—who stole out to the *Resolution* bearing a piece of his corpse:

> They . . . asked us, with great earnestness and apparent apprehension, "When the *Orono* [Lono] would come again? and what he would do to them on his return?" The same inquiry was frequently made afterward by others; and this idea agrees with the general tenour of their conduct toward him, which shewed, that they considered him as a being of a superior nature (Cook and King 1784, 3:69).[9]

Earlier, at the time the high priest Ka'ō'ō came into Kealakekua together with King Kalaniopu'u, the two played out with

[9] This question of the Lono priests followed on another, that had been evoked by the persistent inquiries of the British as to whether the Hawaiians had eaten the rest of Cook. When the British, after many indirect questions, finally demanded if "they had not eat some of it?," the Hawaiians were horrified at the idea "and asked, very naturally, if that were the custom amongst us?" (Cook and King 1784, 3:69).

Captain Cook a complex exchange of objects and courtesies—an "occasion of state" as Samwell called it—that would interpret each to others.[10] Kalaniopu'u put his own feather cloak and helmet on Cook, and in the British commander's hand the flywhisk emblem of the royal tabu status. When it came his turn, however, the high priest of Lono dressed Cook in a mantle of red tapa cloth. ("A sort of religious adoration," as Lt. King had concluded of an earlier performance: "Their idols we found always arrayed with red cloth, in the same manner as was done to Captain Cook" [Cook and King 1784, 3:5].) The King had represented Cook in his own social image as a divine warrior; whereas, the priest represented his own temple image as a divine Cook. King Kalaniopu'u also exchanged names with the Captain, and later received a dinner, a linen shirt, and Cook's naval sword. The vice-versa movement of regalia and personae is a microcosm of the transfers of sovereignty during the New Year rite, by which the king ultimately incorporates Lono. And in a correlated transaction of this occasion of state, the high priest unilaterally gave King Kalaniopu'u a number of iron adzes that had been collected by his fellow Lono priests in return for their generous hospitality to the British. If this again implied a *royal* appropriation of Lono's benefits (at the priests' expense), it was also a material paradigm of the evolving historic structure. The difference in the respective relations of King and Priest to Cook/Lono would unfold as an opposition of practical interests.

"A royal feather robe has the chief, a newly opened bud, a royal child/The offering by night, the offering by day: it belongs to the priest to declare [the] ancient transactions." These lines from a celebrated eighteenth-century chant, perfect caption to the intricate exchanges of the "occasion of state," speak to a difference that continued to distinguish the conduct of the Lono priests toward Cook from that of the warrior chiefs. Projected into history, the difference is that the sense of the totality and immortality of the society conveyed in the priests' transactions with the British was in the chiefs' case conflated with lineage

[10] The "occasion of state" is described in more or less detail by King (in Cook and King 1784, 3:16–19, Beaglehole 1967:512–13), Edgar (Journal: 27 Jan. 1779), Roberts (Log: 27 Jan. 1779), as well as Samuel (Beaglehole 1967:1169), among others.

and their own interest. Even after Cook's death, while a state of hostility prevailed between the British and the chiefs at Ka'awaloa, the Lono priests were daily sending food supplies to the ships. This they had done from the beginning, as also they generously provisioned the astronomical camp near Hikiau temple and the excursion parties traveling inland for work or exploration. Yet "no return was ever demanded," reads the official *Voyage*, "or even hinted at in a most distant manner. Their presents were made with a regularity, more like the discharge of a religious duty, than the effect of mere liberality" (Cook and King 1784, 3:14–15). Still, Cook failed to acknowledge adequately these priestly adorations, as his own rituals interfered with his perceptions of them. "For it was ever his practice to pay his whole attention to pleasing the King or Chief of the Spot where he was," as Mr. King says, so that for a long time he did not even realize that the priests were responsible for "the vast daily supplies of Vegetables and barbacued hogs," and he proceeded to materially compensate the King Kalaniopu'u for the respectful sacrifices of the priest Ka'ō'ō (Beaglehole 1967:564). I use the liturgical terms advisedly. An important Hawaiian text of the 1830s speaks of the people's relation to Cook as *ho'omana*, 'worship', so that "they gave him [Cook/Lono] pigs, taro, tapa and all kinds of things the way these are given to the gods; they bargained not" (Remy 1861:28). By this logic and all evidence, the priests' mode of exchange with Cook was sacrifice.

Yet "in all our dealings with the [warrior chiefs]," says Mr. King, "we found them sufficiently attentive to their own interests" (Cook and King 1784, 3:14–15). The British catered to these interests so far as to suspend trade of iron implements in favor of the daggers affected by the Hawaiian nobility as insignia of their status—the kind of iron dagger that killed Cook. But the chiefs' interests were also dangerous because they were disposed to promote them by theft and chicane. In relation to the god, they were prepared to play the trickster, mythical and ancestral archetype of the usurper. The chiefly mode of exchange with the British alternated opportunistically between *noblesse oblige* and stealing. Cook, King, Ellis, and others remarked on the aristocratic vice from the day the ships entered Kealakekua Bay. The sudden outbreak of stealing could be traced "to the presence and encouragement of their chiefs": a Polynesian sociology of derring-do that continued to plague the foreigners to the day of Cook's death—itself the consequence of the theft of the *Discovery*'s cutter, traceable by all accounts to the chief Palea. But then, the Makahiki was all about the aggressive seizure of Lono's gifts by the warrior chief.

We have to do with what has been called a "structure of the conjuncture": a set of historical relationships that at once reproduce the traditional cultural categories and give them new values out of the pragmatic context (Sahlins 1981). Chiefs, priests, and English were all following their received inclinations and interests. The result was a little social system, complete with alliances, antagonisms—and a certain dynamic. "Here are clearly party matters subsisting between the Laity and the Clergy," Mr. Clerke was moved to remark of the Hawaiians' behavior during the crisis following Cook's death. By then, the British had been drawn into this Hawaiian schismogenesis, which indeed was exacerbated by their own presence. For the more the priests objectified themselves as the party of Lono, the more they marked out for Cook the destiny of the king's victim.[11]

Nevertheless, by virtue of a series of spectacular coincidences, Cook made a near-perfect ritual exit on the night of 3 February. The timing itself was nearly perfect, since the Makahiki rituals would end 1 February ($\pm$ 1 day), being the 14th day of the second Hawaiian month. This helps explain Mr. King's entry for 2 February in the published *Voyage*: "Terreeoboo [Kalaniopu'u] and his Chiefs, had, for some days past, been very inquisitive about the time of our departure"—to which his private journal

[11] It will be seen from this paragraph that I have not used the notion of a conjunctural structure in the Braudelian sense, a point that has justifiably caused some criticism among reviewers of *Historical Metaphors* (Sahlins 1981). Braudel's "structure of the conjuncture" refers to relations of some intermediate duration—as opposed to the *longue durée* on one hand and the event on the other—such as capitalist economic cycles. My own use is more literal (*conjoncture*, '*situation qui résulte d'une rencontre de circonstances*' [Robert]), and while definitely *événementielle* allows more than Braudel does for the structuration of the situation. A "structure of the conjuncture" in this sense is a situational set of relations, crystallized from the operative cultural categories and actors' interests (see chap. 5). Like Giddens's (1976) notion of social action, it is subject to the double structural determination of intentions grounded in a cultural scheme and the unintended consequences arising from recuperation in other projects and schemes.

adds, "& seem'd well pleas'd that it was soon" (1784, 3:26; Beagle-hole 1967:517). Captain Cook, responding to Hawaiian impor-tunities to leave behind his "son," Mr. King, had even assured Kalaniopu'u and the high priest that he would come back again the following year. Long after they had killed him, the Hawai-ians continued to believe this would happen.

With the high priest's permission, the British just before leav-ing removed the fence and certain images of Hikiau temple for firewood. Debate raged in the nineteenth century about the role of this purported "sacrilege" in Cook's death, without notice, however, that following Lono's sojourn the temple is normally cleared and rebuilt—indeed, the night the British left one of the temple houses was seen on fire. Among the other ritual coinci-dences, perhaps the most remarkable was the death of poor old Willie Watman, seaman A. B., on the morning of 1 February. Watman was the first person among Cook's people to die at Kea-lakekua: on the ceremonial day, so far as can be calculated, that the King's living god Kahoali'i would swallow the eye of the first human sacrifice of the New Year. And it was the Hawaiian chief—or by one account, the King himself—who specifically requested that old Watman be buried at Hikiau temple. Messrs. Cook and King read the burial service, thus introducing Christianity to the Sandwich Islands, with the assistance however of the high priest Ka'ō'ō and the Lono "brethren," who when the English had finished proceeded to make sacrifices and perform ceremonies at the grave for three days and nights.

So in the early hours of 4 February, Cook sailed out of Kea-lakekua Bay, still alive and well. The King, too, had survived Lono's visit and incorporated its tangible benefits, such as iron adzes and daggers. In principle, the King would now make sac-rifices to Kū and reopen the agricultural shrines of Lono. The normal cosmic course would be resumed. Hence the ultimate ritual coincidence, which was meteorological: one of the fer-tilizing storms of winter, associated with the advent of Lono, wreaked havoc with the foremast of the *Resolution*, and the Brit-ish were forced to return to Kealakekua for repairs on 11 Febru-ary 1779.

It was "chance;" or in the Western scientific metaphor, "the intersection of two independent chains of causation." The weak link in one of the chains was the "dishonest work" and "slovenly supervision" of the Deptford naval yard (Beaglehole 1967: 1xix). Cook had complained before that his ships had been better equipped when they were in the private service. Given this corrupt system of naval procurement, perhaps we should speak of an unhappy intersection of structures. Certainly the British expedition of discovery had gone out of phase with the Hawaiian ritual cycle. Mr. King remarks that there were not as many hundreds of people at their return to Kealakekua as there had been thousands when they first came in. A tabu was in effect, which was ascribed to the king's absence. By the best evidence, the British had interrupted the annual bonito-fishing rite, the transition from the Makahiki season to normal temple ceremonies. Cook was now *hors cadre*. And things fell apart.

In the mythopolitical crisis occasioned by Lono's inexplicable return, the tensions and ambivalences in the social organization of the previous weeks were now revealed. The King, who came in next day, was furious with the priests for again letting the British use the ground near Hikiau temple. The priests reciprocated with a cordial detestation of the chiefs at Ka'awaloa, an attitude they did not trouble to conceal from their British friends. And to complete the triangle, the King and chiefs "were very inquisitive . . . to know the reason of our return," Mr. Burney says, "and appeared much dissatisfied with it" (Burney MS : 12 Feb. 1779; cf. Burney 1819:256–57). In retrospect, as Lt. King reflected, "it is not very clear, but that some of the chiefs were glad of seeking an occasion to quarrel" (Beaglehole 1967:568). Actually, the chroniclers vary in their assessment of Hawaiian reactions, perhaps due to different experiences of the complex structure of the conjuncture. Samwell, friend to the priests, could find "the abundant good nature which had always characterized [the Hawaiians]" still glowing "in every bosom" and animating "every countenance" (1957:6). For John Ledyard it was evident from the people's appearance, "that our former friendship was at an end, and that we had nothing to do but to hasten our departure to some different island, where our vices were not yet known, and where our extrinsic virtues might gain us another short space of being wondered at" (1963:141).[12]

---

[12] For other general characterizations of Hawaiian attitudes regarding the return of Cook's ships, mostly negative, see: Clerke (in Beaglehole 1967:531–32),

All along, the diverse and delicate relationships between the two peoples had been ordered by the one salient interpretation of Cook as the Makahiki god which the Hawaiian authorities were able to reify, and with which the Great Navigator could comply. Now that reality began to dissolve. For the King and chiefs, it even became sinister. Lt. King records in his journal the touching empiricist belief that once the reasons for the return were explained to the chiefs, their noticeable disapproval would be dispelled (Beaglehole 1967:68). But the problem was not empirical or practical: it was cosmological—in which respect, the state of *Resolution*'s mast was simply not intelligible. "They were constantly asking what brought us back," reads one account, "for they could form no notion of our distress or what was the matter with our mast" (Anonymous [of Mitchell]: 23 Jan. 1781). It would be sinister because the return-out-of-season presented a mirror image of Makahiki politics. Bringing the god ashore during the triumph of the King, it would reopen the whole issue of sovereignty. Hence the ominous notion Hawaiians did form of what brought the British back, according to some of the most reliable journalists (Burney, King, and Gilbert): that it was in order to settle the island, "and deprive them of part if not the whole of their Country" (Gilbert *MS*; Burney 1819:256–57; Beaglehole 1967:509). As in the good Frazerian theory of divine kingship, the ritual crisis was a political threat.

There was an immediate outbreak of theft and violence. "Ever since our arrival here upon this our second visit," wrote Mr. Clerke, "we have observed in the Natives a stronger propensity to theft than we had reason to complain of during our former stay; every day produced more numerous and more audacious depredations" (in Beaglehole 1967:531–32). The day before Cook's death, 13 February, was notable for violent altercations with chiefs. Mr. Trevenen later blamed Cook's death on a chief thrown off the *Resolution* this day for stealing. Chiefs attempted to prevent some commoners from assisting the British who were loading water on shore, near the priests' settlement. In a scuffle involving Palea, the one who was to arrange the theft of the *Discovery*'s boat, two midshipmen (one of them George Vancouver)

Zimmermann (1930:90), Ellis (1782, 2:102), Home (Log: 7 Feb. 1779), Law (Journal: 11 Feb. 1779), etc.

and several seamen were well and truly drubbed. Cook, who had already shown in Tonga and the Society Islands that he would not suffer "the Indians" to think they had the advantage of him, decided after the skirmishes of 13 February that he would again be obliged to use force. So when he went ashore next day to take King Kalaniopu'u hostage, he made sure to land in the company of armed marines.

The scene was strangely reminiscent of the climactic battle of the Makahiki, the *kāli'i*, but played in reverse. The god Lono (Cook) was wading shore with his warriors to confront the King. Rather than the reinstitution of human sacrifice by the King under the aegis of Kū, news came that Lono's people had killed a chief (i.e., Kalimu, shot by Rickman's blockading party). Now the King would be taken off to sea—instead of the canoe of Lono set adrift. And did not the other actors play out their legendary roles? Recall that Kalaniopu'u was prevented from accompanying Cook by the intercession of the favored wife, Kaneikapolei. For one brief and decisive instant, the confrontation returned to the original triad of the god, the man, and the woman, with the issue again determined by the woman's choice.

The supporting characters included the warrior-champions of the *kāli'i* combat. Cook was accompanied everywhere on shore by his second, Lt. of the Marines Molesworth Phillips. Should we not likewise search for the slayer of Cook among the companions of the King's retinue: the one who parries the spear of the god? We have been doing the cultural analysis of an historic event (or vice versa). By all rights, it should lead to a cultural solution of the "murder mystery."

For example, all those among the alleged initial assailants of Cook who are identifiably commoners can be eliminated. The sociological category is wrong; besides, the weapon, the iron trade dagger, was affected by the chiefly coteries only. On the other hand, Trevenen's chief, the one thrown off the *Resolution* for theft, is also unlikely since Trevenen says he was killed in action; whereas, Hawaiian and British testimony, contemporary and later, indicates the slayer lived to tell his story. For similar reasons, the chiefs accused by Mr. Ellis and Mr. King can be dismissed. To make a long forensic argument short, there is one man who best fits the case ritually and historiographically. He is the one identified as Cook's slayer by Samwell, Edgar, Bayly, and the "honest Keali'ikea," priest of Lono, and apparently also the person of the same description and reputation seen by members of the Vancouver expedition in 1793 and 1794. He had a role in life and position in society as the King's defender. His name was Nuha.

A near relative and constant companion of the King, Nuha (or Kanuha) was, Samwell says, a personage of "first consequence" (Beaglehole 1967:1171). He belonged to a notable landholding family of Ka'awaloa, a line of chief's men descended from a secondary royal marriage of a few generations back.[13] The notices from Vancouver's time also suggest he was related affinally to the present King Kalaniopu'u. But as "one of the To'ah or fighting men of the Island," Nuha probably owed his position about the royal person as much to his prowess as to his kinship. Samwell had been singularly impressed with Nuha's physical appearance from first he saw him in the King's retinue: "he was tall and stout, with a fierce look and demeanour, and one who united in his figure the two qualities of strength and agility, in a greater degree, than ever I remembered to have seen before in any other man" (1957:23). Thus Nuha would be one of the *kaukau ali'i* or lesser chiefs of the royal entourage, a man whose privileges were contingent on his service. He was a warrior, and on that day he was everything he should be.

In status and appearance, this is exactly the figure of Cook's assassin depicted by John Webber, artist of the expedition, in his well-known "Death of Captain Cook" (fig. 4:1). We should not ignore the graphic evidence. Indeed, the painting's chief artistic merit is generally acknowledged to be its effort at accuracy. Consider, then, Webber's characterization of Cook's attacker. He is a young man, of exceptional size and athletic build. Perfect for the *kāli'i* part. Besides, he wears—in warrior fashion, over one shoulder—a distinctive cloak, made primarily of blackcock or frigatebird feathers, by contrast to the fine, multicolored feather garments and helmet seen on the right side of the painting. The latter are made of rare mountain birds (fig. 4:2). The difference is

---

[13] Researches in Hawaiian genealogical and land records (Archives of Hawaii) indicate that Kanuha was one of the famous "Moanas" of Hawai'i Island, descended thus from the high chief Keakealani Kane, and related by marriage to the high Kū priest Holoa'e—as well as the father of the well-known early Christian convert and traditional intellectual, Kelou Kamakau.

precisely the one reported by Lt. King between the feather cloaks of "inferior chiefs" and those of the highest nobility (Cook and King 1784, 3:136–37).

But the dagger held menacingly by the warrior in Webber's scene (fig. 4:3) was probably made from an iron spike manufactured at Matthew Boulton's Soho factory in Birmingham—requisitioned by Cook "to be distributed to them in presents toward obtaining their friendship." And in March 1776, just when Cook was taking on such cargo for the expedition, the London publishing house of Strachan and Cadell, which would later issue the official account of the voyage, announced the publication of Adam Smith's *Wealth of Nations*. We are thus reminded—in a brilliant essay by Bernard Smith (1979)—that if Cook died as a Hawaiian god, he was also the avatar of a new kind of European imperialism. One could add that Cook's death made a remarkable juncture of the two theologies, since his spirit was destined to play the same role in the one as in the other. Europeans and Hawaiians alike and respectively were to idolize him as a martyr to their own prosperity.

For Hawaiians Cook had been a form of the god who makes the earth bear fruit for mankind: a seminal god, patron of the peaceful and agricultural arts. Yet on the European side, as "Adam Smith's global agent" he was likewise the spirit incarnate of the peaceful "penetration" of the marketplace: of a commercial expansion promising to bring civilization to the benighted and riches to the entire earth. Cook was to chart the course: determine the routes, the resources, the markets. Harbinger thus of the *Pax Brittanica*, Cook was also a bourgeois Lono.

The convergence of spiritual beliefs was already present in the death of Cook: in the reasons he died and the way he died. Cook's own dispositions in the treatment of "ye Natives"—his concern to secure their friendship, to keep the use of force to a minimum, to trade honestly (if advantageously), to prevent the spread of "the Venereal" and of firearms—all these were ultimately consistent, often consciously so, with the world expansion of commerce that his voyages were designed to make possible. Cook made the new era of capitalist expansion a point of his own personal character (Smith 1979). He was no Cortes— any more than Lono was the conquering Kū. Bernard Smith says that "Cook must have been the first European to practise

Figure 4.1   John Webber, *The Death of Captain Cook* (Dixson Galleries, Sydney, Australia)

Figure 4.2 Webber, *The Death of Captain Cook*, detail

Figure 4.3   Webber, *The Death of Captain Cook*, detail

successfully on a global scale the use of tolerance for the purpose of domination" (1979:179). So if the Hawaiians were willing to receive him as their own god, he was willing to accept the
honors. However he understood it ritually, he would appreciate
it practically. But then, as the poet Cowper wrote when he
learned how Cook had died, "God is a jealous god."[14]

On the other hand, Cook's hubris was as much Polynesian as
it was European. Consider that he had had years of experience
in these islands as "a kind of superior being." So many times
before he had brought himself and his people away from the
edge of disaster. Similarly this time, despite everything that has
been said since of Cook's fatigue or his parasites, by all contemporary accounts he met the crisis with an unhurried confidence.
He seems to walk through his death scene with a certain dream-
like quality. More than one journal speaks of an unaccountable
"infatuation," as if he thought himself invincible. He would
have died, then, a truly Polynesian death: the death reserved for
the man who has accumulated so much *mana*, he is tempted to
defy the rules that govern ordinary men. Maori say of such persons that they

[14] "Cook did not depend much upon God; he kept his powder dry, mentioned
Providence rarely, and performed the Sunday naval service intermittently; but
he was perfectly willing to play God himself, as he did at Hawaii, if the cultiva-
tion of peaceful cultural relations depended on it" (Smith 1979:168).

can only be overcome by some act or default, such as a
disregard or neglect of some religious or warlike obser-
vance, which has been shown by experience to be essential to success in war; but which our warrior, spoiled
by a long career of good fortune, had come to regard as
necessary to ordinary mortals only and of but little consequence to men of *mana* (Gudgeon 1905:62).

Still, as Cook once wrote in his private journal: "Such risks as
these are the unavoidable Companions of the Man who goes on
Discoveries."

5

Structure and History

Well, but do you not see, Cratylus, that he who follows names in the search after things, and analyzes their meanings, is in great danger of being deceived?

Plato, *Diol.*, *Cratylus*.

There had been better times in the relations between Hawaiians and Europeans, such as attended the very first moments of their encounter, more than a year before Cook's death: encounter marked by the *aloha* with which the islanders greeted their "discoverers."

On 20 January 1778, when the *Resolution* and *Discovery* made their initial anchorage at Waimea, Kaua'i, a satisfactory traffic began almost instantaneously between the British and ordinary Hawaiians, both on shore and about the ships.[1] The local people provided foodstuffs in return for iron goods, which they took avidly in any form or shape. The women in the canoes alongside were already making their famous and unmistakable overtures to the seamen, "their intentions of gratifying us in all the pleasures the Sex can give" (King Log: 20 Jan. 1778). As we know, the women soon succeeded in consummating their special de-

[1] In the first section of this paper, I resume briefly certain historic events and processes discussed in somewhat greater detail in *Historical Metaphors* (Sahlins 1981). The object will be to pick up and develop the historical theory of that earlier work.

136

mands, despite the sexual tabus Captain Cook had imposed on his own men. So began a career of tabu violations by women of the people that the Hawaiian chiefs and priests would soon discover applied equally to their own sacred prohibitions.

On the third day of Kaua'i, Captain Cook's ship, the *Resolution*, was driven off to sea by adverse winds while trying to shift her berth in Waimea Bay. The *Discovery* under Captain Clerke remained, and the next morning was once again surrounded by the numerous small vessels of the common people. But this peaceful commerce was suddenly interrupted by the appearance of a large double canoe bearing the most sacred chief of the Island, Kaneoneo by name. Preemptorily, the people's canoes were ordered out of the way so that the chief could make his own exclusive advent in the presence of the British. Here we need to recall that the Hawaiians considered these extraordinary beings who had broken through the sky beyond the horizon were thus, like the chief himself, of a nature divine. They had come from the spiritual homeland of chiefs and gods, Kahiki— or in the Kaua'i dialect "Tahiti"—as indeed the British admitted that "Otaheite" (Tahiti) had been their last port of call.

When the sacred Kaneoneo came out to the ships, however, the Hawaiian common people did not get out of his way fast enough. More than one British journalist records with some surprise that thereupon, and "without endeavouring in the least" to avoid them, the chief simply ran down the people in his way, leaving the occupants of four canoes swimming in the wreckage.[2] Later that day, the incident was repeated when the same royal vessel came out to invite Captain Clerke ashore, where Kaneoneo had prepared an appropriate Polynesian reception (with gifts) for the English captain. On this second occasion, the astronomer Bayly relates, the sight of the chief's canoe was enough to send the commoners flying "with the greates[t] precipitation & we soon found not without reason for as soon as the King's canoe came up with any Canoe they run right over it, knocking down everyone that came within their reach, so that

[2]The incident is described in Cook and King (1784, 2:245–46), King's journal (29 Jan. 1778), and Burney's journal (24 Jan. 1778), among others—notably a good but slightly varying account by Bayly (Journal: 24 Jan. 1778). Clerke's journal also (Adm 55/22: 24 Jan. 1778) describes Kaneoneo's subsequent visit on board the *Discovery*.

the people were obliged to jump & dive to avoid being knocked on the head & leave their canoes to be run down" (Journal: 24 Jan. 1778).

But then, Kaneoneo was a chief of the highest tabus. Offspring of a brother-sister marriage, such a chief is "called divine, akua" (Malo 1951:54). When he goes abroad, the people must fall prostrate on their faces—the kind of homage that Hawaiians also accorded to Captain Cook. And this is why Kaneoneo ran over the people's canoes. The commoners were caught in a Hawaiian double bind: prostrating face down in their canoes when the sacred chief came out, they could not also get out of his way.

I take this incident as a condensed paradigm of the subsequent course of Hawaiian history: of the changing relations between chiefs and common people, marked by unprecedented forms of oppression, that developed out of their respective relations to European adventurers, especially the increasing numbers of venturing merchants. Not only a paradigm, this original collision among the Hawaiians condenses also a possible theory of history, of the relation between structure and event, beginning with the proposition that the transformation of a culture is a mode of its reproduction. In their different ways, the commoners and chiefs responded to the divine strangers according to their own customary self-conceptions and interests. Encompassing the extraordinary event in traditional cultural forms they would thus recreate the received distinctions of Hawaiian status. The effect would be to reproduce Hawaiian culture-as-constituted. But once again: the world is under no obligation to conform to the logic by which some people conceive it. The specific conditions of European contact gave rise to forms of opposition between chiefs and people that were not envisioned in the traditional relations between them. Here is a second proposition of our possible theory: that in action or in the world—technically, in acts of reference—the cultural categories acquire new functional values. Burdened with the world, the cultural meanings are thus altered. It follows that the relationships between categories change: the structure is transformed.

First, then, to show the traditional grounds of Hawaiian responses to the British presence. As for the common people, men and women in their respective ways made spontaneous overtures of exchange with Cook's company, resulting notably in a lively material trade. This simple pragmatism was especially characteristic of the cultural consciousness—the *habitus*—of Hawaiian commoners, in contrast to their chiefs and priests (cf. chapter 2). Specifically, the conduct of the people was appropriate to the interest Hawaiians call *'imi haku*, 'to seek a lord'. And this was counterpart to the heroic system of chiefly domination. The main, global principle of organization was hierarchy itself, expressed in the reciprocal but unequal *aloha* between the people and the chief who held their land as his patrimonial estate. Beyond immediate kinfolk, the people's relations to each other were mediated by the ruling chiefs ("hierarchical solidarity"). Whereas, the chiefs, by their own connections to the realm of spirit (Kahiki), mediated the relations between the social totality and the cosmos. Hence the famous sexual demands of ordinary Hawaiian women on the too-willing crews of Cook's ships. It was their way "to find a lord": upward liaisons that would establish kinship relations with, and claims upon, the powers-that-be. So if the British were greeted with an effusion of traditional *aloha*, as tourists in Hawaii still are, it was with the same interested synthesis of libido and lucre.

On the other hand, consider closely the behavior of the Kaua'i sacred chief, Kaneoneo. The cosmological status of ruling chiefs implied their own privileged intervention with the divine stranger. Cook's advent in 1778 thus put in place a certain historical "structure of the conjuncture": a system of relationships destined to affect the further course of European trade and Hawaiian politics. The British were to Hawaiians in general as the Hawaiian chiefs were to their own people. In the beginning, however, the implications were equivocal or even dangerous. For by the Hawaiian versions of the theory of stranger-kings, the reign of sacred ruler from Kahiki is founded through a usurpation of the existing dynasty. Indeed, at every accession—as at every annual Makahiki ceremony—the king seizes power, "celebrates a victory" as Hocart says, making his predecessor a victim of sacrifice or sorcery. Hence the initial ambivalence of Kaneoneo's approach to Cook's ships: the chief appeared only on the fourth day, for example, long after the common people. Kaneoneo's behavior would be repeated by other important chiefs in the next decades; time and again they approached the shipping some days after the common folks, and with the same ambiguous display of dignity and circumspection. In Kaneoneo's case, when he did finally go on board the *Discovery*, his attendants prevented him from proceeding any further than the gangplank where, forming a protective circle about him, they suffered no Englishman but Captain Clerke to approach him. Problem was that if the foreigners were truly gods, they were also, then, the chief's natural rivals.

But then, Kaneoneo's behavior, his hesitancy, brought him into practical contradictions with his own people. Their collision course can be charted from the categories of the traditional culture, as a vector of the customary differences between the common people and the sacred chief. Not only did it belong to the chief to take priority in relations with the divine stranger. He was first in all things: the firstborn, first to act in war or peace, the one who initiates the agricultural year by appropriate sacrifices and gathers the tributes of the first-fruits. Essential principle of Polynesian hierarchy, this *firstness* is what makes the political functioning of the society the same as the creative action of divinity. And if Kaneoneo's claims to precedence brought him into violent opposition with the people in his way, still the chief's privileged connection with the gods is always maintained by the sacrifice of lawless men, i.e., violators of the royal tabus.

In the decades following Cook's fatal visit, Hawaiian chiefs and commoners, men and women, ritual tabus and material goods, were all engaged in practical exchange with Europeans in ways that altered their customary meanings and relationships. And always the functional revaluations appear as logical extensions of traditional conceptions. The dominant structure of the initial situation, that the chiefs distinguished themselves from their own people in the manner that Europeans were different from Hawaiians in general, became a conceit of personal identity—from which ensued an order of political economy. The chiefs self-consciously appropriated the personages of the European great alongside an appropriate European style of the sumptuary life. The famous Kamehameha, conqueror of the Islands between 1795 and 1810, never tired of asking passing European visitors if he did not live "just like King George." Already by 1793, three of the dominant Hawaiian chiefs had named their sons and heirs "King George" (Bell 1929:64). By the early nineteenth century the putting-on of prominent European identities had become high fashion in Hawaii. Witness this American trader's account of a gathering of Hawaiian notables in 1812:

> At the race course I observed Billy Pitt, George Washington and Billy Cobbet walking together in the most familiar manner . . . while in the center of another group, Charley Fox, Thomas Jefferson, James Madison, Bonnepart, and Tom Paine were seen to be on equally friendly terms with each other (Cox 1832:44).

At that date also Cox (alias Kahekili Ke'eaumoku) was the Governor of Maui, John Adams (alias Kuakini) would soon be Governor of Hawai'i; whereas the aforementioned Billy Pitt (Kalaimoku) was "Prime Minister" of the Kingdom. About the same period, which was marked by the lucrative sandalwood trade, an intense competition for status developed among the Hawaiian aristocracy. It took the form of ostentatious consumption of foreign luxury goods—but then, *mana* had been traditionally associated with a style of celestial brilliance. Fine clothing was the main item, and fashions changed wildly, since as one Boston merchant lamented over a useless cargo of silks, of a kind that had already come out on another ship the past year, the object of the chiefs was to have something "they have never seen before."[3] Soon the finest textiles of China and New England, accumulated in useless superabundance, lay rotting in chiefly storehouses, to be dumped finally in the ocean.

But the people's access to the market remained severely restricted, even as regards practical and domestic equipment. Rather, their products entered European trade as tributes or rents collected by the chiefs on quasi-traditional lines and disposed of on the chiefs' own account. The early history of the iron trade had already proved that the powers-that-be were able

---

[3]The statement appears in a letter from the trader James Hunnewell to J. P. Sturgis & Co., 30 Dec. 1829 (Hunnewell Papers). Aside from the Hunnewell papers and journals of other traders at the Baker Library, a good sense of the American trade during this sandalwood period can be gained from the John C. Jones or Marshall & Wildes correspondence at Houghton Library, Harvard. Excellent résumés of Hawaiian economic history in the late eighteenth century and early nineteenth century may be found in Bradley (1968 [1943]) and Morgan (1948).

to organize commerce for the satisfaction of their own demands, to the neglect of the commoner's necessities. By the mid-1790s, the ruling chiefs had a surfeit of iron tools and would not even look at another axe, so that European trade was diverted notably to muskets and cloth, means and signs of chiefly power, and this well before the people in general had exhausted their need or capacity for productive uses of iron. As late as 1841, an American missionary at Hawai'i Island remarked that there was still not a decent set of carpenter's tools in his district—except those owned by local chiefs (Forbes 1842:155). By this time, the people's resistance had been reduced to creative uses of scatological metaphor, as when the commoners of Waialua, O'ahu mixed goat excrements in the pounded taro (*poi*) destined as tribute for their ruling chief (Emerson to Chamberlain: 19 Oct. 1835). One could say that traditional Hawaiian culture was preserved by logical inversion, since excrement is negative food, thus proper reciprocity for the kind of *aloha* the chiefs were now dumping on the common people.

Serious resistance had long passed. It had been transcended by negotiated uses of the chiefs' tabus, process that ended in a revaluation of the meaning of tabu that can be correlated with the emerging distinctions of class (cf. Sahlins 1981). Early on, the chiefs began to use tabus for the regulation of European trade: an extension from ritual to practical purposes that could be justified by ancient meanings and functions of chiefly precedence. Between 1795 and 1819, the great Kamehameha regularly imposed such interdictions on the times and terms of commerce with European ships, in the interest of forestalling the commoners' trade, or else of ensuring that the demands of political and aristocratic consumption would take priority over the people's interest in domestic goods. In the event, the concept of tabu, as signifying things set apart for the god, underwent a logical extension to the point of a functional transformation. Tabu progressively became the sign of a material and proprietary right. One can still see the final form in Hawai'i today: in the numerous signs that read KAPU and mean 'no trespassing'.

The commercial uses of the tabu by Kamehameha and other chiefs meant that, for the common people, the sacred restrictions which promised divine benefits (when respected) were now directly counterposed to the general welfare. In *Historical*

Metaphors I show that the ordinary Hawaiians did not then hesitate to violate tabus of all kinds, in more or less open defiance of the powers-that-be. Women of the people broke the ritual tabus that would confine them to their houses in order to ply their amorous intercourse with the crews of European ships. This passionate commerce soon became an important means of the people's trade, with a view toward circumventing at once the priests' tabus and the chiefs' business. And when ordinary men found common interest with their women in tabu transgressions, it broke down their own sacral status as men in contrast to women. For in the old days and in the domestic cult, men were tabu by relation to women in the same way that the chiefs were tabu by relation to the people. Crosscutting the distinctions of rank, the tabu could not in this respect become the exclusive privilege of chiefship. Rather, it argued an inclusion of the whole society *in* the chiefship, if in a subordinate way. But now the developing class cleavage revised the ancient proportions of tabu, making salient the radical opposition of ruling chiefs and common people, as respectively tabu and *noa* or 'free' from restrictions. This is a true structural transformation, a pragmatic redefinition of the categories that alters the relationships between them. The tabu now uniquely sacralized the distinctions of class at the expense of gender.

Phenomenology of the Symbolic Life

Now it seems to me there is something more to this tempest in a South Pacific teapot than a possible theory of history. There is also a criticism of basic Western distinctions by which culture is usually thought, such as the supposed opposition between history and structure or stability and change. In our own native folklore as well as academic social science, we constantly use such reified dichotomies to partition the anthropological object. I need not remind you that the antithesis between history and structure has been enshrined in anthropology since Radcliffe-Brown and the heyday of functionalism, and more recently confirmed in the structuralism inspired by Saussure. Yet this brief Hawaiian example suggests there is no phenomenal ground— let alone any heuristic advantage—for considering history and structure as exclusive alternatives. Hawaiian history is throughout grounded in structure, the systematic ordering of contingent circumstances, even as the Hawaiian structure proved itself historical.

What, then, of the corollary opposition between stability and change? Again, Western thought presupposes the two are antithetical: logical and ontological contraries. Cultural effects are identified as continuous with the past or discontinuous, as if these were alternative kinds of phenomenal reality, in complementary distribution in any cultural space. The distinction runs deep, through a whole series of elementary categories that organize the common wisdom: the static vs. the dynamic, being vs. becoming, state vs. action, condition vs. process, and—should we not include?—noun as opposed to verb. From there it is only a small logical step to the confusion of history with change, as if the persistence of structure through time (think of the *pensée sauvage*) were not also historical. But again, Hawaiian history is surely not unique in the demonstration that culture functions as a *synthesis* of stability and change, past and present, diachrony and synchrony.

Every practical change is also a cultural reproduction. As for example, the Hawaiian chiefship, incorporating foreign identities and material means, reproduces the cosmic status of the chief as a celestial being from Kahiki. In this mytho-praxis of hierarchy, the Polynesian *ariki*, the royal firstborn "had started his life at the time the world was created"; or more precisely for Hawaii, his life is the creation (Koskinen 1960:110; cf. chapter 4). Sure of its cosmological privileges, the Hawaiian chiefship was able to include the appearance of Captain Cook in its own mythopractical terms.

In the upshot, the more things remained the same the more they changed, since every such reproduction of the categories is not the same. Every reproduction of culture is an alteration, insofar as in action, the categories by which a present world is orchestrated pick up some novel empirical content. The Hawaiian chief for whom "King George" of England is the model of celestial *mana* is no longer the same chief, nor in the same relation to his people.

I am arguing that this symbolic dialogue of history—dialogue between the received categories and the perceived contexts, between cultural sense and practical reference—puts into question a whole series of ossified oppositions by which we habitually understand both history and cultural order. I mean not only stability and change or structure and history, but also the past as radically distinct from the present, system vs. event, or even infrastructure in contrast to superstructure. So what I propose, if you will bear with me through a semiphilosophical excursion, a kind of naïve phenomenology of symbolic action, is that we self-consciously explore these reified distinctions with a view toward discovering their truer synthesis.

The problem comes down to the relation of cultural concepts to human experience, or the problem of symbolic reference: of how cultural concepts are actively used to engage the world. Ultimately at issue is the being of structure *in* history and *as* history. But I begin more simply by making two elementary observations, neither of them at all novel or my own discovery. The first is the venerable Boasian principle that "the seeing eye is the organ of tradition . . ." Human social experience is the appropriation of specific percepts by general concepts: an ordering of men and the objects of their existence according to a scheme of cultural categories which is never the only one possible, but in that sense is arbitrary and historical. The second proposition is that the use of conventional concepts in empirical contexts subjects the cultural meanings to practical revaluations. Brought to bear on a world which has its own reasons, a world in-itself and potentially refractory, the traditional categories are transformed. For even as the world can easily escape the interpretive schemes of some given group of mankind, nothing guarantees either that intelligent and intentional subjects, with their several social interests and biographies, will use the existing categories in prescribed ways. I call this double contingency the risk of the categories in action.

But first, the continuity of culture in action: the seeing eye as the organ of tradition. I invoke thus a long philosophical tradition, tracing notably to Kant and carried on in linguistics by Saussure and Whorf as well as in the social anthropology of Boas and Lévi-Strauss. All these (and others) have taught that the experience of human subjects, especially as communicated in discourse, involves an appropriation of events in the terms of *a priori* concepts. Reference to the world is an act of classification, in

the course of which realities are indexed to concepts in a relation
of empirical tokens to cultural types. We know the world as logical instances of cultural classes: "Captain Cook is a god." It is not
that, as some have believed, we have a "need" to classify. Formal
classification is an intrinsic condition of symbolic action.

Or as Walker Percy puts it (1958:138), the symbolic character
of consciousness consists in the pairing of a percept and a concept, by means of which the objects of perception become intelligible to ourselves and are transmitted to others. "Every conscious perception," Percy says, "is of the nature of a recognition,
a pairing, which is to say that the object is recognized as being
what it is. . . . it is not enough to say that one is conscious of
something; one is conscious of something as *being something*."
—"He [Cook] is a god." But then recognition is a kind of recognition: the event is inserted in a preexisting category, and
history is present in current action. The irruption of Captain
Cook from beyond the horizon was a truly unprecedented event,
never seen before. But by thus encompassing the existentially
unique in the conceptually familiar, the people embed their
present in the past.

The same thing happens in the logical structure of discourse:
in the way that sentences describe or assert. Assimilating a particular (the grammatical subject) within a more general type (the
kind of act or attribute predicated of it), the propositional clause
unfolds likewise as an act of symbolic classification:

> *He akua ia.*
> A god he
> "He is a god."

The subject identifies a spatiotemporal particular (in a possible
world): "He," "Cook." The predicate describes by means of relative generals: "god." Many philosophers have recognized this
hierarchy of logical types in the structure of discourse. Strawson, for example:

> Two terms coupled in a true sentence stand in referen-
> tial and predicative position, respectively, if what the
> first term designates or signifies is an instance of what
> the second term signifies. Items so related (or the terms
> that designate or signify them) may be said respectively
> to be of lower or higher [logical] type (Strawson 1971:69).

One might summarize thus far by saying that there is no such thing as an immaculate perception. "Far from it being the object that antedates the viewpoint," as Saussure puts it, "it would seem that it is the viewpoint that creates the object." Besides, he adds, "nothing tells us in advance that one way of considering the fact in question takes precedence over others or is in any way superior to them" (Saussure 1959:8).

Saussure here refers to the "arbitrary" character of the symbolic scheme: a certain *découpage* of the possible continuities of sense, implying a segmentation of the world in reference as a function of language-internal relations among signs (linguistic value). The cultural categories by which experience is constituted do not follow directly from the world, but from their differential relations within a symbolic scheme. The contrast in French between the terms *fleuve* and *rivière* entails a different segmentation of fluvial objects from the usual English glosses 'river' and 'stream', inasmuch as the French terms do not turn on relative size as the English do, but on whether or not the water flows into the ocean (cf. Culler 1977). Similarly, the English (or French) distinction between 'god' and 'man' is not the same as the apparent Hawaiian parallel of *akua* and *kanaka*, because *kanaka* as designating '(ordinary) men' thus stands in definitional contrast as well to *ali'i* or 'chief'. In the Hawaiian, 'chief' and 'god' are transitively alike by opposition to men; nor would the difference of gods and men correspond to that between spirits and mortals, since some mortals (chiefs) are also gods. There is no necessary starting point for any such cultural scheme in "reality," as Stuart Hampshire writes, while noting that some philosophers have believed there is (1967:20). Rather, the particular cultural scheme constitutes the possibilities of worldly reference for the people of a given society, even as this scheme is constituted on principled distinctions between signs which, in relation to objects, are never the only possible distinctions. Or to cite Saussure's own predecessor, Michel Bréal:

> it cannot be doubted that language designates things in an incomplete and inexact way. . . . Substantives are signs attached to things: they include just the part of the *vérité* that can be included by a name, a part necessarily all the more fractional as the object has more reality . . . if I take a real being, an object existing in nature, it will

be impossible for language to put into the word all the
notions that that object or being awakens in the mind
(Bréal 1921 : 178–79).

Bréal speaks of the inevitable disproportion between language,
any language, and the world: "our languages are condemned to
a perpetual lack of proportion between the word and the thing.
The expression is sometimes too wide, sometimes too narrow"
(*Ibid.*, p. 107). One could say that it is always both, since the objects of reference are at once more particular and more general
than the expressions used to designate them. The objects are
more particular as tokens in a specific space-time than are the
signs as conceptual categories or classes. On the other hand,
things are more general than their expressions, as presenting
(experientially) more properties and relations than are selectively picked out and valued by any sign. Thus the well-known
principle: it is impossible to exhaust the description of any object.
   So the sign, as sense, becomes doubly arbitrary in reference:
at once a relative segmentation and a selective representation.
And from the arbitrary nature of the sign it follows that culture
is, by its own nature, an historical object. Saussure, who was of
course famous for the distinction of diachronic and synchronic
viewpoints in the study of language, was nevertheless first to
admit, and ever to insist, that a linguistic system is thoroughly
historical. It is historical because it is arbitrary: because it does
not simply reflect the existing world; but, on the contrary, in ordering existing objects by preexisting concepts, language would
ignore the flux of the moment. Both the totality and the particu-
larity of present objects escape it. Conversely, then, the system
is arbitrary because it is historical. It recognizes the present,
whatever it "really" is, as a past. The paradox of certain cultural
orders called "historyless" is that they insist upon a thorough-
going *approche historicisante du monde* (to borrow a phrase from
Délivré [1974]). We have seen that Cook was a tradition for Hawaiians before he was a fact.
   On the other hand, the empirical realities in all their particularities can never live up to the myth, any more than Cook as a
man could live up to the exalted status the Hawaiians intended
him. This brings us to the second general consideration of our
excursion into the elementary forms of the symbolic life: the risk

of cultural action, which is a risk of the categories in reference. In action, people put their concepts and categories into ostensive relations to the world. Such referential uses bring into play other determinations of the signs, besides their received sense, namely the actual world and the people concerned. *Praxis* is, then, a risk to the sense of signs in the culture-as-constituted, precisely as the sense is arbitrary in its capacity as reference. Having its own properties, the world may then prove intractable. It can well defy the concepts that are indexed to it. Man's symbolic hubris becomes a great gamble played with the empirical realities. The gamble is that referential action, by placing *a priori* concepts in correspondence with external objects, will imply some *unforeseen* effects that cannot be ignored. Besides, as action involves a thinking subject (or subjects), related to the sign in the capacity of agent, the cultural scheme is put in double jeopardy, subjectively as well as objectively: subjectively, by the people's interested uses of signs in their own projects; objectively, as meaning is risked in a cosmos fully capable of contradicting the symbolic systems that are presumed to describe it.

The objective gamble thus lies in the disproportions between words and things. Every implementation of cultural concepts in an actual world submits the concepts to some determination by the situation. This is what we have described as the functional revaluation of signs; the revaluation of the Hawaiian tabu-concept, for example. For signs such as "tabu" are notoriously polysemic: as virtual or in the society in general, they have many possible meanings. But when actualized, when ventured in a particular context such as the regulation of trade, "tabu" is valorized in some selective sense. One meaning is foregrounded, made salient by relation to all possible meanings. At the same time, reference is made to concrete particulars that are not the same as in all previous uses. In the event, the structure of the "semantic field" is revised (cf. Lyons 1977, 1:250 f.). The idea of tabu has been objectified as a commercial and proprietary right, a sense that may well be rendered general by the powers of the people imposing it—with reciprocal effects on definitions and relations of these persons and their powers. "Tabu" thus emerges from action with an empirical residue. The idea is burdened with the world.

The subjective risk consists in the possible revision of signs by acting subjects in their personal projects. Contradiction arises from the inevitable difference between the value of a sign in a symbolic system, i.e., its semantic relations to other signs, and its value to the people using it. In the cultural system, the sign has a conceptual value fixed by contrasts to other signs; whereas, in action the sign is determined also as an "interest," which is its instrumental value to the acting subject. Recall that the word "interest" derives from a Latin impersonal construction (*inter est*) meaning 'it makes a difference'. Yet if an interest in something is the difference it makes for someone, so in a parallel way and on another plane Saussure would thus define the sign as a conceptual value. As a concept, the sign is determined by differential relations to other signs. The meaning of "blue" is determined by the coexistence in the language of other words such as "green." If, as is true in many natural languages, there were no "green," the term "blue" (or "grue") would have a greater conceptual and referential extension: it would also cover the field we call (in English) "green." The same goes for God the Father, a dollar bill, motherhood, or filet mignon: each has a conceptual sense according to its differential place in the total scheme of such symbolic objects. On the other hand, the symbolic object represents a differential interest to various subjects according to its place in their life schemes. "Interest" and "sense" are two sides of the same thing, the sign, as related respectively to persons and to other signs. Yet my interest in something is not the same as its sense.

Saussure's definition of linguistic value helps make the point, as it is framed on an analogy to economic value. The value of a 5-franc piece is determined by the dissimilar objects with which it can be exchanged, such as so much bread or milk, and by other units of currency with which it can be contrastively compared: 1 franc, 10 francs, etc. By these relationships the significance of 5 francs in the society is determined. Yet this general and virtual sense is not the value of 5 francs *to me*. To me, it appears as a specific interest or instrumental value, and whether I buy milk or bread with it, give it away, or put it in the bank depends on my particular circumstances and objectives. As implemented by the subject, the conceptual value acquires an intentional value—which may well be different also from its conventional value.

Because as ventured in action, the sign is subjected to another kind of determination: to processes of human consciousness and intelligence. No longer a disembodied or virtual semiotic system, meaning is now in contact with the original human powers of its creation. There is no reason to believe—although the belief is the *a priori* of certain forms of linguistic relativism— that such creative powers are suspended once people have a culture. On the contrary, in action signs are subsumed in various logical operations, such as metaphor and analogy, intensional and extensional redefinitions, specializations of meaning or generalizations, displacements or substitutions, not to neglect creative "misunderstandings." And because signs are engaged by interests in projects, thus in temporal relations of implication not simply simultaneous relations of contrast, their values are risked so to speak syntagmatically as well as paradigmatically. Such interested uses are not imperfect merely, by relation to the Platonic cum cultural ideals, but potentially inventive. We have seen how Hawaiian chiefs were able to recognize their traditional *mana* in the fancy goods of European merchants, as opposed to coarser stuffs or domestic utilities. The goods offered in trade were factored according to the chiefs' self-conceptions. By an interested metaphor on celestial brilliance, whose logic was motivated in the traditional culture, as discovered however in the existing situation by a certain intentionality, the meaning of *mana* was changed.

Antithesis and Synthesis

Given these phenomenological understandings, certain critical reflections follow concerning the Procrustean dichotomies of the academic wisdom.

In a certain structuralism, history and structure are antinomies; the one is supposed to negate the other. Whereas, in the nature of symbolic action, diachrony and synchrony coexist in an indissoluble synthesis. Symbolic action is a duplex compound made up of an inescapable past and an irreducible present. An inescapable past because the concepts by which experience is organized and communicated proceed from the received cultural scheme. An irreducible present because of the world-

uniqueness of any action: the Heraclitean difference between
the unique experience of the river (or *fleuve*) and its name. The
difference lies in the irreducibility of specific actors and their empirical contexts, which are never precisely the same as other actors or other situations—one never steps into the same river
twice. As responsible for their own actions, people do become
authors of their own concepts; that is, they take responsibility
for whatever their culture might have made them. For if there is
always a past in the present, an *a priori* system of interpretation,
there is also "a life which desires itself" (as Nietzsche says). This
is what Roy Wagner (1975) must mean by "the invention of culture": the particular empirical inflection of meaning that is given
to cultural concepts when they are realized as personal projects.

Again it is necessary to insist that the possibility that the present will transcend the past, while at the same time remaining
true to it, depends on the cultural order as well as the practical
situation. Just for starters, there are all degrees of *approches his-
toricisantes du monde*. In Hopi, as Whorf showed, it is not grammatical to suppose that "tomorrow is another day": it is merely
the same day, grown older and come back again. Besides, there
is the social system. And in social systems there are differential
powers. We have seen that in Hawaii, whatever the interpretation the run of ordinary folk may have put on Captain Cook, the
priests and chiefs could not only objectify their own opinions by
ritual performances, but also oblige the people to render material tributes to such opinions. Or again, everything that was said
about heroic polities (chapter 1) suggests the differential capacity of powers-that-be to make general understandings of their
personal innovations. Giddens (1976) puts the dialogue of action ("structuration") in a general way by referring to the "duality of structure" as preexisting concept and unintended consequence—not forgetting either the *intended* consequences of
people in power. The phenomenology we have been discussing
will remain "naïve" insofar as it ignores that symbolic action is
communicative as well as conceptual: a social fact that is taken
up in the projects and interpretations of others. Here thus enters
the "structure of the conjuncture," the situational sociology of
cultural categories, with the motivations it affords to risks of reference and innovations of sense. In contrast to any phenomenological reduction, a full anthropological practice cannot neglect

that the precise synthesis of past and present is relative to the cultural order, as manifested in a specific structure of the conjuncture.

Still, the Hawaiian case, for all its historicization of the world, has already shown that there is no ground either for the exclusive opposition of stability and change. Every actual use of cultural ideas is some reproduction of them, but every such reference is also a difference. We know this anyhow, that things must preserve some identity through their changes, or else the world is a madhouse. Saussure articulated the principle: "What predominates in all change is the persistence of the old substance; disregard for the past is only relative. That is why the principle of change is based on the principle of continuity" (1959: 74). Yet in a certain anthropology, also notoriously in the study of history, we isolate some changes as strikingly distinctive and call them "events," in opposition to "structure."

This is really a pernicious distinction, structure and event. If only for the relatively trivial reason that all structure or system is, phenomenally, evenemential. As a set of meaningful relations between categories, the cultural order is only virtual. It exists *in potentia* merely. So the meaning of any specific cultural form is all its possible uses in the community as a whole. But this meaning is realized, *in presentia*, only as events of speech and action. Event is the empirical form of system. The converse proposition, that all events are culturally systematic, is more significant. An event is indeed a happening of significance, and *as significance* it is dependent on the structure for its existence and effect. "Events are not just there and happen," as Max Weber said, "but they have a meaning and happen because of that meaning." Or in other words, an event is not just a happening in the world; it is a *relation* between a certain happening and a given symbolic system. And although as a happening an event has its own "objective" properties and reasons stemming from other worlds (systems), it is not these properties *as such* that give it effect but their significance as projected from some cultural scheme. The event is a happening interpreted—and interpretations vary.

Consider again the apotheosis of Englishmen in Hawaii, and also their eventual fall from such grace. Captain Cook was truly a great man (or at least we think so), but there was nothing inherently divine in the navigation of his ships into an Hawaiian bay, let alone that it represented the return of Lono, the ancient god of the people and of fertility, which was what Hawaiians supposed. Thus the 10,000 people in Kealakekua Bay singing and rejoicing in Cook's return of 1779. Rarely has colonialism enjoyed a more auspicious beginning. On the other hand, when Hawaiian women began to live and eat with the crews aboard Cook's or Vancouver's ships, serious doubts were cast on the foreigners' divinity. Now, there is nothing in the act of eating with women that is inherently ungodly—except that in the Hawaiian system it is polluting of men and destroys their tabu. Events thus cannot be understood apart from the values attributed to them: the significance that transforms a mere happening into a fateful conjuncture. What is for some people a radical event may appear to others as a date for lunch. So here we are conscientiously separating system and event by heroic acts of academic theory, whereas the human symbolic fact is: no event *sans* system.

Clearly, the twin anthropological (or historical) errors of materialism and idealism consist in attempts to link the meaningful significance and the worldly happening in some mechanical or physicalist relation of cause and effect. For materialism the significance is the direct effect of the objective properties of the happening. This ignores the relative value or meaning given to the happening by the society. For idealism the happening is simply an effect of its significance. This ignores the burden of "reality": the forces that have real effects, if always in the *terms* of some cultural scheme.

The same goes for theory and practice, taken as phenomenal alternatives: this objectified distinction between cultural concepts and practical activities that is itself untrue in practice and absurd as theory. All *praxis* is theoretical. It begins always in concepts of the actors and of the objects of their existence, the cultural segmentations and values of an *a priori* system. Therefore, there is no true materialism that is not also historical. Marx said as much, but a certain current and trendy Marxism, bemused by the opposition of theory and practice, would deny it. Consider this assertion by Hindess and Hirst:

> Historical events do not exist [in] and can have no material effectivity in the present. The conditions of existence

of present social relations necessarily exist in and are constantly reproduced in the present. It is not the "present" which the past has vouchsafed to allow us but the "current situation" . . . All Marxist theory, however abstract it may be, exists to make possible the analysis of the current situation. . . . An historical analysis of the "current situation" is impossible (Hindess and Hirst 1975:312).

Yet culture is precisely the organization of the current situation in the terms of a past. Nor is there, then, any infrastructure without superstructure, since "in the final analysis" the categories by which objectivity is defined are themselves cosmological—just as for Hawaiians the advent of the British was an event of universal dimensions whose guiding expressions were concepts of *mana, atua* (or divinity), and the celestial geography of Kahiki (the spiritual origins). If practice, then, put in place the structural correspondence between Hawaiian chiefs and prominent Europeans, while opposing both to the Hawaiian people-in-general, this became the organization of material trade as well as personal identity—not to mention that it figures decisively in historical events, such as the rivalry between Captain Cook and the Hawaiian King that proved disastrous to the Great Navigator. *Praxis* thus unfolded as the relative exclusion of the common people from European goods, notably the goods placed in the Hawaiian category of prestige items, to present such scenes as "Billy Pitt" Kalaimoku and "John Adams" Kuakini disporting themselves in Chinese silk dressing gowns and European waistcoats, in chambers decorated with fine teak furniture and gilded mirrors, or at dinners served on solid-silver table settings, while the commoners progressively sank into an immiseration from which they have not yet recovered. Nor is it that practice is simply resumed in its effects by the superstructure, as a distorted consciousness of the material realities arriving on the stage of history as it were *post festum*. For as we have seen, the utilities of trade were constantly subject to definition by the demands of chiefly consumption. So that what appears in the account books and letters of Boston merchants in Hawaii, documenting the shifting demands for guns, naval stores, or this or that type of cashmere fabric, are politically contextual intimations of Polynesian divinity. The market was an irreducible condition of material *praxis*, where prices were set according to inescapable conceptions of Polynesian *mana*.

One could go on to make similar observations ("deconstructions") about the historical synthesis of such radical dichotomies as the "individual" and the "collective" or the "real" and the "ideological." But enough said, since these oppositions are so many analogous expressions of the same misplaced concreteness. The truer issue lies in the dialogue of sense and reference, inasmuch as reference puts the system of sense at the risk of other systems: the intelligent subject and the intransigent world. And the truth of this larger dialogue consists of the indissoluble synthesis of such as past and present, system and event, structure and history.

Bibliography

Abbreviations

AH	Archives of the State of Hawaii, Honolulu.
BM	British Museum Library, London.
ML	Mitchell Library (Library of New South Wales), Sydney.
PRO-Adm	Public Records Office: Office of the Admiralty, London.
SOAS	School of Oriental and African Studies Library, University of London, London.

Adler, Alfred. 1978. Le pouvoir et l'interdit, in *Systèmes de signes*, pp. 25–40. Paris: Hermann.
————1982. The ritual doubling of the person of the king, in *Between belief and transgression*, ed. M. Izard and A. Adler, pp. 180–92. Chicago: University of Chicago Press.
Andrews, Lorrin. 1836. Letters from Mr. Andrews at Lahaina-luna, 2 Dec. [1835]. *Missionary Herald* 33:390–91.
Anonymous (of Mitchell). MS copy of a letter to Mrs. Strachan of Spithead (ML: Safe 1/67).
Bakhtin, Mikhail. 1968. *Rabelais and his world*, trans. from the Russian by Helene Iswolsky. Cambridge: MIT Press.
Balandier, Georges. 1967. *Anthropologie politique*. Paris: Presses Universitaires de France.
Barber, James. MS. Some accᵗ of the death & remains of Capᵗ Cook . . . recᵈ from Joshua Lee Dimsdell Quarter Master of the Gunjara. Dixson Library (Library of New South Wales).
Barnes, J. A. 1951. The Fort Jameson Ngoni. In *Seven tribes of*

British Central Africa, ed. Elizabeth Colson and Max Gluckman, pp. 194–252. London: Oxford University Press.

———1967. *Politics in a changing society*. 2d ed. Manchester: Manchester University Press.

Barraclough, Geoffrey. 1978. *Main trends in history*. New York: Holmes and Meier.

Barrère, Dorothy B., Mary Kawena Pukui, and Marion Kelly 1980. *Hula: Historical perspectives*. Pacific Anthropological Records No. 30. Honolulu: Bishop Museum.

Bayly, William. MS. A log and journal, kept on board His Majesties sloop Discovery by Wm Bayly astronomer. PRO-Adm 55/20.

Beaglehole, J. C. 1967. *The journals of Captain James Cook on his voyages of discovery, III: The voyage of the* Resolution *and* Discovery *1776–1780*. Parts 1 and 2. Cambridge: Cambridge University Press (for the Hakluyt Society).

———1974. *The life of Captain James Cook*. Stanford, Calif.: Stanford University Press.

Beckwith, Martha. 1970. *Hawaiian mythology*. Honolulu: University of Hawaii Press.

———1972. *The Kumulipo*. Honolulu: University of Hawaii Press.

Bell, Edward. 1929. Log of the Chatham, *Honolulu Mercury* 1(5): 55–69.

Benveniste, Émile. 1969. *Le vocabulaire des institutions Indo-Européenes*. 2 vols. Paris: Les Editions de Minuit.

Best, Elsdon. 1902–3. Notes on the art of war, Parts 2, 5. *Journal of the Polynesian Society* 11:47–75; 12:32–50.

———1976 [1924]. *Maori religion and mythology*, vol. 1. Dominion Museum Bulletin 10. Wellington: Government Printer.

———1925. *Tuhoe: The children of the mist*, vol. 1. New Plymouth: Avery.

———1929. *The whare kohanga and its lore*. Dominion Museum Bulletin 13. Wellington: Government Printer.

Bingham, Hiram. 1969 [1855]. *A residence of twenty-one years in the Sandwich Islands*. New York: Praeger.

Binney, Judith. 1968. *The legacy of guilt: A life of Thomas Kendall*. Christchurch: Oxford University Press for the University of Auckland Press.

Bird, John. 1888. *The annals of Natal, 1495–1845*, vol. 1. Pietermaritzburg: P. Davis and Sons.

Bloch, Marc. 1966. *French rural history*, trans. Janet Sondheimer. Berkeley: University of California Press.

Bloxam, (Rev.) R. MS. A narrative of a voyage to the Sandwich Islands in H.M.S. Blonde, 1824–1825–1826. National Library of Australia (MS. 4255).

Bonte, Pierre, and Nicole Echard. 1976. Histoire et histoires: Conception du passé chez les Hausa et les Tuareg (République du Niger). *Cahiers d'Études Africaines* 16:237–96.

Bott, Elizabeth. 1972. Psychoanalysis and ceremony, together with appendix. In *The Interpretation of Ritual*, ed. J. S. La Fontaine, pp. 205–37, 277–82. London: Tavistock.

————1981. Power and rank in the kingdom of Tonga. *Journal of the Polynesian Society* 90:7–82.

Bourdieu, Pierre. 1977. *Outline of a theory of practice*. Cambridge: Cambridge University Press.

Bradley, Harold W. 1968 [1943]. *The American frontier in Hawaii*. Gloucester: Peter Smith.

Braudel, Fernand. 1980. *On history*. Chicago: University of Chicago Press.

Bréal, Michel. 1921. *Essai de sémantique*. 5th ed. Paris: Hachette.

Brewster, A. B. MS. The chronicles of the Noikoro tribe. National Archives of Fiji (CS2195 FSB2).

Broughton, William R. 1804. *A voyage of discovery in the North Pacific Ocean . . . in the years 1795, 1796, 1797, 1798*. London: Cadell and Davies.

Bryant, A. T. 1929. *Olden times in Zululand and Natal*. London: Longmans, Green.

————1949. *The Zulu people*. Pietermaritzburg: Shuter and Shooter.

Buick, T. Lindsay. 1926. *New Zealand's first war, or the rebellion of Hone Heke*. Wellington: Skinner, Government Printer.

————1936. *The treaty of Waitangi*. 3d ed. New Plymouth (N.Z.): Thomas Avery and Sons.

Burney, Lt. James. MS. Journal of Lieutenant James Burney with Captain Ja^s Cook, 1776–1780. BM: Add MS. 8955.

————MS. Journal of the proceedings of His Maj^{ies} sloop, the Discovery . . . ML.

————1819. *Chronological history of North-eastern voyages*. London: Payne & Foss.

Burrows, R. 1886. *Extracts from a diary kept by Rev. R. Burrows during Heke's war in the North in 1845*. Auckland: Upton.

Byron, George. 1826. *Voyage of H.M.S. Blonde to the Sandwich Islands, in the years 1824–1825*. London: Murray.

Calvert, James. MS. Journals of Rev. James Calvert. Methodist Missionary Society Papers, SOAS.

Capell, A. 1973. *A new Fijian dictionary*. 4th ed. Suva: Government Printer.

Carleton, Hugh. 1874. *The life of Henry Williams*. 2 vols. Auckland: Upton.

Chadwick, H. Munro. 1926. *The heroic age.* Cambridge: Cambridge University Press.

Churchward, C. M. 1938–39. Rotuman legends. *Oceania* 9: 462–73.

Clastres, Pierre. 1977. *Society against the state,* trans. from the French by Robert Hurley. New York: Urizen Books.

Clerke, Capt. James. MS. Log and proceedings, 10 Feb. 1776–12 Feb. 1779. PRO-Adm 55/22, 23.

Clunie, Fergus. 1977. *Fijian weapons and warfare.* Suva: Fiji Museum.

Colenso, F. W. 1882. Contributions toward a better understanding of the Maori race. *N.Z. Inst. Trans.* 14:33–48.

Colnett, James. MS. The journal of James Colnett aboard the *Prince of Wales* and *Princess Royal* . . . PRO-Adm 55/146.

Commissioner of Public Lands. 1929. *Indices of awards made by the board of commissioners to quiet land titles in the Hawaiian Islands.* Honolulu: Star-Bulletin Press.

Cook, James, and James King. 1784. *A voyage to the Pacific Ocean . . . in His Majesty's Ships* Resolution *and* Discovery. 3 vols. Dublin: Chamberlaine et al.

Corney, Peter. 1896. *Voyages in the Northern Pacific.* Honolulu: Thrum.

Council of Chiefs. 1881. Notes of proceedings of a Native Council, held at Mualevu . . . 1880 . . . 1881, *Proceedings of the Native Council of Chiefs, Sept. 1875–26 August 1960.* Microfilm, Western Pacific High Commission, National Archives of Fiji.

Cowan, James. 1922. *The New Zealand wars.* Vol. 1:1845–64. Wellington: R. E. Owen, Government Printer.

Cox, Ross. 1832. Adventures on the Columbia River. New York: Harper.

Cross, William. MS. Diary of Rev. William Cross, 28 Dec. 1837–1 Oct. 1842. Methodist Overseas Mission Papers No. 336, ML.

Culler, Jonathan. 1977. *Ferdinand de Saussure.* New York: Penguin.

Cunnison, Ian. 1951. *History on the Luapula.* Rhodes-Livingstone Paper, No. 21. Manchester: Manchester University Press.

————1957. History and genealogies in a conquest state. *American Anthropologist* 59:20–31.

————1959. *The Luapula peoples of Northern Rhodesia.* Manchester: Manchester University Press.

Dampier, Robert. 1971. *To the Sandwich Islands on H.M.S. Blonde,* ed. Pauline King Joerger. Honolulu: University of Hawaii Press.

Davis, C. O. 1876. *The life and times of Patuone.* Auckland: J. H. Field.

Délivré, Alain. 1974. *L'histoire des rois d'Imerina: Interpretation d'une tradition orale*. Paris: Klincksieck.

Derrick, R. A. 1950. *A history of Fiji*. 2d ed. Suva: Printing and Stationery Department.

Diapea, William. 1928. *Cannibal Jack*. London: Faber and Gwyer.

Dibble, Sheldon. 1909 [1843]. *A history of the Sandwich Islands*. Honolulu: Thrum. (Reissue)

Diderot. 1972 [1772/80]. Supplement au voyage de Bougainville ou dialogue entre A et B. In *Le neveu de Rameau et autres textes*. Paris: Livre de Poche.

Dorson, Richard M. 1968. *The British folklorists*. Chicago: University of Chicago Press.

Dorton, Lilikalā. 1981. MS. *'O ka le'ale'a o ka mele ma'i*, or The joy of genital chants. Unpublished course paper, University of Hawaii (Anthropology 498, Spring 1981).

Dranivia, Solomone. MS. Nai tukutuku mai na gauna makawa. Methodist Overseas Mission 164, Fiji Museum. (Xerox of original in ML)

Dumézil, Georges. 1948. *Mitra-Varuna*. Paris: Gallimard.

———1949. *L'heritage Indo-Européen à Rome*. 4th ed. Paris: Gallimard.

———1958. *L'ideologie tripartite des Indo-Européens*. Brussels: Latomus.

———1968. *Myth et épopée*. 3 vols. Paris: Gallimard.

———1977. *Les dieux soverains des Indo-Européens*. Paris: Gallimard.

Dumont, Louis. 1970. *Homo hierarchicus*. Chicago: University of Chicago Press.

Dumoulin, Jerome, and Dominique Moisi, eds. 1973. *The historian between the ethnologist and the futurologist*. Paris: Mouton.

Durkheim, Émile. 1905–6. Compte-rendu de *Sociologia e storia*, A. D. Zenopol. *L'Année Sociologique* 9:140.

Edgar, Thomas. MS. A log of the proceedings of His Majesty's Sloop Discovery, Charles Clerke, Commander. PRO-Adm 55/21, 55/24.

Elbert, Samuel H. 1962. Symbolism in Hawaiian poetry. *ETC.: A Review of General Semantics* 18:389–400.

Elbert, Samuel, and Noelani Mahoe. 1970. *Na mele o Hawai'i nei*. Honolulu: University of Hawaii Press.

Elbert, Samuel H., and Mary Kawena Pukui. 1979. *Hawaiian grammar*. Honolulu: University of Hawaii Press.

Eliade, Mircea. 1954. *The myth of the eternal return*. Bollingen Series 46. Princeton, N.J.: Princeton University Press.

Ellis, William, 1782. *An authentic narrative of a voyage performed by Captain Cook*. 2 vols. London: Goulding.

Ellis, (Rev.) William. 1828. *Narrative of a tour through Hawaii, or Owhyhee*. London: Fisher and Jackson.

———1969 [1842]. *Polynesian researches: Hawaii*. Rutland, Vt.: Tuttle.

Emerson, (Rev.) J. S. MS. Missionary letters. Hawaiian Mission Children's Society Library.

Emerson, Nathaniel B. 1965 [1909]. *Unwritten literature of Hawaii: The sacred songs of the hula*. Rutland, Vt., and Tokyo: Tuttle. (Reissue)

Endicott, W. 1923. *Wrecked among cannibals in the Fijis*. Salem: Marine Research Society.

Erskine, John Elphinston. 1967 [1853]. *Journal of a cruise among the islands of the Western Pacific*. London: Dawsons of Pall Mall. (Reissue)

Evans-Pritchard, E. E. 1954. *Social anthropology*. Glencoe, Ill.: Free Press.

———1962. *Essays in social anthropology*. London: Faber and Faber.

Feeley-Harnik, Gillian. 1978. Divine kingship and the meaning of history among the Sakalava of Madagascar. *Man* n.s. 13: 402–17.

Firth, Raymond. 1959. Economics of the New Zealand Maori. Wellington: R. E. Owen, Government Printer.

———1971. *Elements of social organisation*. London: Tavistock.

Fison, Lorimer. 1904. *Tales from old Fiji*. London: Moring.

Forbes, Cochrane. 1842. Report from Kaelakekua. *Missionary Herald* 38:154–56.

Fornander, Abraham. 1916–19. *Memoirs*, vols. 4–6. Fornander Collection of Hawaiian Antiquities and Folklore. Honolulu: Bishop Museum.

———1969 [1878–85]. *An account of the Polynesian race*. 3 vols. Rutland, Vt.: Tuttle. (Reissue)

Fox, James J. 1971. A Rotinese dynastic genealogy. In *The translation of culture*, ed. T. Beidelman. London: Tavistock.

Frankfort, Henri. 1948. *Kingship and the gods*. Chicago: University of Chicago Press.

Frazer, Sir James G. 1900. *The golden bough*. 2d ed. 3 vols. London: Macmillan.

———1905. *Lectures on the early history of kingship*. London: Macmillan.

———1911–15. *The golden bough*. 3rd ed. 13 vols. London: Macmillan.

————1963. *The golden bough.* 1 vol. abridged ed. (reissue of the 1922 ed.). New York: Macmillan.

Freud, Sigmund. n.d. *Totem and taboo.* New York: Random House.

Freycinet, Louis Claude de Saulses de. 1978. *Hawaii in 1819: A narrative account,* trans. Ella Wiswell from *Voyage autour du monde . . . ,* ed. Marion Kelly. Pacific Anthropological Records 26. Honolulu: Bishop Museum.

Furet, François. 1972. Quantitative history. In *Historical studies today,* ed. Felix Gilbert and Stephen R. Graubard. New York: Norton.

Gardiner, John. 1898. The natives of Rotuma. *Journal of the Royal Anthropological Institute* 37:457–524.

Geertz, Clifford. 1961. *The social history of an Indonesian town.* Cambridge: MIT Press.

————1980. *Negara: The theatre state in nineteenth-century Bali.* Princeton, N.J.: Princeton University Press.

Giddens, Anthony. 1976. *New rules of the sociological method.* London: Hutchinson.

Gifford, Edward Winslow. 1929. *Tongan society.* Bernice P. Bishop Museum Bulletin No. 61. Honolulu: Bishop Museum.

Gilbert, Felix, and Stephen Graubard, eds. 1972. *Historical studies today.* New York: Norton.

Gilbert, George. MS. Journal of George Gilbert [Cook's third voyage]. BM Add MS. 38580.

Gluckman, Max. 1963. *Order and rebellion in tribal Africa.* London: Cohen and West.

Goldie, W. H. 1905. Maori medical lore. *Transactions of the New Zealand Institute,* 1904, 37:1–120.

Goldman, Irving. 1970. *Ancient Polynesian society.* Chicago and London: University of Chicago Press.

Grey, Sir George. 1956 [1855]. *Polynesian mythology.* New York: Taplinger.

Gudgeon, Lt. Col. C.M.G. 1905. Mana Tangata. *Journal of the Polynesian Society* 14:49–66.

Guidieri, Remo. 1973. Il *Kula,* ovvero della truffa. *Rassegna Italiana di Sociologia* 559–93.

Hammatt, Charles H. MS. Journal of Charles H. Hammett [in the Sandwich Islands, 6 May 1823–9 June 1825]. Baker Library, Harvard University.

Hampshire, Stuart. 1967. *Thought and action.* New York: Viking.

Handy, E. S. Craighill. 1927. *Polynesian Religion.* Bernice P. Bishop Museum Bulletin 34. Honolulu: Bishop Museum.

————1965. Government and society. In *Ancient Hawaiian civilization*. Rutland, Vt., and Tokyo: Tuttle.

Handy, E. S. Craighill, and Mary Kawena Pukui. 1972. *The Polynesian family system in Ka'-u, Hawai'i*. Rutland, Vt., and Tokyo: Tuttle.

Henry, Teuira. 1928. *Ancient Tahiti*. Bernice P. Bishop Museum Bulletin 48. Honolulu: Bishop Museum.

Heusch, Luc de. 1958. *Essais sur le symbolisme de l'inceste royal en Afrique*. Bussels: Université Libre de Bruxelles.

————1962. Le pouvoir et le sacré. *Annales du Centre d'Étude des Religions*, No. 1. Brussels: Institut de Sociologie, Université Libre de Bruxelles.

————1972. *Le roi ivre ou l'originie de l'État*. Paris: Gallimard.

————1982. *Rois nés d'un coeur de vache*. Paris: Gallimard.

Hexter, J. H. 1972. Fernand Braudel and the Monde Braudelien. *Journal of Modern History* 44:480–541.

Hindess, B., and P. Hirst. 1975. *Pre-capitalist modes of production*. London: Routledge, Kegan Paul.

Hiroa, Te Rangi (Sir Peter Buck). 1977 [1949]. *The coming of the Maori*. Wellington: Maori Purposes Fund Board, Whitecoulls.

Hocart, A. M. FN (MS). Fijian field notes. Microfilm copy in the University of Chicago Libraries of originals in the Turnbull Library, Wellington.

————HF (MS). The heart of Fiji. Microfilm copy in the University of Chicago Libraries of original in the Turnbull Library, Wellington.

————WI (MS). The windward islands of Fiji. Manuscript original of *The Lau Islands, Fiji*. Wellington: Turnbull Library.

————1914. Mana. *Man* 14(46):97–101.

————1915. Chieftainship and the sister's son in the Pacific. *American Anthropologist* 17:631–46.

————1929. *Lau Islands, Fiji*. Bernice P. Bishop Museum Bulletin 62. Honolulu: Bishop Museum.

————1933. *The progress of man*. London: Methuen.

————1936. Sacrifice. *Encyclopedia of the Social Sciences* 13.

————1950. *Caste*. New York: Russell and Russell.

————1952. *The northern states of Fiji*. Royal Anthropological Institute of Great Britain and Ireland, Occasional Publication 11. London: The Institute.

————1969 [1927]. *Kingship*. Oxford: Oxford University Press. (Reissue)

————1970 [1936]. *Kings and councillors*. Chicago: University of Chicago Press. (Reissue)

Home, Alexander. MS. Log book of Captain Alex: Home, R.N.

. . . while with Captain Cook on his last voyage. National Library of Australia (MS. 690).

Howard, Alan. 1971. Households, families and friends in a Hawaiian-American community. *Working Papers of the East-West Population Institute*. No. 19. Honolulu: East-West Center.

Huber, Peter B. 1980. The Anggor bowman: Ritual and society in Melanesia. *American Ethnologist* 7:43–57.

Hunnewell, James. MS. Papers of James Hunnewell. Baker Library, Harvard University.

Hunt, John. MS. Journals of the Rev. John Hunt. Methodist Missionary Society (Box 5). SOAS.

I'i, John Papa. 1959. *Fragments of Hawaiian history*, trans. Mary Kawena Pukui. Honolulu: Bishop Museum Press.

Isaacs. Nathaniel. 1970. *Travel and adventures in eastern Africa*, ed. Louis Herman and Percival R. Kirby. Capetown: Struik.

Izard, Michel, and Pierre Smith (eds.). 1979. *La fonction symbolique*. Paris: Gallimard.

Jaggar, Thomas James. MS. Diaries of Thomas James Jaggar, 1837–1843. Microfilm copy of manuscript original in the National Archives of Fiji, Adelaide University Library.

Jarré, Raymond. 1946. Mariage et naissance chez les Fidjiens de Kadavu. *Journal de la Société des Océanistes* 2(2):79–92.

Johansen, J. Prytz. 1954. *The Maori and his religion*. Copenhagen: Munksgaard.

———1958. Studies in Maori rites and myths. *Historiskfilosofiske Meddelelser* 37(4). Copenhagen.

Kaawa, P. W. 1865. MS. The ancient tabus of Hawaii (*Na kapu kahiko o Hawaii nei*), trans. from the newspaper *Kuokoa*, 25 Nov., 2 Dec., 9 Dec.

———1865. Thrum collection, Ka Hoomana Kahiko, 29. Honolulu: Bishop Museum Library.

Kamakau, Samuel M. MS. Na Mo'olelo Hawai'i. Bishop Museum Library.

———1961. *Ruling chiefs of Hawaii*. Honolulu: Kamehameha Schools Press.

———1964. *Ka po'e kahiko: The people of old*, trans. Mary Kawena Pukui, ed. Dorothy Barrère. Honolulu: Bishop Museum Press.

———1976. *The works of the people of old*, trans. Mary Kawena Pukui, ed. Dorothy Barrère. Honolulu: Bishop Museum Press.

Kamokuiki. MS. Genealogy, AH (G33).

Kanoa, P. (attributed). 1839. Crime in the Sandwich Islands. *Hawaiian Spectator* 2:234.

Kapiti, Pita. 1913. Kumara lore. *Journal of the Polynesian Society* 22:36–41.

Keesing, Felix M. 1936. Hawaiian homesteading on Molokai. In *University of Hawaii research publications*, vol. 1 (3). Honolulu: University of Hawaii Press.

Kekoa, E. 1865. Birth rites of Hawaiian children in ancient times, trans. from *Ka Nupepa Ku'oko'a*, 14 Oct. 1865, by T. Thrum. Thrum Collection 23, Bishop Museum Library.

Kennedy, Gavin. 1978. *The death of Captain Cook*. London: Duckworth.

Kepelino, Z. 1932. *Kepelino's traditions of Hawaii*, ed. M. Beckwith. Bernice P. Bishop Museum Bulletin 95.

—————1977. Kepelino's 'Hawaiian Collection'; His Hooiliili Hawaii, Pepa I, 1858, trans. Basil F. Kirtley and Esther T. Mookini. *Hawaiian Journal of History* 11:39–68.

King, Lt. James. MS. Log and proceedings [of Cook's third voyage, HMS Resolution, 1776–1778]. (Photostat of PRO-Adm. 55/116 in Cook Collection, AH)

Koskinen, Aarne A. 1960. *Ariki, the first-born*. Folklore Fellows Communications No. 181. Helsinki: Suomalainen Tiedeakatemia Scientiarum Fennica.

Kotzebue, Otto von. 1830. *A new voyage of discovery round the world in the years 1823, 24, 25, and 26*. 2 vols. London: Colburn and Bentley.

Krige, Eileen Jensen. 1936. *The social system of the Zulus*. London: Longmans, Green.

Krige, Eileen Jensen, and J. O. Krige. 1943. *The realm of the Rain-Queen*. London: Oxford University Press.

Kuper, Hilda. 1947. *An African aristocracy: Rank among the Swazi*. London: Oxford University Press.

Law, John. MS. Journal of John Law. BM Add MS. 37327.

Leach, Edmund. 1972. The structure of symbolism, together with appendix. In *The interpretation of ritual*, ed. J. S. La Fontaine, pp. 239–76, 283–84. London: Tavistock.

Ledyard, John. 1963 [1783]. *John Ledyard's journal of Captain Cook's last voyage*, ed. James Kenneth Munford. Corvallis: Oregon State University Press.

Le Goff, Jacques. 1972. Is politics still the backbone of history? In *Historical studies today*, ed. Felix Gilbert and Stephen R. Graubard, pp. 337–55. New York: Norton.

Le Goff, Jacques, and Pierre Nora (eds.). *Faire l'histoire*. Paris: Gallimard.

Lester, E. H. 1941–42. Kava-drinking in Viti Levu, Fiji. *Oceania* 12:97–121.

Lévi-Strauss, Claude. 1963. *Totemism*. Boston: Beacon.
———1966. *The savage mind*. Chicago: University of Chicago Press.
Lisiansky, Urey. 1814. *A voyage around the world in the years 1803, 1804, 1805, and 1806*. London: Booth.
Lyons, C. J. 1875. Land matters in Hawaii. *Islander*: 16 July, 30 July, 6 Aug., 13 Aug.
Lyons, John. 1977. *Semantics*. 2 vols. Cambridge: Cambridge University Press.
Lyth, Richard Burdsall. MS. Tongan and Feejeean reminiscences. ML (B549).
———MS. Reminiscences, 1851–1853. ML (B548).
Makemson, Maud W. 1941. *The morning star rises*. New Haven: Yale University Press.
Malo, David. 1839. On the decrease of population in the Hawaiian Islands. *Hawaiian Spectator* 2 : 121–30.
———1951. *Hawaiian antiquities*, trans. Nathaniel B. Emerson. Honolulu: Bishop Museum Press.
Manby, Thomas. 1929. Journal of Vancouver's voyage to the Pacific Ocean. *Honolulu Mercury* 1(1) : 11–15; 1(2) : 33–45; 1(3) : 39–55.
Maning, F. E. 1906. *Old New Zealand*. Christchurch: Whitcombe and Tombs.
Martin, John (ed.). 1817. *An account of the natives of the Tonga Islands . . . from the extensive communications of Mr. William Mariner*. 2 vols. London: Murray.
McIntyre, W. David, and W. J. Gardner. 1971. *Speeches and documents on New Zealand history*. Oxford: Oxford University Press.
Meek, C. K. 1931. *A Sudanese kingdom*. London: Kegan Paul, Trench, Trubner.
Menzies, Archibald. MS. Archibald Menzies journal of Vancouver's voyage. BM Add. MS. 32641.
Metge, Joan. 1976. *The Maoris of New Zealand, Rautahi*. 2d ed. London: Routledge and Kegan Paul.
Methodist Missionary Society. MS. Feejee District Minutes and Reports, 1835–1852. SOAS.
Morgan, Theodore. 1948. *Hawaii: A century of economic change, 1778–1836*. Cambridge: Harvard University Press.
Oliver, Douglas. 1974. *Ancient Tahitian society*. 3 vols. Honolulu: University of Hawaii Press.
Percy, Walker. 1958. Symbol, consciousness, and intersubjectivity. *Journal of Philosophy* 55 : 631–41.
Pocock, David. 1964. The anthropology of time-reckoning. *Contributions to Indian Sociology* 7 : 18–29.

"The Polynesian" (Hawaiian newspaper). 1845. Obituary of Kekauluohi, 21 June.

Portlock, Nathaniel. 1789. *A voyage around the world . . . in 1785, 1786, 1787, and 1788*. London: Stockdale.

Préaux, Jean-G. 1962. La sacralité du pouvoir royal à Rome. In Luc de Heusch et al., *Le pouvoir et le sacré*, Annales du Centre d'Étude des Religions 1:103–21. Brussels: Institut de Sociologie, Université Libre de Bruxelles.

Puget, Peter. MS. Fragments of journals, 1792–1794. BM Add MSS. 17546–17548.

————MS. A log of the proceedings of His Majesty's armed tender *Chatham*, 1793–1794. PRO-Adm. 55/17.

Pukui, Mary Kawena, and Samuel Elbert. 1965. *Hawaiian-English dictionary*. Honolulu: University of Hawaii Press.

Pukui, Mary Kawena, et al. 1972. *Nānā i ke kumu* (Look to the source). 2 vols. Honolulu: Hui Hānai. (Second vol. issued 1979)

Pukui, Mary Kawena, and Alfons L. Korn. 1973. *The echo of our song*. Honolulu: University of Hawaii Press.

Putnam, Hilary. 1975. *Language, mind, and reality*. Vol. 2. Cambridge: Cambridge University Press.

Quain, Buell. 1948. *Fijian village*. Chicago: University of Chicago Press.

Rabuka, Niko. 1911. Ai sau ni taro me kilai. *Na Mata*: 154–58, 172–76.

Reid, A. C. 1977. The fruit of the Rewa: Oral traditions and the growth of the pre-Christian Lakeba state. *Journal of Pacific History* 12:2–24.

Remy, Jules. 1861. *Ka Mooolelo Hawaii (Histoire Hawaiienne)*. Paris: Clave. (A French translation and Hawaiian text of the Lahainaluna Students' *Mo'o'olelo* of 1838.)

Rickman, Lt. John (attributed). 1781. *Journal of Captain Cook's last voyage to the Pacific*. London: E. Newberry.

Ricoeur, Paul. 1980. *The contributions of French historiography to the theory of history*. Oxford: Clarendon Press.

Riou, Edward. MS. A log of the proceedings of His Majesty's Sloop *Discovery*, 1778–1779. PRO-Adm. 51/4529.

Roberts, Helen H. 1926. *Ancient Hawaiian music*. Bernice P. Bishop Museum Bulletin 29. Honolulu: Bishop Museum.

Roberts, Henry. MS. A log of the proceedings of His Majesties Sloop *Resolution* . . . Dixson Library (Library of NSW).

Robertson, George. 1948. *The discovery of Tahiti. A journal of the second voyage of H.M.S. "Dolphin."* London: Hakluyt Society.

Rokowaqa, Epeli. n.d. Ai tukutuku kei Viti. Suva: n. pub. (A copy of this rare book is available in the National Archives of Fiji.)

Rosaldo, Renato. 1980. *Ilongot headhunting, 1883–1974*. Stanford, Calif.: Stanford University Press.

Rutherford, J. 1961. *Sir George Grey*. London: Cassell.

Sahlins, Marshall. 1962. *Moala*. Ann Arbor: University of Michigan Press.

————1979. L'apothéose du captaine Cook. In *La fonction symbolique*, ed. Michel Izard and Pierre Smith, pp. 307–39. Paris: Gallimard.

————1981. *Historical metaphors and mythical realities: Structure in the early history of the Sandwich Islands kingdom*. Association for the Study of Anthropology in Oceania, Special Publication No. 1. Ann Arbor: University of Michigan Press.

————1983. Raw women, cooked men, and other "great things" of the Fiji Islands. In *The Ethnography of Cannibalism*, ed. Paula Brown and Donald Tuzin, pp. 72–93. Special Publication, Society for Psychological Anthropology.

————In press. Hierarchy and humanity in Polynesia. In *Transformations of Polynesian Culture*, ed. Anthony Hooper. The Polynesian Society, Special Publication.

Samwell, David. 1957 [1786]. *Captain Cook and Hawaii*. San Francisco: Magee. (Reissue of 1786, *A Narrative of the Death of Captain James Cook*.)

Sartre, Jean-Paul. 1968. *Search for a method*, trans. Hazel E. Barnes. New York: Vintage Books.

Saussure, Ferdinand de. 1959. *Course in general linguistics*. New York: McGraw-Hill.

Sayes, Shelly Ann. 1982. Cakaudrove: Ideology and reality in a Fijian confederation. Ph.D. dissertation, The Australian National University.

Schütz, Albert J. (ed.). 1977. *The diaries and correspondence of David Cargill, 1832–1843*. Canberra: Australian National University Press.

Schwimmer, Eric. 1963. Guardian animals of the Maori. *Journal of the Polynesian Society* 72:397–410.

————1966. *The world of the Maori*. Wellington: Reed.

————1978. Lévi-Strauss and Maori social structure. *Anthropologica*, n.s., 20:201–22.

Shortland, Edward. 1856. *Traditions and superstitions of the New Zealanders*. 2d ed. London: Longman, Brown, Green, Longmans and Roberts.

————1882. *Maori religion and mythology*. London: Longmans.

Simmons, David. 1976. *The great New Zealand myth*. Wellington: Reed.

Sinclair, Keith. 1972. *The origins of the Maori wars*. Wellington: New Zealand University Press.

Skinner, W. H. 1911. The ancient fortified *Pa*. *Journal of the Polynesian Society* 20:71–77.

Smith, Bernard. 1979. Cook's posthumous reputation. In *Captain James Cook and his times*, ed. Robin Fisher and H. Johnston. Seattle: University of Washington Press.

Smith, Jean. 1974–75. Tapu removal in Maori religion. *Journal of the Polynesian Society* (Memoirs Supplement) 83:1–43; 84:44–96.

Smith, S. Percy. 1910. *Maori wars of the nineteenth century*. Christchurch: Whitcombe and Tombs.

———1913–15. Lore of the Ware Wananga. *Polynesian Society Memoirs*, vols. 3 and 4.

Stern, Gustaf. 1968 [1931]. *Meaning and change of meaning*. Bloomington: University of Indiana Press.

Stewart, C. S. 1970 [1830]. *Journal of a residence in the Sandwich Islands during the years 1823, 1824, 1825*. Honolulu: University of Hawaii Press.

Stone, Lawrence. 1981. *The past and the present*. Boston: Routledge and Kegan Paul.

Strawson, P. F. 1971. *Logico-linguistic papers*. London: Methuen.

Swayne, C. R. MS. Lau papers (mostly from Swayne). Cambridge University Museum of Archaeology and Ethnology.

Tambiah, S. J. 1976. *World conqueror and world renouncer*. Cambridge: Cambridge University Press.

Thomas, John. MS. Tonga or the Friendly Islands. Methodist Missionary Society (Box 653), School of Oriental and African Studies Library, University of London.

Thompson, E. P. 1977. Folklore, anthropology and social history. *The Indian Historical Review* 3:247–66.

Thompson, Laura. 1940. *Southern Lau, Fiji: An ethnography*. Bernice P. Bishop Museum Bulletin 232. Honolulu: Bishop Museum.

Thurston, Asa. MS. Missionary letters. Hawaiian Mission Children's Society Library, Honolulu.

Tippett, A. R. 1973. *Aspects of Pacific ethnohistory*. Pasadena: William Carey Library.

Toganivalu, Ratu Deve. MS. A history of Bau. Transcript in the National Archives of Fiji (F62/247).

Tregear, Edward. 1969 [1891]. *The Maori-Polynesian comparative dictionary*. Oosterhout: Anthropological Publications. (Reissue)

Trevenen, James. MS. Marginal notes to the published account

(Cook and King) of Cook's third voyage. Typescript copy in Sinclair Library, University of Hawaii.

Turner, Victor. 1969. *The ritual process*. Chicago: Aldine.

Valeri, Valerio. 1972. Le fonctionnement du systeme des rangs a Hawaii. *L'Homme* 15:83–107.

———1982. The transformation of a transformation: A structural essay on an aspect of Hawaiian history (1809–1819). *Social Analysis* 10:3–41.

———In press. *The human sacrifice: Ritual and society in ancient Hawaii*. Chicago: University of Chicago Press.

Vancouver, Captain George. 1801. *A voyage of discovery to the North Pacific Ocean . . . in the years 1790, 1791, 1792, 1793, 1794 and 1795*. New edition, 5 vols. London: Stockdale.

Vansina, J. 1964. *Le royaume Kuba*. Musée Royal de l'Afrique Centrale, Annales, Sciences Humaines, No. 49.

Vernant, Jean-Pierre. 1979. *Mythe et société en grèce ancienne*. Paris: Maspero.

———1982. *The origins of Greek thought* (translation of *Les origines de la pensée grecque*, 1962). Ithaca: Cornell University Press.

Wagner, Roy. 1975. *The Invention of Culture*. Englewood Cliffs, N.J.: Prentice-Hall.

Wallis, Mary David Cook. 1851. *Life in Feejee, or, five years among the cannibals*, (By a Lady). Boston: Heath.

Wallis, Samuel. 1824. An account of a voyage round the world, in the years 1776, 1767, and 1768. In *General history and collection of voyages and travels*, ed. Robert Kerr, 12:120–241. Edinburgh and London: Blackwood and T. Cadell.

Wards, Ian. 1968. *The shadow of the land*. Wellington: A. R. Shearer, Government Printer.

Waterhouse, Joseph. 1866. *The king and people of Fiji*. London: Wesleyan Conference.

Watt, Sir James. 1979. Medical aspects and consequences of Cook's voyages. In *Captain Cook and his times*, ed. Fisher and Johnston. Seattle: University of Washington Press.

White, John. 1874. *Te Rou; or, the Maori at home*. London: Low, Marston, Low, and Searle.

———1855. Maori customs and superstitions. In *The history and doings of the Maoris*, by Thomas Wayth Gudgeon, pp. 95–225. Auckland: Brett.

———1887–90. *Ancient history of the Maori*. 6 vols. Wellington: Government Printer.

Whitney, Samuel. MS. Journal of Samuel Whitney. Hawaiian Mission Children's Society Library, Honolulu.

Wilkes, Charles. 1845. *Narrative of the United States exploring expeditions*. Vols. 2 and 3. Philadelphia: Lea and Blanchard.

Williams, Herbert W. 1975. *A dictionary of the Maori language.* 7th ed. Wellington: A. R. Shearer, Government Printer.

Williams, Thomas, and James Calvert. 1859. *Fiji and Fijians.* 2 vols. New York: Appleton.

Williams, William. 1867. *Christianity among the New Zealanders.* London: Seeley, Jackson, and Halliday.

Wilson, Monica. 1969. The Nguni people. In *The Oxford history of South Africa,* ed. Monica Wilson and Leonard Thompson, 1: 75–130. Oxford: Clarendon Press.

Wise, John H. 1965. The history of land ownership in Hawaii. In *Ancient Hawaiian civilization,* by E. S. Craighill Handy, Kenneth P. Emory, et al. Rutland and Tokyo: Tuttle.

Wolf, Eric. 1982. *Europe and the peoples without history.* Berkeley: University of California Press.

Wright, Harrison M. 1959. *New Zealand, 1769–1840: Early years of Western contact.* Cambridge: Harvard University Press.

Wyllie, R. C. (ed.). 1846. *Answers to questions proposed by His Excellency, R. C. Wyllie, His Hawaiian Majesty's Minister of Foreign Relations* . . . Honolulu: Government Printer.

Young, Michael W. 1966. The divine kingship of the Jukun: A reevaluation of some theories. *Africa* 36: 135–52.

Zimmermann, Heinrich. 1930. *Zimmermann's Captain Cook: An account of the third voyage of Captain Cook around the world, 1776–1780,* trans. Elsa Michaelis and C. French, ed. F. W. Howay. Toronto: Ryerson Press.

Index

Abortion, 23
Action (*praxis*), xiv; cultural categories risked in, ix–x, 145–51; as performative, xi, 27–31; theory versus, 154–56
Aeneas, 82
Africa, divine kingship in, 42–43, 44, 46, 75, 77, 79, 92
Agamemnon, 82
Akua (divine), 30–31, 146
Aloha, 3, 12, 24, 116, 136, 139
Amita, 83
Andrews, Lorrin, 10
Anggor, of New Guinea, 30n
Anonymous of Ngapuhi, 63n, 66, 67–68, 70
"Anthropology of Time Reckoning, The" (Pocock), 50
Antigonus, 121
A priori categories, 145–46, 154
Ao (day), 59, 110–11
Athens, 33–34
Australian Aboriginals, xii, xviii

Bakhtin, Mikhail, 92
Balandier, Georges, 75, 76n
Barnes, J. A., 44
Barraclough, Geoffrey, 33n
Barrère, Dorothy B., 5, 15
Bau. *See* Fiji

Bayly, William, 129–30, 137
Beaglehole, J. C., 1–7, 106–9, 120–30
Beauty, in Hawaii, 17–19, 23
Barkcloth, ceremonial use of, 85–87, 90, 99
Beckwith, Martha, 110, 111
Bell, Edward, 140
Benveniste, Émile, 46
Best, Elsdon, 13, 55, 59, 60, 62, 63–64
Bird, John, 49
Birth chants, Hawaiian, 22, 25, 109–10
Birth rituals, Tahitian, 100
Bloch, Marc, ix, 20, 31
Boas, Franz, 145
Bohannan, P., 75
Bonte, Pierre, 51
Botoni, of Koro, 99–100
Bott, Elizabeth, 45n, 47
Bougainville, Louis Antoine de, 6
Bourdieu, Pierre, 29, 51
Braudel, Fernand, xiv, 125n
Bréal, Michel, 147–48
Brewster, A. B., 79
British: in Hawaii, xiii, 104–35, 136–43; in New Zealand, viii, 60–71; in Tahiti, 74
Broughton, William R., 43n

Bryant, A. T., 42, 49
Buick, T., 62, 65, 66n, 68–69
Burney, Lt. James, 106, 127, 128, 137n
Burrows, R., 61, 62, 65n, 70

Calcul sauvage, 30
Calvert, James, 37, 39, 41n, 98
Cannibalism: in Fiji, 86, 89, 96, 97–103; in Hawaii, 112–13; Maori, 57. See also Human sacrifice
Capell, A., 101n
Capitalism, viii, 52, 131
Carleton, Hugh, 61, 62–63, 66n
Celeritas, 90–92, 97, 99
Chadwick, H. Monro, 42, 46
Change versus stability, 143–45, 153. See also Structure
Chaos, ritual of, 43–44, 80, 116
Charisma, 35
Children of the land (kama'āina), xi–xii, 28–31
Christ, Passion of, 92n, 96n
Christianity: in Fiji, 37–40; in Hawaii, 39n, 126
Clastres, Pierre, 75–76, 79
Clerke, Capt. James, 125, 128, 137, 140
Colenso, F. W., 68, 112
Conception rites, 59
Cook, Capt. James, 1–31; arrival of, in Hawaii, 1–5, 30–31, 104–5, 120–21, 136–38; death of, xiii–xiv, 74, 76, 94, 104–35; as god, x, 4–5, 31, 73–74, 81, 93–94, 104–35, 144–55 passim
Cooked versus raw, 99–103, 113
Coronation ceremonies: in Fiji, 84–87, 93, 95–99, 119; in Hawaii, 21, 80, 93, 116–17, 119; significance of, 80
Cosmogony: Hawaiian, 14, 109–12; Maori, 13–14, 55–60, 80n, 110
Cosmology, xv
Cowper, William, 134
Cox, Ross, 141

Creation chants, 14
Cronos, 79
Cross, William, 38
Crow Indians, 53
Culture. See Structure
Cunnison, Ian, 47, 50

Dahomey, kingship in, 77
Davis, C. O., 66n
Délivré, Alain, 148
Derrick, R. A., 37, 40n, 41n, 94n
Descent and lineage: Crow/ Omaha, 53; in Fiji, 48; Hawaiian, xii, 14, 19–22, 24–25, 44, 49, 51, 111; heroic versus segmentary modes of, 44; Maori, 13–14, 45n, 59, 67; Nguni, 44–45; performative versus prescriptive structure in, xii
Diarchy, 90–91
Diderot, Denis, 6
Dingiswayo, 42
Dionysius of Halicarnassus, 82–83
Discovery (ship), 1, 2n, 104–6, 120–21, 136–37, 140
Divine kingship, x–xi, xv, 77; African, 42–43, 44, 46, 75, 77, 79, 92; duality of, 90–91; in Fiji, 36, 37, 48, 75–103, 119; in Hawaii, xiii–xv, 16–19, 21, 39n, 43–44, 75, 77, 79–80, 92–94, 109, 114, 138, 139, 147; of Latins, 81–84; of Maori, 35, 36, 48; Scythian, 33–34; sociological aspects of, 44–54
Division of labor: in cultural and historical consciousness, 49; linguistic, ix–x
Dolphin (ship), 74
Dorton, Lili, 15n, 16, 18n
Dumézil, Georges, xv, 33, 57, 73, 77–78, 80n, 81, 84, 99
Dumont, Louis, 35, 114
Durkheim, Émile, 29, 34, 45

Earth Mother (Papa), 13–14, 58–64, 80n, 115

Echard, Nicole, 51
Edgar, Thomas, 2n, 129–30
Elbert, Samuel, 11–12
Eliade, Mircea, 58–59
Ellis, William, 6n, 7, 39n, 104–5, 124, 129
Emerson, J. S., 5, 10, 142
Eskimo, xi, xii, 26
Etruscans, 99
Evans-Pritchard, E. E., xviii
Event: anthropology versus history, and, 72; as final form of cosmic myth, 58; as individual and collective representation, 108; and structure, vii, xiii–xiv, 138, 153
Exogamy, 22
Exploit, Heusch on, 79

Feeley-Harnik, Gillian, 49–50
Fiji: awareness of history in, 49; divine kingship in, 36, 37, 48, 75–103, 119; marriage in, 27, 48, 87
Firth, Raymond, xiv, 70
Forbes, Cochrane, 142
Fornander, Abraham, 5, 18, 118
Fornication, 116
Fox, James J., 50
Frazer, Sir James, xv, 35, 77, 81, 97, 109, 120–21, 128; his Golden Bough, 44, 92n, 105, 112
French, in New Zealand, 63
Freud, Sigmund, 12, 97
Friendship, performative and prescriptive, xi, 27
Fronting, 28
Functional revaluation of cultural categories, ix, 149. See also Structure
Furet, François, 58

Geertz, Clifford, vii, 76, 108
Genital chants (mele ma'i), 15–16
George III, King of England, 140, 144
German tribes, 40, 42, 46
Giddens, Anthony, 152

Gifford, Edward Winslow, 45n
Gilbert, George, 128
Gluckman, Max, 92
Golden Bough, The (Frazer), 44, 92n, 105, 112
Goldie, W. H., 55, 59
Gravitas, 90–92, 97, 99
Gray, Thomas, 32, 33n
Greece, ancient, 33–34, 82
Grey, Sir George, 54, 56, 60, 64n
Gudgeon, Lt. Col. C. M. G., 135

Habitus, 29, 51, 53, 139
Hampshire, Stuart, 147
Handy, E. S., 79, 116
Hānai (feeding), 7, 28
Hawaii, 1–31, 104–35, 136–43; chiefs versus common people in, 138–43; Christianity in, 39n, 126; descent and lineage in, xii, 14, 19–22, 24–25, 44, 49, 51, 111; divine kingship in, xiii–xv, 16–19, 21, 39n, 43–44, 75, 77, 79–80, 92–94, 109, 114, 138, 139, 147; Kumulipo chant in, 14, 109–10, 115; Makahiki festival in, 4–5, 92–94, 105, 110, 114–29, 139; performative structure in, x–xii, 19–20, 26–31; regicide in, 94n; sexuality in, xi, 3–26, 29, 139; tabu in, x, 8–9, 10, 18–21, 25, 43, 80, 114, 115, 117, 127, 136–37, 142–43, 149, 154. See also Cook, Capt. James
Hawaiki, 58, 60, 64, 71
Hazelwood, Brother, 89
He'a-o-ke-koa, 115
Heke, Hone, viii, 60–71
Henry, Teuira, 74
Herodotus, 33
Heusch, Luc de, 42, 77, 79
Hierarchical solidarity, 45–46, 139
Hierarchy, concept of, 35, 50, 114–15
Hindess, B., 154–55
Hiroa, Te Rangi, 62
Hirst, P., 154–55

Historical Metaphors (Sahlins),
142–43
History: anthropology and, x,
xvii, 72; awareness of, by common people, 49–52; heroic,
x–xi, 34–54, 152; Maori concept of, 58–59; "new," x–xi,
32–33, 49; performative versus
prescriptive structure and, xii–
xiii; structure versus, vii–viii,
143–45, 151. *See also* Event
Hocart, A. M., xv, 14, 35, 37–38,
42n, 48, 49, 75–103 passim, 139
Homosexuality, 10
Hone Heke, viii, 60–71
Hongi Hika, 65, 66n, 67
Hoohokuokalani, 80n
Hopi, 9, 152
"Hot Fire" (song), 11
Huber, Peter, 30n
Hula, 5, 15, 116
Human sacrifice: in Fiji, 95–103;
in Hawaii, 19, 93, 115–16, 119–
20, 129, 139, 140; in Tahiti, 74.
See also Cannibalism
Hunnewell, James, 141n
Hunt, John, 49
Hypergamy, 7, 10, 22, 117
Hypogamy, 10, 22

Idealism, 154
Illuminated Sky (Wakea), 14, 80n
Ilongot, 53
Imperialism, xiii, 131
Incwala ceremonies, 92
Incest, 22, 79–80
India, kingship in, 77
Indians, American, 9, 36–37, 53,
77–78, 152
Indo-European kingship, xv, 33–
34, 77, 90, 97
Infanticide, 23
Installation rituals. *See* Corona-
tion ceremonies
Interest, concept of, ix–x, xvi–
xvii, 29–30, 150–51
Ireland, kingship in, 77

Jaggar, Thomas James, 39
Jarré, Raymond, 100n
Johansen, J. Prytz, 35, 47n, 54,
58, 59, 60, 112
Jupiter, 84, 92

Kaawa, P. W., 75
Kahiki, 73–74, 120, 137, 139, 144,
155
Kahoali'i, 19, 119–20, 126
Ka-'I-i-mamao, King, 109–10,
115
Kalakaua, King, 12, 19n
Kalaniopu'u, King, 22, 106,
121–30
Kāli'i, 118–19, 122, 130
Kamakau, Samuel M., 114, 117–
18
Kamapua'a, 114
Kamba, battle, 40–41
Kamehameha, King, 9, 16, 18n,
19, 43n, 50–51, 80, 140, 142
Kanaka, 147
Kane (man), 111
Kaneikapolei, 106–7, 129
Kaneoneo, 137–40
Kant, Immanuel, 145
Kaona (hidden meanings), 12–13,
14–15
Ka'ō'ō, 122–23, 124, 126
Kapiti, Pita, 112
Ka'upu, 117
Kava, 36, 75, 85–87, 89, 95–97
Kazembe, Kingdom of, 47
Kekoa, E., 26
Keoua, 19
Kepelino, Z., 111
Ki'i (man), 111
Kila, 18, 21
King, Lt. James, 1, 2, 4n, 6n, 9,
105, 107, 121–31, 136
Kingship. *See* Divine kingship
Kinship, perpetual, 47. *See also*
Descent and lineage
Kipling, Rudyard, 10
Kiwala'o, King, 79–80
Kororareka, flagstaff at, 60–71

Koskinen, Aarne A., 144
Kū, 113–15, 121–22, 129, 131
Kuba, 36
Kumulipo chant, 14, 109–10, 115
Kūnui'ākea, 16, 18n

La'ila'i, 111
Laka, 5, 116
Lakeba, 85
Language: Hawaiian, 28; logical structure of, 146. *See also* Sign
Lasakau, 99–100
Latins, 81–84, 91–92
Latinus, King, 82–83
Lau. *See* Fiji
Le'a, 3–4, 29
Leach, Edmund, 94
Ledyard, John, 127
Lelemahoalani, 3n
Lester, E. H., 36
Lévi-Strauss, Claude, xi, xiii, 13, 71, 81, 98–99, 112
Levuka, 99–100
Lili'uokalani, Queen, 16
Lineage. *See* Descent and lineage
Linguistic value, 150. *See also* Language
Lono, xvii, 4–5, 31, 73–75, 93–94, 105–35, 153–54
Lono-at-the-Makahiki, 115, 117
Love. See *Aloha*; *Le'a*; Sexuality
Luapala, 47, 50
Lupercalia, 92
Lyons, John, 149
Lyth, Richard Burdsall, 98n

Madagascar, history in, 49
Mahoe, Noelani, 11–12
Makahiki ceremony: and Cook, 4–5, 93–94, 105, 110, 114–29, 139; described, 92–93
Malani of Lakemba, 49
Malo, David, 14, 75, 138
Mana: in Fiji, 37–38; in Hawaii, 8, 18, 30, 74, 134–35, 144, 151, 155–56; and Maori, 65, 70–71, 134–35

Manaia, myth of, 64
Maning, F. E., 63n, 66n, 70
Maori, 107, 115; cosmogony of, 13–14; 55–60, 80n, 110; and divine kingship, 35, 36, 48; lineage and descent among, 13–14, 45n, 59, 67; and *mana*, 65, 70–71, 134–35; mytho-praxis of, and 1844–46 revolt, viii, 54–72; sweet potato ritual of, 112, 113, 114
Marquesans, 116
Marriage: Crow/Omaha, 53; elementary and complex forms of, 53; in Fiji, 27, 48, 89; in Hawaii, 5, 14, 22–25, 116–17, 138; of immigrant king, as form of reciprocal exchange, 82–83; 87–88; prescriptive, 27; Roman, 82–83. *See also* Descent and lineage; *specific forms of marriage, as* Hypergamy
Marx, Karl, 38, 52, 70, 76, 154
Marxism, 154–55
Materialism, 154
Maui, 55
Mbau, 37–40
Meaning, ix–x, xiv, 145–47
Mexico, kingship in, 77
Moala. *See* Fiji
Mo'ikeha, 18
Mongolia, kingship in, 46
Mycaenian god-kings, 33–34

Ndabele, 45
Nemi, 81, 112
Net of Maoloha, 120
New Guinea, 26; Anggor of, 30n
Ngapuhi, 56, 60–71
Ngatiawa, 62
Nguni, 42–43, 44–45, 46
New Zealand. *See* Maori
New Zealand Company, 68
Nietzsche, Friedrich, 152
Noikoro, 79, 87
Nopera Panakareau, 70
Nuha, 108, 130

Numa, 91
Numitor, 83

Oedipus, 80
Oliver, Douglas, 74
Orou, 6

Papa. *See* Earth Mother
Parricide, 47, 59–60, 79, 86
Peloponnesian War (Thucydides),
    54, 55
Pelops, 82
Pensée sauvage, xii, 14, 30, 144
Percy, Walker, 146
Perpetual kinship, 47
Persia, kingship in, 77
Philippines, Ilongot in, 53
Phillips, Lt. Molesworth, 107, 129
Plato, quoted, 136
Plutarch, 84
Pō (darkness), 59, 64, 110–11
Pocock, David, 50
Polis, 33–34
Polyandry, 22, 23
Polygamy, 23
Polygyny, 22, 46, 48
Polynesia: divine kingship in, xv,
    46, 73, 77–78; lineage and de-
    scent in, 20, 44, 81. *See also*
    Fiji; Hawaii; Maori; Tahiti;
    Tonga
Polynesian Mythology (Grey), 54,
    56–57
Polynesian wars, 54–55
Pomare, 68n
Positional succession, 47
Power, theories of origin of, 75–
    76. *See also* Divine kingship
Praxis. See Action
Préaux, Jean-G., 82
Prthu, 78
Pukui, Mary Kawena, 5n, 12n,
    15, 79
Pul Eliya, 26
Purim festival, 92n
Putnam, Hilary, ix

Quirinus, 91

Radcliffe-Brown, A. R., xii, 27,
    28, 143
Rangi (Sky Father), 13, 56–64,
    115
Rebellion, ritual of, 92
Remus, and Romulus, 79, 83
Resolution (ship), xiv, 1–4, 9, 94,
    105, 121–22, 126–29, 136–37
Rewa, 38–41
Riou, Edward, 1, 105
Robertson, George, 74
Rokowaqa, Epeli, 87, 96, 101
Rome, 77, 79, 81–84, 91–92, 99
Romulus, 76, 79, 81–84, 89
Rongo, 112, 113–14
Rosaldo, Renato, 53
Rou, 56–57
Rousseau, Jean-Jacques, 3, 35
Rutulians, 82–83

Sabines, 84, 89, 90, 91
Sacaea festival, 92n
Sahlins, Marshall, xiv, 8, 9, 31,
    75, 94n, 114, 121, 125, 142–43
Samwell, David, 1–3, 5, 15, 108n,
    116, 120, 122–23, 127, 128–29
Sartre, Jean Paul, 72
Saturnalia, 92
Saussure, Ferdinand de, ix, xv–
    xvi, 77, 103, 143, 145, 147–48,
    150, 153
Sayes, Shelly Ann, 36
Scandinavians, and kingship, 77
Schütz, Albert J., 38
Scythian kings, 33–34
Sea people, 99–102
Search for a lord (*'imi haku*), 24–
    25, 139
Search for a Method (Sartre), 72
Service, Elman, 36–37
Sexuality: Fiji, 89–90; Hawaiian,
    xi, 3–26, 29, 139; Maori, 55, 59
Shaka, 42
Shakespeare, William, his *Henry
    V* quoted, 51, 94
Shortland, Edward, 55, 65, 66n,
    113
Sign: functional revaluation of,

ix, 149–51; thing versus, ix, 147–48
Simmons, David, 58
Sinclair, Keith, 70
Sioux Indians, 9
Skinner, W. H., 62, 65
Sky Father. *See* Rangi
Smith, Adam, 131
Smith, Bernard, 131–34
Smith, Jean, 55, 60, 113
Smith, S. Percy, 60, 66
Social contract, 35, 76
Sociobiology, 76–78
South America, chiefship in, 75
Splashing-water (*hi'uwai*) ceremony, 117
Stern, Gustaf, x
Stone, Lawrence, 32
Stranger-king. *See* Divine kingship
Strawson, P. F., 146
Structuralism, xv–xvi, 81, 143, 151
Structure: of the conjuncture, xiv, xvii, 67, 125, 127, 152–54; in convention and action, ix; history versus, vii–viii, 143–45, 151; meaning of, vii, 89; prescriptive versus performative, x–xiii, 19–20, 26–31; reproducing itself, viii, xii–xiii, 81, 138, 144–45; structuring, of *habitas*, 29; subconscious versus explicit, 53–54; synchronic versus diachronic, xv, 72, 77, 102–3, 144, 151; trace, 66n
Supplément au voyage de Bougainville, 6
Sutton, Bruce, 72n
Swazi, 45, 92
Sweet potato ritual, 112, 114
Symbolic object, 150

Tabu: in Fiji, 97; in Hawaii, x, 8–9, 10, 18–21, 25, 43, 80, 114, 115, 117, 127, 136–37, 142–43, 149, 154; of Maori, 112, 113
Tacitus, 40

Tahiti, 7, 68, 137; Wallis in, 74, 75
Tāne, myth of, 13–14, 58, 59–60, 80n
Tantalus, 82
Taro, 14, 113, 142
Tarpeia, 84
Tarquin, 82
Tatius, King, 91
Ta'ufa'āhau, King, 47
Thakombau, 37–41, 94n
Theogamy, 5–6, 25
Thomas, John, 50n
Thompson, E. P., 49
Thompson, Laura, 100n
Thucydides, 54, 66
Thurston, Asa, 22
Tikanga, 59
Tippett, A. R., 84
Tiv, 75
Toko, 64–65
Toganivalu, Ratu Deve, 100n
Tonga, 1, 38, 40, 129; heroic segmentation in, 45n; historical-genealogical knowledge in, 50n; and kava, 75, 95; positional succession in, 47
Trace structure, 66n
Totemism, 13–14, 81, 112
Trade: with Fiji, 39, 88; with Hawaii, 6–8, 124, 131, 136, 139–43, 151, 155–56; with Maori, 66–67, 68, 70
Tregear, Edward, 65
Trevenen, James, 8n, 128, 129
Trojans, 82–84
Tswana, 26
Tū, 57, 112–15
Tūāhu, 61–71
Tuareg, 51
Tūhoe, 62
Tui Nayau, 84–87
Turner, V., 43n

Valeri, Valerio, 18, 21, 22, 93, 106, 116, 119
Valery, P., 76n
Vancouver, Capt. George, 9, 128–29, 130, 153

Vansina, J., 36
Vernant, Jean-Pierre, 33–34, 54
Vico, Giambattista, 32, 35
Viwa Island, 38–39
Voltaire, 32, 33n
Vunivalu, 84n, 97–98

Wagner, Roy, 152
Waitangi, Treaty of, 62, 67–71
Wakea (Illuminated Sky), 14, 80n
Wallis, Capt. Samuel, 74, 75
Wards, Ian, 70, 71
Waterhouse, Joseph, 38, 39n, 75
Watman, Willie, 126
Watt, Sir James, 109
Wealth of Nations (Smith), 131

Webber, John, 130–31
Weber, Max, 153
White, John, 56–57, 66
Whorf, Benjamin Lee, 28, 145, 152
Wilkes, Charles, 68n
Williams, Henry, 69–70
Williams, Herbert W., 59, 64, 65
Williams, Thomas, 37, 39, 98
Wolf, Eric, viii
World-system theory, viii
Wright, Harrison M., 66n

Zeus, 33, 79
Zimmerman, Heinrich, 3n
Zulu, 42–43, 44, 45, 49